Thirty years after two alcoholics met in Akron, this huge throng at the A.A. International Convention in Toronto, Ontario, joined in saying words that sum up the spirit behind the worldwide growth of A.A., before and since: "I am responsible. When anyone, anywhere, reaches out for help, I want the hand of A.A. always to be there. And for that, I am responsible" (preceding pages).

DR. BOB
and the Good Oldtimers

DR·BOB
and the
Good
Oldtimers

A biography, with recollections
of early A.A. in the Midwest

1980
Alcoholics Anonymous World Services, Inc., New York, N.Y.

This is A.A. General Service Conference-approved literature

Library of Congress Catalog Card No. 80-65962

ISBN 0-916856-07-0

Printed in the United States of America

Foreword

The preparation of this book began after the April 1977 A A General Service Conference approved the project. Originally, a joint biography of the two co-founders was planned. When this proved impracticable, it became apparent that Dr. Bob's biography should be written first, before Bill W.'s.

The end of the last century was the setting for all of Dr. Bob's childhood and youth. Even with the most thorough research, this early period includes months and years of which only the barest account can be given, and that in the memories of but a few men and women. Undramatic as these recollections are, they give glimpses into the innate character that would help to shape the Fellowship of Alcoholics Anonymous.

For Dr. Bob's adult years—as an active and then as a recovering alcoholic—the material is far richer. In the course of research, the book naturally expanded from biographical limits into a memoir of early A.A. in the Midwest. Our co-founder was in the same position as any other A.A. member: Without the

Fellowship and its program, his life would have been only a short story with a tragic ending.

Both the individual and the larger history unfolded partially from A.A. literature and material in the archives at the A.A. General Service Office in New York City—but chiefly from face-to-face talks with relatives, friends, and acquaintances of Dr. Bob and with pioneer members of Midwestern A.A. The locales of these interviews included, not only Ohio and Dr. Bob's native Vermont, but California, the D.C. area, Florida, North Carolina, New York, and Texas. The section headed "Sources" (page 349), serving as both footnotes and bibliography, gives the origins and availability of quoted matter.

The interviews yielded a greater wealth of historical material than could be included in one book; but the complete records are now in the A.A. archives. To all the people who shared their memories, the Fellowship owes a debt of gratitude.

Contents

1. Childhood and college years

Robert Holbrook Smith—eventually to be known to grateful alcoholics as Dr. Bob, co-founder of Alcoholics Anonymous— was born August 8, 1879, in the front bedroom of a large, 19th century clapboard house at Central and Summer Streets in St. Johnsbury, Vermont.

He was the son of Judge and Mrs. Walter Perrin Smith. Influential in business and civic affairs, Judge Smith sat on the Caledonia County (Vermont) Probate Court. He was also, at various times, state's attorney, member of the state legislature, superintendent of St. Johnsbury schools, director of the Merchants National Bank, and president of the Passumpsic Savings Bank. In addition, he taught Sunday school for 40 years.

Dr. Bob, who rarely discussed family background, described his father as being a typical Vermont Yankee— reserved and taciturn on first acquaintance, with a lively if somewhat dry sense of humor.

Many years later, Dr. Bob's son, Robert R. Smith (nick-named Smitty), was to describe his father in much the same way. "Upon your first contact, he was very reserved and formal in his relationships, but when you became his friend, he showed a personality which was just the opposite—friendly, generous, and full of fun," Smitty said.

Under the granite surface, Judge Smith betrayed a good deal of warmth and compassion, with perhaps a touch of indulgence, toward his only son. Certainly, he made an attempt to understand and control the malady that threatened to destroy Bob's life and work. Many times, with varying degrees of temporary success, he tried to rescue Bob from the effects of his drinking. Unfortunately, Judge Smith, who died in 1918, did not live to see Dr. Bob attain permanent sobriety.

Mrs. Smith, who did live to see Dr. Bob get sober, was described as a stern, tight-lipped, churchgoing lady who busied herself with the countless social and religious activities of St. Johnsbury's towering, gray stone North Congregational Church.

"Grandma Smith was a cold woman," said Suzanne Windows, Dr. Bob's adopted daughter. "Once, she came to the house, and we were all sick with the flu. Instead of pitching in, she went to bed, too!"

Mrs. Smith felt that the way to success and salvation lay through strict parental supervision, no-nonsense education, and regular spiritual devotion.

"Mom [Anne Ripley Smith] blamed her for Dad's drinking," said Sue. "She felt the stern upbringing nearly ruined him. When he got the chance, he just broke loose."

Dr. Bob (who, as we know, was not one to "louse it all up

Healthy Vermont boyhood behind him, medical career ahead, young Dr. Bob already had a second career—alcoholic.

with Freudian complexes") merely said, "I just loved my grog." But he could look back and see certain long-range influences in his childhood.

Although he had a much older foster sister, Amanda Northrup, of whom he was quite fond, he grew up as an only child. In his middle years, Dr. Bob said he considered this unfortunate, because it may have "engendered the selfishness which played such an important part in bringing on my alcoholism."

And he did find one source of future rebellion: "From childhood through high school, I was more or less forced to go to church, Sunday school and evening service, Monday-night Christian Endeavor, and sometimes to Wednesday-evening prayer meeting," he recalled. "This had the effect of making me resolve that when I was free from parental domination, I would never again darken the doors of a church." Dr. Bob kept his resolution "steadfastly" for the next 40 years, except when circumstances made it unwise.

Another sign of rebellion came at an early age. Young Bob was sent to bed every evening at five o'clock. He went with a quietly obedient air that might have led some parents to suspect the worst. When he thought the coast was clear, Bob got up, dressed, and slipped stealthily downstairs and out the back door to join his friends. He was never caught.

From 1885 to 1894, Bob went to the two-story, red brick Summer Street elementary school, two blocks from the Smiths' house in St. Johnsbury. By the Passumpsic River in northeastern Vermont, St. Johnsbury was, and is, a typical New England village with about 7,000 people then and only about 8,400 by the 1970's. It is approximately 100 miles northeast of East Dorset, Vermont, where Bill Wilson—Dr. Bob's partner-to-be in founding A.A.—was born, grew up, and is now buried.

Dr. Bob described the general moral standard of St.

Johnsbury as "far above the average." And the consumption of alcohol was considered a question of morality. No beer or liquor was legally sold except at the state liquor agency. And the only way you could purchase a pint or so was to convince the agent that you really needed it.

"Without this proof," Dr. Bob said, "the expectant purchaser would be forced to depart empty-handed, with none of what I later came to believe was the great panacea for all human ills."

What about those who sought to circumvent the spirit, if not the letter, of the law? "Men who had liquor shipped in from Boston or New York by express were looked upon with great distrust and disfavor by most of the good townspeople," Dr. Bob said.

But some of the townspeople had local sources of supply. Young Bob had his first drink one summer day when he was just turning nine years old. He was at a neighbor's farm, helping the men bale hay. Wandering off, he found a jug of hard cider hidden by one of the farmhands in a corner of the barn.

He pulled the cork and sniffed. He gasped, and his eyes watered. Powerful! Still, he took a drink—probably, more because it was forbidden than for any other reason.

He liked the taste, but he was evidently able to "take it or leave it" at the time, for his reminiscences included no mention of further drinking until some ten years after that first drink.

As a youngster, Bob had other ways of escaping discipline. From his earliest years, he loved the outdoors, a refuge from the stuffy schoolhouse he was forced to attend each day—until summer. Freedom from some of the musts came with vacations. Bob was released then to wander the hills, to fish and hunt and swim.

Close as he was (and remained throughout his life) to his

foster sister, it was chiefly during these vacations that he could
spend time with Amanda. In the summer, they picnicked,
hiked, and swam together. They also spent many hours building and sailing their own boat at the Smith summer cottage on
Lake Champlain, on the Vermont-New York border. After
one of these visits with the Smiths, Amanda, who later became
a history professor at Hunter College in New York City, received from ten-year-old Bob the following note on lined
paper:

St. Johnsbury Vt
May 4 1890

Dear Miss Northrup

I have been meaning to write you every day but have
been putting it off till now. I thank you very much for sending
me the pictures and book. I have enjoyed the book very much
and hope you will read it when you come up here again. I
went over to Mr Harrington and played with Rover the dog.
They have a bull calf and he said he would sell it to me for a
dollar. Mama says if theres anything we need it is a bull. I
went fishing Wednesday and caught about ten fish and a lizard. I have got the lizard in a pan of water and I expect to put
him in alcohol. Pa got me a new bridle and saddle blanket and
I ride every day. I enjoy it very much. Come up here as soon
as you can.

With much love
Robert H Smith

(Even in adulthood, Dr. Bob never developed into much
of a correspondent. His letters to Bill Wilson were one-
pagers, short and to the point, with the words scrawled across
the sheet.)

During these summers, young Bob became an expert
swimmer and at one time saved a girl from drowning. (This
convinced him that children should learn to swim at an early

age. He taught Smitty and Sue to swim when they were five years old. The three of them would set out every vacation morning to swim the channel near their summer cottage at West Reservoir, Akron, Ohio. Misled by the sight on one occasion, an alarmed neighbor called Anne Smith to tell her that her children had fallen out of a boat in the middle of the channel.)

As the boy grew older, he wandered farther afield. Once, he and some friends went to Canada on a hunting trip. Game was so scarce that they lived on eels, blueberries, and cream-of-tartar biscuits for three weeks. Finally, they flushed a particularly large woodchuck. When they had him within range, they started blazing away.

After being shot at for some time, the woodchuck disappeared into its burrow. This episode later caused Judge Smith to remark that the woodchuck probably went in to get away from the noise.

Another time, the boys were wandering in the woods. As they sauntered along, kicking at stones, laughing and joking, they suddenly came upon a huge bear. The bear, probably more frightened than the boys, lumbered deeper into the forest. The young hunters were hard on its heels, yelling and shouting encouragement to one another. Still, the bear got away. "However, I don't believe we ran after him as fast as we might have," Dr. Bob used to say.

Vacation time shrank as childhood faded. In his teens, Bob began to spend summers either working on a Vermont farm or juggling trays and carrying suitcases as a bellhop at a summer hotel in New York's Adirondack Mountains.

In 1894, the 15-year-old entered St. Johnsbury Academy. Now an impressive, ten-building complex, the academy was established with the philanthropic aid of Fairbanks Morse Company as an independent secondary school "for the intellectual, moral, and religious training of boys and girls in

northeastern Vermont." One of its alumni was Calvin
Coolidge, the 30th President of the United States.

Bob was to become an avid reader in later years, but he
rarely cracked a book throughout his scholastic career. There
were repercussions and accusations of "waywardness" from
parents and teachers. Nonetheless, he managed to maintain
passing, even creditable grades.

Although his scholastic neglect may have disgraced him
with his elders, Bob was popular with his schoolmates. Perhaps his sometimes adventurous revolts against authority
gave him a glamorous aura. Maybe his contemporaries sensed
some special traits of character obscure to adults. Or maybe
he was just a likable fellow. Whatever the attraction, he had
many friends, then and throughout his life.

It was in his senior year at St. Johnsbury, at a dance in the
academy gym, that Dr. Bob first met Anne Robinson Ripley of
Oak Park, Illinois. A student at Wellesley, Anne was spending
a holiday with a college friend.

She was small and reserved but had a cheerfulness,
sweetness, and calm that were to remain with her throughout
the years. She had been reared within a family of railroad
people. It was a very sheltered atmosphere, although there
wasn't much money at that time. Anne, who abhorred ostentation and pretense, always pointed out that she attended
Wellesley on a scholarship, because her family couldn't have
afforded to send her there otherwise.

Bob's meeting with Anne was the beginning of what
could hardly be described as a whirlwind courtship; it was to
culminate in marriage after 17 years. No one today can be
absolutely certain of the reason for the delay. There were
years of schooling, work, and internship ahead for Bob.
There was also the possibility that Anne had a healthy fear of
entering the state of holy matrimony with a drinking man.
Perhaps she waited until Bob gave evidence of being sober for

a time before she agreed to marry him. However, they saw each other and corresponded regularly during this period, while Anne taught school.

After his graduation from St. Johnsbury Academy, in 1898, young Bob set off for four years at Dartmouth College, sixty miles south at Hanover, New Hampshire.

The photograph in his college yearbook shows a young man with strong, classic features, who could have posed for an Arrow collar advertisement—the standard for masculine good looks early in this century. Bob grew to be more than six feet in height, with wide, athletic shoulders and big bones.

Reminiscing about the Dr. Bob of later years, several people recalled that what first struck them was the size of his hands, which appeared to be uncommonly large and strong— seemingly too awkward to have handled the delicate business of medical surgery with such skill. And not even those horn-rimmed glasses could hide the penetrating gaze.

Dr. Bob had a deep and resonant voice, which never lost its New England twang but undoubtedly got huskier and raspier as his intake of whiskey increased.

Emma K., who, with her husband, Lavelle (an A.A. member), cared for Dr. Bob and Anne Smith in their last years, on Ardmore Avenue in Akron, Ohio, described Dr. Bob as "very Eastern. Nobody could understand what he said half the time.

"When I said 'aunt,' he used to tell me, 'Don't say "ant." That's something that crawls on the ground. Say "ahnt." ' Imagine saying 'ahnt.' Or he was at the telephone ordering something. When he'd get ready, he'd look at me and laugh and he would say—I can't say it—but he would say, 'Doctah Ah H. Smith, 855 Ahdmaw. No, I said *Ahdmaw* — Aahdmoah!' "

In Bob's Dartmouth years, of course, his New England accent hardly set him apart. He embarked on college life with zest. Freed from his parents' restraining supervision, he saw this as a time to seek out and enjoy new experiences without the necessity of having to give an accounting.

Dartmouth had a name then for being a rugged backwoods school where the 800 or so students spent the long winters ignoring their books and drinking as much beer and hard cider as they could hold. It seems, however, that the real rebels and rakehells in this "wilderness college where there is an unaccountable degree of immorality and vice" were those periodically admonished in the school paper for wearing sweaters, "which cover a multitude of sins," to church and dinner.

Joe P., an Akron A.A. who went to Dartmouth several years after Bob, recalled, "Dartmouth was the drinkingest of the Ivy League schools when I went there. New Hampshire was dry and you couldn't get whiskey, so you'd take the train down to a little town in Massachusetts. Everybody ran over and loaded up, then drank all the way back home. Sometimes, we'd go up to Canada for liquor—or have the brakemen on the trains bring it back to us.

"The natives would have hard cider. Every window in Dartmouth had a jug of hard cider sitting on it. On those horribly cold days, they'd drill down through the ice and take the alcohol out. A cupful would knock the hat right off your head.

"It was a school way up in the mountains, and there was nothing else to do. There were about six girls in town who were waitresses at the Hanover Inn. We were known as the Dartmouth animals, and we tried to act the part. You were supposed to be rough. There was no way to get rid of your exuberance, except when you finally got to go down to Smith, or to Wellesley down near Boston."

Bob's first discovery in his search for the facts of campus life probably did not come about by accident. More likely, it was exactly what he hoped to find: that drinking seemed to be the major extracurricular activity.

"Almost everyone seemed to do it," Bob said, using the time-honored words that "almost everyone" uses to justify heavy drinking in a particular place, profession, or society. So, with a combination of dedication, perseverance, and natural ability, he set out to become a winner in this new sport.

In the beginning, he drank for the sheer fun of it and suffered little or no ill effects. "I seemed to be able to snap back the next morning better than most of my fellow drinkers, who were cursed (or perhaps blessed) with a great deal of morning-after nausea," he said. "Never once in my life have I had a headache, which fact leads me to believe that I was an alcoholic almost from the start."

At Dartmouth, the oncoming illness was no more apparent to classmates than it was to Bob himself. E. B. Watson, who was president of Bob's class of 1902, later became a professor at the college. Still later, as a professor emeritus, he commented in a letter that Bob had been friendly and well liked at Dartmouth for his frank and unpretentious ways of speech. "Although he indulged somewhat excessively in beer (the only beverage then obtainable in New Hampshire), he did not become a slave to alcohol until his graduate schooling."

"I roomed with him in my junior year," recalled Dr. Philip P. Thompson. "I remember him as a tall, lanky gentleman, a little bit abrupt in manner. He was restless. I have no recollection of ever seeing him study, although he was always up in his classes."

Dr. Thompson described his roommate as "rather quick-spoken," remembering a Saturday when several members of the class were having a seemingly endless discussion about where they would go and what they would do that afternoon. Evidently, alcohol was mentioned a time or two, for Bob said,

"Well, if we're going to get drunk, why don't we get at it?"

In that junior year, Dr. Thompson noted, Bob was devoting more and more of his time to playing billiards and drinking beer. "He told me he had liked the taste of liquor ever since he had had some hard cider as a small boy," Dr. Thompson said, noting that Bob could drink liquor in quantities "that the rest of us could not stand."

In addition to learning his way around a billiard table at Dartmouth, it was probably there that Bob started to attain his eventual high proficiency with a deck of cards—whether bridge, poker, or gin rummy. In these and any other games, Dr. Bob was highly competitive and always played to win.

He even learned to pitch horseshoes somewhere along the line. One of the pioneer members in Akron A.A., Ernie G., recalled that a number of A.A.'s including Dr. Bob used to go up to a Minnesota fishing camp in the early 1940's.

"You couldn't get him in a boat to go fishing," Ernie remembered. "I'd say, 'You ought to get away from that card table.' Then I said, 'I'll beat you in a game of horseshoes.' He said, 'Okay, we'll just see about that. How much are we going to play for?'

"I said, 'I won't make it tough on you. Let's make it a quarter.' Hell, I didn't know he was a horseshoe pitcher. He could throw ringers like nobody's business. I thought I was pretty good, too, but he took me two out of three. If he had been in practice, I wouldn't've stood a chance."

Smitty often remarked jokingly that his father's skill at pool, cards, and other games of chance was the result of a misspent youth. Dr. Bob would just smile and say nothing.

Another trick Bob picked up along the way was an ability to chugalug a bottle of beer without any apparent movement of his Adam's apple. "We said he had a patent or open throat," said Dr. Thompson.

Dr. Bob never lost the knack of not swallowing, a barroom trick that must have been good for a free shot or two here and there in his drinking years. In his sober years, he would take a day's supply of vitamins or medicines and toss them down his open throat all at one time, without water. "What's the difference?" he'd say. "They all go the same place."

In addition to describing Bob's proficiency at chugalugging, Dr. Thompson told of two incidents, with a significant detail that foreshadowed the future.

"Bob and I liked to take long walks. One day, we walked to White River Junction. As we approached through the rail yard, a voice came out of a freight car: 'Hey, Bub, get me a sandwich, will you?'

"It was dusk and we couldn't see who it was, but we went into the restaurant and bought a couple of sandwiches, which we put in the car door. 'Thank you,' said the voice. We asked him where he was going, and he said Portland, Maine.

"Later that year, Admiral Dewey returned from Manila to his home state of Vermont, and there was to be a great reception for him in Montpelier. Bob had the idea of going up there and said that since we didn't have any money, we should try to hop a freight the way that tramp did.

"We found a car with an open door and jumped in, not knowing whether the train was going to Montreal or Boston, upriver or down. Fortunately, it went up the Connecticut River, stopping at every little station along the way as it got colder and darker.

"We made it to Montpelier the next day. When we arrived, covered with straw and somewhat disheveled, Bob decided we needed a few beers, though it was only around breakfast time.

"Going out into the street, we met a Dartmouth man whose father happened to be Governor of Vermont. When we told him we had come to see Admiral Dewey, he invited us to view the parade with the Governor at the State House. So, in spite of our appearance, we were honored by sitting with the Governor (in the background, of course) and watching the procession in real state."

On the whole, that seems to be a harmless escapade; a youngster who would flout his parents' five-o'clock curfew by sneaking out of the house might be expected to grow up into a young man who would hop a freight on impulse.

But the boy who savored a first taste of hard cider, on the sly, had also grown up into a man who considered "a few beers" to be perfectly sensible refreshment at breakfast time.

Dr. Bob spent his last years at Dartmouth doing, by his own account, "what I wanted to do, without regard for the rights, wishes, or privileges of others, a state of mind which became more and more predominant as the years passed."

He was graduated in 1902—" 'summa cum laude' in the eyes of the drinking fraternity," in his own words, but with a somewhat lower estimate from the dean. (More formally, he was a member of Kappa Kappa Kappa.)

In most Dartmouth classmates' recollections of Bob, there was a notable gap of almost 35 years—for reasons that eventually became obvious.

The *Alumni Magazine* of November 1936 included this brief note: "Some of you fellows have been wondering about Bob Smith, but you can let up on it now. Bob says that while he has been in Hanover many times, he could never make it at reunion time. He hopes now to be present in June 1937."

In November 1942, the class reporter noted: "Bob Smith as we know him is now Dr. Robert Smith. [He still hadn't made the reunion.] He has sent me a book, 'Alcoholics Anonymous.' In the past few years, he has been very interested and, I judge, a prime worker in the field of rescuing the pitiable souls who have lost themselves in drink, so far having rescued over 8,000. I know of no more splendid work in the world. 1902 is proud of you, Bob." And in March 1947: "Bob is one of the founders and prime movers of Alcoholics Anonymous, and the story of its growth and achievements is inspiring—especially when I can dig it out of Bob in his own picturesque language. A physician has grateful patients, but Bob has people coming here from all about who worship him. He has redeemed them from worse than death."

(In 1947, A.A.'s Twelve Traditions — including the Eleventh, on maintaining anonymity in the public media—had not yet been accepted formally by the Fellowship as a whole.)

Professor Watson, in a 1958 letter to the A.A. General Service Office in New York, eight years after Dr. Bob's death, mentioned that he had been a subject of discussion among five classmates at a house party on Cape Cod. Two of them had known Bob intimately in college and had later met him on and off in Chicago, Florida, California, and Ohio.

Professor Watson wrote, "We think there has hardly ever been a more widely beneficial uplift effort of any sort so genuine, so fruitful in human rescue, and so practically sensible as your wonderful Alcoholics Anonymous." Using language more flowery than Dr. Bob might have liked, Professor Watson described his late classmate as "a great reformer of himself and others.

"As a class, we are proud to have had as a fellow member so dynamic and socially beneficial a creative figure as Dr. Robert Holbrook Smith, whose influence now extends to the ends of the earth," he said.

But to the youthful Dartmouth graduate of 1902, such a far future would have been even less imaginable than the decades of painful experience that lay immediately ahead.

II. Postgraduate work: M.D. and alcoholic

Now that Bob held a diploma, it was suggested that he set out to make a living and carve a solid, secure future for himself. When it came to things he really wanted, Bob was hardworking. He was also ambitious, and he wanted to become a medical doctor like his maternal grandfather. For some reason we have never learned, however, his mother opposed this quite strongly. He had no choice at the time but to get a job.

Thus, Bob spent the next three years in Boston, Chicago, and Montreal, in a business career that was short, varied, and unsuccessful. For the first two years out of Dartmouth, he was employed by Fairbanks Morse, the St. Johnsbury scales manufacturing company for which his father had once been an attorney.

Arba J. Irvin, another Dartmouth classmate, recalled seeing Bob occasionally when he came to Chicago on business for Fairbanks Morse (and probably to see Anne, who was then teaching school at nearby Oak Park). "Bob wasn't interested in business," Mr. Irvin said. "In fact, every weekend he usually went on a bit of a binge."

After two years with Fairbanks Morse, Bob went to Montreal to sell railway supplies, gas engines, and other items of heavy hardware. A few months later, he moved to Boston, where he worked for a short time at Filene's department store, "which he didn't like and wasn't good at," according to his son, Smitty.

Although Bob's friends were aware of only occasional binges, he was drinking as much as he could afford throughout this period. Signs of progression in his illness appeared as he began to wake up with what he called "the morning jitters." Yet he would boast that he lost only half a day's work during those three years.

If he ignored, denied, or was unaware of his alcoholic progression, he did not deny the lack of progression in his business career. He still wanted to be a doctor, and somehow managed to persuade his family to let him pursue that aim. In the fall of 1905, when he was 26 years old, he entered the University of Michigan as a premedical student.

In spite of Bob's high goals and good intentions, all restraints seemed to ease as he once again set foot on a college campus. He was elected to membership in a drinking society, of which, as he put it, he "became one of the leading spirits . . . drinking with much greater earnestness than I had previously shown." All went well for a time. Then the shakes began to get worse.

On many mornings, Bob went to class and, even though fully prepared, turned away at the door and went back to the fraternity house. So bad were his jitters that he was afraid he would cause a scene if he should be called on.

This happened again and again, going from bad to worse. His life in school became one long binge after another, and he was no longer drinking for the sheer fun of it.

Dr. Bob didn't mention having had blackouts at this time. He said nothing about compulsion, nameless fears, guilt, or the morning drink. Nonetheless, the shakes, missed classes, and binge drinking would have been more than enough to qualify him for A.A. But this was 1907, the spring of his second year at Michigan, and A.A. was 28 years in the future.

Still, Bob did make a surrender of sorts that year. He decided he could not complete his education and tried a "geographic cure" instead. He packed his bags and headed south to recuperate on a large farm owned by a friend.

The hospitality extended to him might have been part of his problem. All through the years of drinking, Bob could call on friends and colleagues to bail him out one more time. They rescued him, covered for him, smoothed things over for him.

After a month on the farm, the fog began to clear, and Bob realized that he might have acted hastily in leaving school. He decided to return and continue his work. The faculty had other ideas, however. They felt that the University of Michigan might survive, even prosper, without the presence of Robert Holbrook Smith. After long discussions, with promises and protests on one side, threats and admonitions on the other, Bob was allowed to return and take his exams.

That he did well might be considered a sign of natural ability and intelligence. It might also be considered a mark of the determination some alcoholics have to work harder, longer, and better than everyone else—for a while.

Following the exams, there were further painful discussions in the dean's office. Despite his good last-minute showing, Bob was asked to leave. But he was given his credits, so that he was able to transfer as a junior in the fall of 1907 to Rush University, near Chicago.

There, his drinking became so much worse that fraternity brothers sent for his father. The judge made the long journey in a vain effort to get him straightened out. In later years, Dr. Bob recalled that his father always met these situations quietly, with an attempt at understanding. "Well, what did this one cost you?" he would ask. And that would only heighten Bob's feelings of remorse.

He kept drinking, with hard liquor replacing the beer. He went on longer and longer binges, waking up with even more intense shakes. Just before final exams, Bob went on a particularly rough drunk. When he came in to take his tests, his hand trembled so badly that he could not hold a pencil. As a result, he handed in three absolutely blank examination booklets.

He was, of course, called on the carpet once again. More promises and protestations. The dean of this medical school decided that if Bob wished to graduate, he must come back for two more quarters, remaining completely dry

This he was able to do, and as a result, he was given his medical degree in 1910, when he was 31 years old. In fact, his scholarship and deportment were both considered so meritorious that he was able to secure a highly coveted two-year internship at City Hospital, Akron, Ohio.

The two years as an intern were problem-free. Hard work took the place of hard drinking, simply because there wasn't time for both. "I was kept so busy that I hardly left the hospital at all. Consequently, I could not get into any trouble," Dr. Bob said.

At one time during his internship, Bob ran the hospital pharmacy. This, added to other duties, took him all over the building. Because the elevators were too slow, he was in the habit of running up and down the stairs, rushing as if the devil were after him. This frenzied activity often brought about an explosive "*Now* where is that cadaverous young Yankee!" from one of the older doctors, who became particularly fond of him.

In 1912, when his two years of internship were completed, the 33-year-old M.D. opened an office in the Second
National Bank Building, Akron, where he was to remain until
he retired from practice in 1948.

Perhaps as a result of the irregular hours and tense work
of a new general practitioner, Dr. Bob developed considerable
stomach trouble. "I soon discovered that a couple of drinks
would alleviate my gastric distress, at least for a few hours at a
time," he said. It didn't take him long to return to the old
drinking habits.

Almost immediately, he began to "pay very dearly physically," to know the real horror and suffering of alcoholism. "I
was between Scylla and Charybdis now," he wrote. "If I did
not drink, my stomach tortured me, and if I did, my nerves
did the same thing." (Smitty noted, incidentally, that the stomach trouble disappeared after his father stopped drinking—
although there was then a bit of insomnia, which led to his
reading a lot at night.)

When things got too bad and Bob was unable to function,
he put himself into one of the local drying-out spots—not
once, but at least a dozen times.

After three years of this nightmare existence, the young
doctor ended up in one of the smaller local hospitals, which,
like other drying-out places and sanitaria in the vicinity, ca-
tered to patients with such socially unacceptable ailments as
alcoholism, drug addiction, and mental illness.

The hospital staff did its best, but Bob couldn't or
wouldn't allow himself to be helped. He persuaded well-
meaning friends to smuggle in whiskey by the quart. When
that source of supply failed, it wasn't difficult for a man who
knew his way around a hospital to steal medicinal alcohol. He
got rapidly worse.

Early in 1914, Judge Smith dispatched a doctor from St.
Johnsbury with instructions to bring Bob home. (In a way, St.

Johnsbury was always home for Dr. Bob. Although he lived and worked in Akron for the rest of his life, he continued to go back to Vermont every year, drunk or sober.)

Somehow, the Vermont doctor managed to get Bob back to the house on Summer Street where he was born. There, he remained in bed for two months before he dared venture out. He was utterly demoralized. Then, it was two more months before he returned to Akron to resume his practice. "I think I must have been thoroughly scared by what had happened, or by the doctor, or probably both," Dr. Bob said.

He was still sober at the beginning of the following year. Perhaps he believed he was that way for good, and perhaps Anne Ripley believed this, too. He went to Chicago to marry her. The ceremony took place in the home of her mother, Mrs. Joseph Pierce Ripley, "at half after eight o'clock" (as the wedding invitation read) on January 25, 1915.

Dr. Bob brought his bride back to Akron and a house on a corner at 855 Ardmore Avenue, a tree-lined street in the fashionable west end of town. The $4,000 house was new then, a two-story clapboard structure with large, airy rooms.

The kitchen was modern and fitted with all the latest conveniences, but Smitty remembered it as being long and narrow. "Dad had one particular chair he sat in. He never varied. That was his seat. Every time someone wanted something from the refrigerator, he would have to stand up. But he wouldn't change.

"Mom was a good cook," he said, "but she didn't care for it. She always wanted to dine by candlelight, and Dad wanted to see what he was eating. We practically had a spotlight overhead.

"He was no help around the house—worse than that. Once, Mother prevailed on him to take the wallpaper off the living-room wall. He stuck a garden hose in the window and turned it on. The house was carpeted. Mother almost fainted.

And he had the worst mechanical ability in the world. I did all the fixing."

The first three years of the Smiths' married life were ideal, free from any of the unhappiness that was to come later. Dr. Bob continued to stay sober, and any lingering doubts Anne might have had were stilled. They were then, as always, an extremely devoted couple. ("Mother was always deeply in love with Dad," Smitty recalled. "I never heard them have an argument." Sue concurred, but did admit to over-hearing what might be called "discussions.")

Dr. Bob's professional life was going smoothly, too; he was developing a reputation as a physician, work he loved. He inspired confidence in his patients. A bit authoritative and difficult to approach, he was sympathetic and understanding once you started talking. And he had a way of looking at you over the top of his glasses. "He was a great one for that," said Emma K. (close to the Smiths in their final years). "Just how you expect a doctor to be."

As Dr. Bob's practice grew, the Smiths made many friends and became respected members of the community. And in 1918, they became parents.

But the year of Smitty's birth was also the year of a national event that had a very different impact on Dr. Bob's life. The 18th Amendment was passed—Prohibition.

At the prospect of the whole country's going dry, "I felt quite safe," Dr. Bob recalled. A few drinks at that point would make little difference, he thought; if he and his friends managed to lay in a modest supply of liquor while it was still legal, it would soon be gone.

And that would be that, he reasoned. He could come to

Anne Ripley was a Wellesley student when she and Bob met; during their 17-year courtship, she taught school.

no harm. His thinking, if not quite logical (except by alcoholic logic), was quite typical at that time. Dr. Bob and the rest of the country were soon to learn the results of the Great American Experiment.

Before the amendment went into effect, he was not aware that the government would oblige him by allowing doctors almost unlimited supplies of grain alcohol for "medicinal purposes." Many times during those "dry" years, Dr. Bob went to the phone book, picked out a name at random, then filled out the prescription that would get him a pint of medicinal alcohol.

Soon, a newly accredited member of American society, the bootlegger, appeared on the scene. Quality was not always his long suit. Yet the family bootlegger was more obliging than a liquor store. He delivered at any hour, day or night, including Sundays and holidays. Sorry, though; no checks or credit.

Dr. Bob started out moderately. Within a relatively short time, he drifted out of control again, but not back into the old pattern, for the progression of his disease was evident.

He soon "developed two distinct phobias," in his own words: "One was the fear of not sleeping; the other was the fear of running out of liquor. Not being a man of means, I knew that if I did not stay sober enough to earn money, I would run out of liquor."

This irrefutable logic led him into a squirrel-cage existence — a 17-year "nightmare." Staying sober to earn money to get drunk . . . getting drunk to go to sleep. Then over again—and again!

Instead of taking the morning drink, which he craved, Dr. Bob turned to what he described as "large doses of sedatives" to quiet the jitters, which distressed him terribly. He contracted what in later years would be called a pill problem, or dual addiction.

Whenever Bob did yield to the craving for the morning drink instead, there was a major disaster. First, he was unfit for work within a few hours. Second, he lost his usual skill in smuggling home enough liquor to put him to sleep. This led to a night of "futile tossing around in bed followed by a morning of unbearable jitters."

There were also occasional binges. Sometimes, he hid out at the City Club or registered at the Portage Hotel under a fictitious name. After all, who would believe "Robert Smith"? "But my friends usually found me, and I would go home if they promised that I should not be scolded," he said.

And yet Dr. Bob managed to keep functioning as a physician. "I had sense enough never to go to the hospital if I had been drinking, and very seldom did I receive patients."

Indeed, his career even advanced during these years. After his start as a general practitioner, Dr. Bob developed an interest in surgery. Following further training at Mayo Clinic in Rochester, Minnesota, and Jefferson Medical School in Philadelphia, he began in 1929 to specialize as a proctologist and rectal surgeon. He was also first-call surgeon in Akron for the Baltimore and Ohio Railroad for many years—that is, if there was illness or accident in the area, he was the first doctor called. This provided him with some extra money and a railroad pass.

But as the drinking years went by, the effort it took to do his work and keep up a façade of normality became more and more grueling. His usual pattern was to stay dry but well-sedated every day until four o'clock, then go home. In this way, he hoped to keep his drinking problem from becoming common knowledge or hospital gossip.

Gradually, the façade was crumbling. Dr. Bob may have thought no one knew, but there is considerable evidence that quite a few people were aware of his problem with alcohol. For instance, at the start of his recovery, when he announced to a nurse at City Hospital that he had a "cure" for alcoholism, her first remark was: "Well, Doctor, I suppose you've already tried it yourself?"

Anne C., an A.A. member who knew Dr. Bob before she ever took her first drink, remembered how he would come down to the lunch counter in the Second National Bank Building and order Bromo Seltzer, tomato juice, and aspirin. "I never saw him eat. One day, I asked Bill, the owner, what was wrong with that man. 'Does he have palsy?' 'No, he has a perpetual hangover,' Bill said."

III. Husband, father, and drunk

Dr. Bob's drinking had its inevitable effect on family life, as well as on professional practice. But his two children were unaware of it in their early years, and their memories of childhood are mostly happy.

In Anne's mid-forties, she was advised that she could not have any more children. Sue was adopted then, five years after the birth of the Smiths' son. "They didn't want to raise Smitty as an only child and spoil him rotten," said Sue. "So they got me and spoiled us both rotten. Oh, we got spankings all right. Not often, but when we did, we really deserved it. We learned early that the louder we yelled, the sooner it was over."

Sue, who was five years old when she was adopted, recalled that she was more frightened than anything else when she first met her father. "I didn't know what to expect. I remember him driving up the big circular driveway at City Hospital and telling me to wait while he went inside for a minute. I thought that was where I was going to live. The first night, I picked a fight with a neighborhood girl and got bawled out. I remember I didn't think that was right at all."

There was only five months' difference in the children's ages. Since school authorities didn't know Sue was adopted, this was hard for them to understand. And both Sue and Smitty remembered their father's answer when they said their teacher had asked them how old their parents were. Dr. Bob said, "Tell them we're 70." They did, causing further mystification.

With his stern, rather forbidding appearance, Dr. Bob was not the type children would flock to. And he wasn't exactly comfortable around them, either. But he made the effort. He would go out and play ball with the neighborhood kids. "We'd have a lot of fun," said Sue, "with 15 or 20 people out there, him six-foot-two and a little kid three years old."

"He *appeared* to be stern," said Smitty. "But he was a real confidant. He would come home and talk to us."

This was echoed by Sue. "He looked stern, but he was really quite a softy."

Smitty also noted that he was 21 years old before he knew that there was any medicine but bicarbonate of soda. "I used to ask Dad for medicine," Smitty recalled, "and he told me, 'Why, hell, son, these are for selling, not for taking.' "

"As a father, he was the best," Sue said. "He was loving and at the same time would want to be obeyed. He was fun to be with. I enjoyed many an evening playing cards and had as good a time with him as I have ever had with anyone."

Sue felt that Dr. Bob's strict upbringing not only was responsible for his stubborn resistance to authority, but also led him to give more freedom to his own children. "As I look back on it," she said, "I see he was ahead of his time, or didn't want us to go through what he did when he was a child, having to go to bed at five o'clock in the evening."

Dr. Bob had tremendous drive and great physical stamina, according to Smitty, who said that except for the effects of drinking, he was never sick a day in his life up until his last illness. "I remember when he was 56 years old, he played six sets of tennis with my sister and me. It wore us both down. He had more steam at that age than anyone I ever knew."

"He wasn't idle much of the time," said Sue. "And he always took off at a run. We often used to take long hikes in the woods—Dad, my brother, myself, and a dog. We had great times like that. He loved to take his car down a dirt road to see where it went."

Their recollections of their mother also show deep affection. "She was quiet and unassuming—a lady in the true sense of the word," Smitty recalled in correspondence with Bill Wilson. "She was of medium build and always battling to keep her weight down. She had a delightful sense of humor and a melodious laugh. All of us spent a good deal of time playing tricks on her, because she took it so well."

One trick that their mother never even suspected was played on her after she started to smoke—at 56! Sue and Smitty were not only stealing her cigarettes, but swiping the butts as well, since all Anne ever did was take a few puffs and lay the cigarette down before lighting another. "If she ever inhaled, it was a mistake," said Sue, who felt that the chain smoking was a sign of the tension created by Dr. Bob's alcoholism. "She was broiling inside. She had to be."

It was the middle of the Depression, and Anne bought a roll-your-own machine. "We thought this was beneath our dignity," said Smitty. "We volunteered to roll her some and mixed pencil shavings with the tobacco. When she lit one, it flamed up, and she had to blow it out. The same thing happened with the next. Finally, she said, 'You know, these don't taste as good as the ones you get in the package.' "

Smitty also remembered that his mother chided him

when she found he had started to smoke. "What about you?" he replied. "You smoke."

"Don't you say anything to me about smoking *now*," Anne replied. "And if you wait until you're 50 years old before you start, I won't say anything to you, either."

Dr. Bob also smoked, but would say, "Me? I don't smoke. Anne's the one who smokes in this family."

"Mom was easily shocked, and her shyness and un-worldliness were a source of constant delight to Dad, who loved to bring home some items of unconventional action and watch her reaction," said Smitty.

"After being involved with drunks for a while, however, nothing could surprise or shock her," he said, as his memories moved ahead to the A.A. years. "Even though their ways might be foreign to her own upbringing, Mother was ex-tremely tolerant of others. She just would not criticize. She always sought to excuse their actions.

"Her advice was never given on the spur of the moment, but was reserved until she had time to pray and think about the problem," Smitty said. "As a result, her answer was given in a very loving, unselfish way and served to steady Dad to a very great degree.

"Mother always had a very deep loyalty to our family, and later to the A.A., which made no personal sacrifice too great. She just would not spend any money on herself, in order to help the family get the things she thought they needed.

"By nature a rather timid person, she could nevertheless rise to great heights if she thought the occasion warranted," said Smitty. "I am thinking of the times when she thought the A.A. program was in danger. When this happened, Mother would be ready to do battle with anyone for the principles she believed were right. I have also seen her rise out of her quiet disposition in defense of Dad or myself personally."

But memories of the family's last pre-A.A. years are naturally darker. As the children were growing up, the Smiths became more or less ostracized by their friends. They couldn't accept invitations—because Bob was sure to get drunk and cause a scene. And Anne, to whom hospitality was second nature, didn't dare ask people to their home for the same reason.

Dr. Bob's alcoholism became more and more noticeable to the children as they grew older. He began to promise them, as well as Anne and their few remaining friends, to stop drinking. "Promises," he said, "which seldom kept me sober even through the day, though I was very sincere when I made them."

Smitty's earliest recollections of his father's drinking, as recorded by Bill Wilson in 1954, a few years after Dr. Bob's death, were mostly about its effect on his mother.

"She was very much opposed to it and had quite a problem with Dad in that when he got on a real toot, he wouldn't come home. I imagine I was 13 or 14. I know I wasn't old enough to drive, so I couldn't go looking for him.

"Mother tried time after time to extract promises from him. He was always going to give it up. He said he would never touch another drink in his life.

"I remember one time she became so desperate that she took me upstairs and said, 'Now I'm going to take a drink of whiskey, and when he comes home tonight, you tell him I'm drunk.' She took a drink of it and tried to act like she was drunk. It ended up in quite an uproar and didn't accomplish much. I don't think he thought she was drunk. He was just embarrassed by the show she was putting on. But you can see how desperate she was to show him what he was doing to himself. I don't think she ever had a drink before or after.

"It was 1933, and times were awful hard," Smitty continued, "not only with Dad, but with everybody. Akron was a one-industry town, and when the rubber shops were down, everything was down. We had a second car, but not enough money to license it. The mortgage moratorium was all that saved our house. And we ate enough potato soup to float that.

"Dad had almost no practice left. He would be in hiding, or home and indisposed. Mother lied to his patients, and so did Lily, his office girl.

"He very seldom drove when he had been drinking," Smitty said. "He had the boys in the central garage trained to drive him home.

"Mother always tried to frisk him when he came in. She wanted to see if she could possibly keep him in good shape for the next morning. But Dad had ways of getting around it. He wore heavy driving mittens during the winter, car heaters being very poor then. He'd put half a pint of medicinal alcohol in one of them and toss it up on the second-story sun porch.

"After Mother had frisked him, he would go upstairs and get his whiskey. When he came down again, it would be obvious he had been drinking. She never did figure that one out."

That wasn't the only trick Dr. Bob had up his glove. Like many another alcoholic before, after, and yet to come, he was expert at obtaining and maintaining his supply.

"If my wife was planning to go out in the afternoon, I would get a large supply of liquor and smuggle it home and hide it in the coal bin, the clothes chute, over doorjambs, over beams in the cellar and in cracks in the cellar tile," he said. "I also made use of old trunks and chests, the old-can container, and even the ash container."

He never used the water tank on the toilet, because "that looked too easy." It was a good thing, too, for if Bob was

Number 855 faced Ardmore Avenue in full respectability. Its rear provided discreet spots for hiding bottles.

expert at hiding, Anne was expert at seeking. This was one place she inspected regularly.

Bob also told the bootlegger to hide booze at the back steps, where he could get to it at his convenience.

"Sometimes I would bring it in my pockets," he said. "I used also to put it up in four-ounce bottles and stick several in my stocking tops. This worked nicely until my wife and I went to see Wallace Beery in 'Tugboat Annie' [where Beery pulled the same stunt in an attempt to deceive Marie Dressler], after which the pant-leg and stocking racket was out."

When beer became legal in early 1933, Dr. Bob thought this might provide a solution to satisfy everybody. And he would not actually have to stop drinking. "It was harmless," he said. "Nobody ever got drunk on beer."

Perhaps Bob had superhuman powers of persuasion. Perhaps Anne was in such a state of desperation, she was willing to try anything. In any case, it was with her permission that he filled the cellar with beer.

"It was not long before I was drinking at least a case and a half a day," he said. "I put on 30 pounds of weight in about two months, looked like a pig, and was uncomfortable from shortness of breath."

Then it occurred to him that if he was "all smelled up with beer," nobody could tell what he had been drinking. So he began to needle the beer with straight alcohol. There were the usual results. "And that ended the beer experiment," Dr. Bob said.

During this beer-drinking phase, in 1934, Smitty had gone with his father to visit Dr. Bob's mother and old friends in Vermont. "I was 16," Smitty recalled, "and got to do most of the driving, because he was drinking. I remember that he was afraid Vermont might still be dry, so we loaded up with cases and cases of beer at the New York line. Then we found out it was wet."

Sue was about the same age, in high school, when her father's problem with alcohol dawned on her. "I remember Mom worrying about where he was, or making excuses," she told Bill Wilson in 1954. "But it really hit me when my friends came to the house. Dad got irritable, and I couldn't understand why. I finally asked Mom, and she told me. He never appeared to be tight, but my friends and I would be downstairs, and he would get annoyed because we were in his way when he wanted to get to his supply in the cellar. My friends just thought he was cross.

"Later, when I knew what was going on, he would get touchy about the subject and would get into little arguments with you. They weren't anything serious. Just enough. Well, he was New England and bullheaded. And I was bullheaded. Dad's drinking never made him mean. He was mostly irritable. He sort of snuck in most of the time. Or he was in bed resting. It got worse and worse. We were in debt, and he was sick many mornings until noon."

The money problems grew. Sue remembered how her mother would have to pay debts with money received for Christmas or birthdays. Emma K. recalled commenting on a beautiful little statuette that had been a Christmas present during this period, only to hear Anne reply, "Oh, my dear, if only they had sent food instead!"

"No, I didn't get annoyed at him, but he did put you on the spot a lot of times," Sue said. "You couldn't be loyal to him and Mom both. I felt that put me in the middle.

"I remember once he asked me to get his bottle for him. I wouldn't do it, and he offered me money. He finally got up to ten dollars, and I still wouldn't do it. That was when I realized I didn't know much about what was going on with him—how much he wanted it.

"I think he felt guilty about things, and he began to make promises to us after he knew we were aware of the problem. I had a dime bank, and of course, I knew how to get the dimes out. I'd open it and find maybe two or three extra dollars there. I think he tried to make it up to me that way."

IV. The physician as co-workers see him

Those who worked with Dr. Bob, while he was drinking and while he was recovering, saw different aspects of the man and his problem.

Starting in the late 1920's, Dr. Bob had been going quite often to St. Thomas Hospital (where he was appointed to the courtesy staff in 1934). It was on one of his first visits, in 1928, that he met Sister Mary Ignatia. She had taught music, but after being ill, was assigned less strenuous duties in the admitting office at St. Thomas, which was run by the Sisters of Charity of Saint Augustine, as it is today.

"Doctor would call and say, 'Sister, may I have a bed?' remembered Sister Ignatia. "I would always recognize his voice with its rich New England accent. He rarely came to the hospital without visiting the admitting office.

"He loved to use slang words. If he was at some big dinner, he'd say, 'Well, we put on the nosebag yesterday.' Or he would come into the admitting office, where I'd have many other people around, and ask about his patient. I'd say, 'I put Mrs. Jones in 408, but there's another patient there.' 'Another patient, Sister?' 'Yes, Doctor, another patient.' 'You mean a frail, Sister.' So the next time I would say, 'Doctor, your Mr. Brown is in 241, and there's a frail in 218.' He would just enjoy it."

Dr. Bob was also in the habit of calling almost everyone by a nickname. "He always called me Abercrombie," said one of the early A.A.'s. Bill Wilson was Willie or, on state occasions presumably, Sir William. Alcoholics in general were U.D.'s, for "unknown drunks." And according to Smitty, the good sister had her nickname as well—Ig. However, he was doubtful that his father ever had the nerve to use it in her presence.

As Sister Ignatia recalled, their first meeting seemed of no particular consequence. She knew nothing of Dr. Bob's problem. "He just always seemed different from the rest," she said. "He brought something with him when he came into a room. I never knew what it was. I just felt it."

Another who thought Dr. R. H. Smith was different— "wonderfully different"—was Betty B., then a young student nurse at City Hospital. "He was known to us as Dr. R. H. S., because there were two other Smiths at City Hospital," she said.

In 1934, Betty had no idea that Dr. R. H. S. was an alcoholic, although she was aware that his hands sometimes shook when he did a dressing and that his eyes were bloodshot. Only years later, when she herself came into the A.A. program, did she learn that City Hospital's Dr. R. H. Smith and A.A.'s Dr. Bob were one and the same.

Yet the problem of alcoholism among staff members was

Some colleagues at City Hospital were unaware of Dr. Bob's drinking problem. Slowly, it became obvious.

not unknown even to student nurses. Betty heard that one doctor who had been chief of surgery was dismissed for this reason. She was told they allowed him to operate surreptitiously. And once, when she was on call, he wheeled someone into the operating room in the middle of the night.

Betty saw Dr. R. H. S. as neither pompous nor condescending at a time when student nurses were at the lowest level in a hospital hierarchy where doctors were demigods, at least in their own estimation.

"He didn't ignore me or any other student," she recalled. "When we'd step aside, as required, at an elevator or door so a doctor could precede us, we all knew Dr. R. H. S. would push us ahead, just as he'd stare above his glasses and growl, 'Sit down, woman,' when we automatically started to rise upon his entrance to the chart room. Most unusual of all, he'd thank us after we'd made rounds with him or helped change a dressing.

"His patients loved him. So did the nurses," Betty said, remembering a time when, in her huge white apron and bib, she was still in awe of doctors and afraid of most of them. But not Dr. R. H. S. "I learned that beneath his abrupt and sometimes gruff exterior, he was kind and understanding, even a little shy."

He called all student nurses "woman," a term that made her feel a little less gauche, a bit more mature. She thinks he knew this and that was why he had chosen this incongruous term for student nurses. A select few, charge nurses he had known and respected a long time, were called "sugar."

Betty remembered that he wore purple striped socks beneath his always-too-short surgical trousers. And his surgical cap, instead of being snugly fitted, was perched high above his ears like that of a rakish baker.

"He kept it simple before A.A., and the nurses who scrubbed for him loved him for it," she said. "His surgical

skills were admired by nurses and doctors alike, yet he used
fewer instruments and other operating paraphernalia than
any other surgeon.

"Over the years, I learned to admire and respect some
doctors," Betty said, "but I didn't like many of them, because
of their attitude. It is hard to find a doctor who is good
professionally and is also a decent, fine man with humility.
This is a very special sort of person, and Dr. Smith was that
kind of man.

"When I became a surgical nurse, I learned that most
surgeons are prima donnas. They have temper tantrums and
they throw instruments. They are arrogant and can make it
pretty rough, especially for a student nurse.

"If things started to go bad in an operation, Dr. R. H. S.
would remain very calm. He made us all feel comfortable,
and there was nothing hurried. His somewhat raspy voice
would become soft and low. Orders were given quietly. The
rougher the going, the more calm he became. This attitude
infected us all.

"There was no screaming, no swearing. He was not snide,
and he did not make off-color remarks to embarrass the students. Others would try to belittle us and would sometimes be
really cruel. Dr. Smith was not that way, and because of that,
we all loved him. I never heard an unkind thing said about
Dr. Smith."

Betty saw him as innately kind and possessed of an inner
strength, and recalled his telling students that pain was the
greatest leveler and that suffering patients should be treated
with equal solicitude and compassion whether they were in
charity wards or private rooms.

Above all, Betty remembers assisting Dr. Bob with a lum-
bar puncture, then dropping the specimen. Instead of reporting her, he merely said, "Well, we'll just have to get some
more." And when her supervisor inquired why they were go-

ing through the complicated and tedious procedure again,
Dr. Bob replied that *he* had "dropped the damn thing" before
Betty could get hold of it, saving her from severe reprimand.

"I don't know whether the supervisor believed that, but
she couldn't say he was lying," Betty said. "So I just . . . well, I
could have kissed the ground that man walked on."

Betty also recalled that Dr. Bob could be blunt. "I got a
call to the O.R. one Sunday afternoon. There was just Dr.
Bob, an intern, the anesthetized patient, and me. Dr. Bob was
not garrulous, and none of us were saying anything.

"The patient was turned over on his abdomen. Dr. Bob,
who was a rectal surgeon, felt there was no point in prepping
them there.

"The intern, who was a rather shy young man with his
head in the clouds most of the time, was sort of leaning on the
patient, using a hemostat to pull hairs out of the rectal area. It
was as though he was plucking petals from a flower—'She
loves me, she loves me not.'

"I'll always remember Dr. Bob saying, 'Um, Doctor?' And
the intern said, 'Yes, Dr. R. H.?' And Dr. Bob said, 'Just how
the hell would you like someone pulling hairs out of your ass?'

"Yes, he was blunt. But there was nothing cross or phony
about that man. I knew that long before I knew anything else
about him. He was just a real guy."

Lily, Dr. Bob's receptionist-nurse, was equally devoted,
according to Sue, who remembered her mother's comment
that Lily "had nothing but praise for him, but said she had a
hard time getting him to tell who was indebted to him. He
didn't like to send out bills, and there were many people he
didn't charge at all."

"That's true," agreed Smitty. "He did more charity work
than he did for his regular patients. I remember how he'd
say, 'Well, I've got three operations this morning—two for the
Lord and one for R. H.' Not only that, but people would come

into his office in desperate straits, and he would literally give them his last cent. He might only have 50 cents, but he'd give it to them."

In 1933-34, of course, there were probably fewer and fewer bills to send out. Dr. Bob's position at City Hospital became precarious, to say the least. There are some who say he was actually dismissed, but no record of dismissal has been found. It is likely that discussion of the matter was in a preliminary or "informal" stage when Bob stopped drinking—just in time. However, his surgical practice had dwindled, and he was supplementing his income through catch-as-catch-can general practice.

More light was thrown on this crucial period by Dr. Thomas Scuderi, later the medical director of what is now Ignatia Hall, the alcoholic ward at St. Thomas Hospital.

Dr. Scuderi, a young intern in 1934 when he first met Dr. Bob, described him as "a big hulk of a man, well built, with a husky voice. He was very good to the interns and residents. Couldn't do enough for you. And when he laughed, you couldn't help but laugh with him."

Dr. Scuderi was not then aware of Dr. Bob's drinking problem, "because everything was on the Q.T. in those days." But he later found out that others knew. He advanced several reasons why Dr. Bob might not have been more severely disciplined than he was.

First, Dr. Scuderi felt Dr. Bob was a better surgeon than most, even though disabled by alcohol. Second, Dr. Bob was extremely well liked by his colleagues, who probably did what they could to cover up for him. Third, there was (and to some extent, still is) a tacit agreement in the medical profession to deny that such problems as alcoholism existed among doctors.

Dr. Scuderi (who in 1977, at the time of these reminiscences, was in his seventies and never did start to drink) said

Dr. Bob always gave help and guidance to younger men. Furthermore, he himself became interested in alcoholism through the example of Dr. Bob and Sister Ignatia, when they established the alcoholic ward at St. Thomas.

"I remember he used to tell the young interns, 'Stay away from alcohol if you're smart. Look at it but don't touch it, because it won't get you anywhere.' He said, 'The older you get, the more tempted you are to drink. Stay away from it.'

"Doctors work under a lot of stress," Dr. Scuderi said. "Alcohol is a temptation. They go to a lot of parties, and they don't think they're mixing with the other doctors unless they have a drink in their hand.

"I don't know anything about him being dismissed from City Hospital. All I know is that he made a terrific comeback in surgery at St. Thomas. And he'd get up at two or three in the morning to help another alcoholic.

"R. H. Smith used to visit the alcoholic ward every day. This was in addition to his regular practice—it was entirely voluntary A.A. work. He couldn't do enough for them. He talked to them in short sentences, very simply. He was very approachable, and he would talk to everybody the same way, whether they were the highest or lowest level.

"When I went to Italy last year, I looked up A.A. in the telephone directory. I said to my brother, 'If only Dr. Smith knew how it is—all over the world today.'"

v. The alcoholic in the Oxford Group

In 1934-35, Dr. Bob's wife and children were existing on the bare necessities and living in a shambles of broken promises, given in all sincerity.

Anne did what she could to hold the family together and prayed that her husband would somehow find an answer to his problem. "How my wife kept her faith and courage during all those years, I'll never know," Bob said. "If she had not, I know I would have been dead a long time ago.

"For some reason, we alcoholics seem to have the gift of picking out the world's finest women," he said. "Why they should be subjected to the tortures we inflict upon them, I cannot explain."

In early 1933, about the time of the beer experiment, Dr. Bob and Anne had come into contact with the Oxford Group. It was a spiritual movement that sought to recapture the power of first-century Christianity in the modern world. Its founder, Frank Buchman, had brought followers into his

First Century Christian Fellowship two decades earlier. His Oxford Group Movement, started in 1921, was based upon the same principles. (In 1939, he changed the name to Moral Rearmament.)

Members of the Oxford Group sought to achieve spiritual regeneration by making a surrender to God through rigorous self-examination, confessing their character defects to another human being, making restitution for harm done to others, and giving without thought of reward—or, as they put it: "No pay for soul surgery." They did, however, accept contributions.

Emphasis was placed on prayer and on seeking guidance from God in all matters. The movement also relied on study of the Scriptures and developed some of its own literature as well.

At the core of the program were the "four absolutes": absolute honesty, absolute unselfishness, absolute purity, and absolute love.

(In 1948, Dr. Bob recalled the absolutes as "the only yardsticks" Alcoholics Anonymous had in the early days, before the Twelve Steps. He said he still felt they held good and could be extremely helpful when he wanted to do the right thing and the answer was not obvious. "Almost always, if I measure my decision carefully by the yardsticks of absolute honesty, absolute unselfishness, absolute purity, and absolute love, and it checks up pretty well with those four, then my answer can't be very far out of the way," he said. The absolutes are still published and widely quoted at A.A. meetings in the Akron-Cleveland area.)

In addition to the four absolutes, the Oxford Groupers had the "five C's" and the "five procedures." The C's were confidence, confession, conviction, conversion, and continuance, while the procedures were: Give in to God; listen to God's direction; check guidance; restitution; and sharing—

for witness and for confession. There were slogans as well: "Study men, not books"; "Win your argument, lose your man"; "Give news, not views." In addition, a member recalled how Groupers would go around smiling enthusiastically and asking each other, "Are you maximum?"

Undisputed leader (as well as founder) of the Oxford Group Movement, Frank Buchman was a Lutheran minister from Pennsylvania, who did not drink or smoke. Buchman looked askance at A.A. in later years, and was never quite comfortable with its members.

Oxford Groupers sought to "change" community leaders, with the idea that their example would motivate others. Thus, there was a great deal of publicity and fanfare when new converts achieved spiritual rebirth. Dr. Buchman himself was often interviewed and widely quoted.

A rubber-company president, grateful because the Oxford Group had sobered up his son, brought some 60 Oxford Group leaders and "team members" to Akron for a ten-day "house party," as their gatherings were called. They held meetings throughout the day, and it all culminated in a dinner for 400 prominent citizens of the community.

This had a substantial impact in local church circles and attracted many new members, who subsequently set up weekly meetings in various neighborhoods (much as A.A. members do today).

Oxford Group influence later waned in Akron for various reasons, including the fact that the rubber-company heir got drunk again. But by this time, the team had moved on to St. Louis to sober up a beer baron's son, a situation that undoubtedly posed ticklish publicity problems for the groupers.

It was Anne who persuaded Dr. Bob to go to Oxford Group meetings in the first place, but he later found himself attracted to members of the group "because of their seeming poise, health, and happiness.

"These people spoke with great freedom from embar-
rassment, which I could never do," he said. "They seemed
very much at ease." Above all, Dr. Bob was impressed because
"they seemed to be happy. I was self-conscious and ill at ease
most of the time, my health was at the breaking point, and I
was thoroughly miserable."

Dr. Bob realized that these newfound friends "had something I did not have." He thought he might profit from an
association with them. If he did not, it wouldn't do him any
harm.

Probably because of his earlier church experiences, his
enthusiasm cooled somewhat when he found that their program had a spiritual aspect. However, it was reassuring to
know that they did not meet in a church, but at the Mayflower
Hotel and in private homes.

Dr. Bob and Anne were regular attenders at the West Hill
group, which met on Thursday nights. He and a few others
might have been alcoholics, but he would not admit this in the
beginning, when "I at no time sensed that it might be an
answer to my liquor problem."

For the next two and a half years, Bob attended Oxford
Group meetings regularly and gave much time and study to
its philosophy. It might be said, in fact, that he then embarked on a spiritual search destined to last for the rest of his
life.

"I read everything I could find, and talked to everyone
who I thought knew anything about it," Dr. Bob said. He read
the Scriptures, studied the lives of the saints, and did what he
could to soak up the spiritual and religious philosophies of
the ages. Still, he got drunk.

Another of the regular attenders at the West Hill meeting
was Henrietta Seiberling, daughter-in-law of Frank A.
Seiberling, founder and first president of Goodyear Tire and
Rubber Company. A graduate of Vassar College, Henrietta

was at the time a young housewife with three teenage children, who were also members of the Oxford Group.

As she recalled it (in 1978, the year before her death), a friend named Delphine Weber asked her one night in March or April 1935, "What are we going to do about Bob Smith?"

"What's wrong with him?" Henrietta asked.

"He's a terrible drinker," Delphine replied, noting that he was having problems at the hospital and was practically bankrupt because of his drinking.

"I immediately felt guided that we should have a meeting for Bob Smith, before Bill [Wilson] ever came to Akron," said Henrietta. She went to fellow Oxford Groupers T. Henry and Clarace Williams and asked whether it would be possible to use their home as a meeting place. They readily agreed.

T. Henry, who was a quite well-to-do inventor responsible for a new process in tire-making, was said to look more like a drunk than most alcoholics, because of his ruddy complexion. He was kidded about this a great deal but took it good-naturedly.

Though T. Henry and Clarace undoubtedly had their own spiritual problems, they were regarded as a saintly couple who freely gave of themselves out of a kind of sustained natural goodness that surfaces for only brief moments in most of us.

Unlike others who shared their memories of the Smiths, Henrietta came close to criticizing Anne, stating that she never shared deeply at meetings and was "very sensitive." Henrietta told of an incident in which Anne was speaking about a situation and using the third person. "I said, 'Anne, would you put that in the first person singular?' She burst into tears. First-person sharing was costly to her pride. But she knew me well enough to know my motive, and she trusted it. You know, we must hold them to the highest.

"Bob was very restrained in his conversation," said

Henrietta. "He was absolutely honest and never gossiped. I hardly know what to say his shortcomings might have been except for drink. He had a strong character—like the Rock of Gibraltar." In his A.A. days, she said, "He never spoke as a 'founder.' He always said, 'I just work here.'"

Having found a place to meet, Henrietta then gathered some Oxford Group members to attend. "I decided that the people who shared in the Oxford Group had never shared very costly things to make Bob lose his pride [through their example] and share what I thought would cost him a great deal," she said.

"I warned Anne that I was going to have this meeting. I didn't tell her it was for Bob, but I said, 'Come prepared to mean business. There is going to be no pussyfooting around.'

"We all shared very deeply our shortcomings and what we had victory over. Then there was a silence, and I waited and thought, 'Will Bob say anything?'

"Sure enough, in that deep, serious tone of his, he said, 'Well, you good people have all shared things that I am sure were very costly to you, and I am going to tell you something which may cost me my profession. I am a secret drinker, and I can't stop.'

"We said, 'Do you want us to pray for you?'

"Then someone said, 'Should we get on our knees?'

"And he said, 'Yes,' so we did." (This was the beginning of the Wednesday-night meeting at the home of the Williamses, who, according to Dr. Bob, "allowed us to bang up the plaster and the doorjambs, carting chairs up- and downstairs." Meetings continued at T. Henry's until 1954, long after the alcoholics had "spun off.")

"The next morning," Henrietta continued, "I, who knew nothing about alcoholism (I thought a person should drink like a gentleman and that's all), was saying a prayer for Bob.

"I said, 'God, I don't know anything about drinking, but I

told Bob that I was sure that if he lived this way of life, he could quit drinking. Now I need Your help, God.' Something said to me—I call it 'guidance'; it was like a voice in my head—'Bob must not touch one drop of alcohol.'

"I knew that wasn't my thought. So I called Bob and told him I had guidance for him. 'This is very important,' I said. He came over at ten in the morning, and I told him that my guidance was that he mustn't touch one drop of alcohol. He was very disappointed, because he thought guidance would mean seeing somebody or going someplace.

"Then he said, 'Henrietta, I don't understand it. *Nobody* understands it.' He said, 'Some doctor has written a book about it, but he doesn't understand it. I don't like the stuff. I don't want to drink.'

"I said, 'Well, Bob, that is what I have been guided about.' And that was the beginning of our meetings, long before Bill ever came."

Later, in 1948, Dr. Bob described what might have been the same conversation with Mrs. Seiberling: "I would go to my good friend Henri and say, 'Henri, do you think I want to stop drinking liquor?' She, being a very charitable soul, would say, 'Yes, Bob, I'm sure you want to stop.' I would say, 'Well, I can't conceive of any living human who really wanted to do something as badly as I think I do, who could be such a total failure. Henri, I think I'm just one of those *want*-to-want-to guys.' And she'd say, 'No, Bob, I think you want to. You just haven't found a way to work it yet.'"

T. Henry Williams thought that Bob's drinking slowed down a good bit after he came to the Oxford Group—from every night to once every two or three weeks—but that he didn't quite find an answer until he met Bill.

This impression of an "improved pattern" was probably created by Bob's desire and ability to hide his drinking, even after he admitted that he had a problem. For, as he said later,

"They told me I should go to their meetings regularly, and I did, every week. They said that I should affiliate myself with some church, and we did that. They also said I should cultivate the habit of prayer, and I did that—at least, to a considerable extent for me. But I got tight every night. . . . I couldn't understand what was wrong."

Sue remembered sitting on the steps at a few Oxford Group meetings and recalled that her mother seemed to talk more freely about her father's problem at this time, although no answer had yet been provided.

She also recalled that there had not been much in the way of religious observance in their own home up to that time. "I know we went to Sunday school every Sunday, but they didn't. Dad made a pledge that he wouldn't go to church and almost kept it until they started to go to J. C. Wright's church once in a while, through Oxford Group connections."

This was the situation on May 11, 1935, the Saturday when Henrietta Seiberling received a telephone call from an absolute stranger.

"It was Bill Wilson, and I'll never forget what he said," she recalled. "'I'm from the Oxford Group, and I'm a rum hound from New York.'

"Those were his words. I thought, 'This is really like manna from heaven.' I (who was desperate to help Bob in something I didn't know much about) was ready. 'You come right out here,' I said. And my thought was to put these two men together.

"So he came out to my house and stayed for dinner. I told him to come to church with me the next morning and I would get Bob, which I did."

Active in the Oxford Group, Henrietta Seiberling hoped that its program would relieve Dr. Bob's alcoholism.

Church Directory
BAPTIST
CATHOLIC
EPISCOPAL
JEWISH
LUTHERAN
NAZARENE

VI. Two alcoholics meet

Bill had called Henrietta out of his own desperation when, after pacing up and down the lobby of the Mayflower Hotel on South Main Street in downtown Akron, he suddenly realized that he needed to talk to another drunk in order to keep from drinking himself.

The Mayflower, with its sleek Art Deco façade, was practically new—the best, most modern hotel in Akron. And on Saturday night, people came downtown to shop, maybe eat at a restaurant, and go to a movie. Ginger Rogers and Fred Astaire were starring in "Roberta" at the Rialto, and James Cagney was featured in "G-Men" at another theater.

There was a festive air in the Mayflower lobby that night—with the warm, tempting laughter Bill remembered

In the lobby of the Mayflower Hotel, a stranger in town turned to this directory, to stay out of the bar.

coming from the bar. Probably, the bar was unusually
crowded and many private parties were being held in the
hotel suites, because guests were gathering for the annual
May Ball given by the St. Thomas Hospital Guild. Sister Ignatia would have been there, along with the young doctor Tom
Scuderi. As a member of the courtesy staff, Dr. Bob, too,
might well have put in an appearance, had he been sober.

Instead of joining the merrymakers at the bar, "Bill got
the guidance to look at the ministers' directory in the lobby,"
Henrietta said. "And a strange thing happened. He just
looked there, and he put his finger on one name—Dr. Walter
Tunks.

"So Bill called Dr. Tunks, and Dr. Tunks gave him a list of
names. One of them was Norman Sheppard, who was a close
friend of mine and knew what I was trying to do for Bob.
Norman said to Bill, 'I have to go to New York tonight, but
you call Henrietta Seiberling. She will see you.' "

As Bill described it, he had already called nine names on
his list of ten, and Henrietta's was the last. Bill remembered
having once met a Mr. Seiberling, former president of Goodyear Tire and Rubber Company, assumed that this was his
wife, and couldn't imagine calling her with such a plea. "But,"
Bill recalled, "something kept saying to me, 'You'd better call
her.'

"Because she had been enabled to face and transcend
other calamities, she certainly did understand mine," Bill said.
"She was to become a vital link to those fantastic events which
were presently to gather around the birth and development
of our A.A. Society. Of all the names the obliging rector had
given me, she was the only one who cared enough. I would

*The Reverend Walter Tunks played important roles in the
beginning of Dr. Bob's sober life—and the end.*

like here to record our timeless gratitude," Bill concluded.

Henrietta, of course, was not the wife of the rubber-company president, but his daughter-in-law. She lived in the gatehouse of the Seiberling estate on Portage Path, a short distance from the Smiths' home.

Henrietta tried to get Bob and Anne over to her house that Saturday. Could they come over to meet a friend of hers, a sober alcoholic, who might help Bob with his drinking problem?

At the moment, Bob was upstairs in a stupor, after having brought home a large Mother's Day plant, putting it on the kitchen table, and collapsing on the floor. It had been all Anne and the children could do to get him upstairs.

Anne merely said at first that she didn't think it would be possible for them to make it that day. But as Dr. Bob recalled, "Henri is very persistent, a very determined individual. She said, 'Oh, yes, come on over. I *know* he'll be helpful to Bob.'

"Anne still didn't think it very wise that we go over that day," Dr. Bob continued. "Finally, Henri bore in to such an extent that Anne had to tell her I was very bagged and had passed all capability of listening to any conversation, and the visit would just have to be postponed."

Henrietta called the Smiths again on Sunday. "Will Bob be able to make it today?"

"I don't remember ever feeling much worse, but I was very fond of Henri, and Anne had said we would go over," Bob went on. "So we started over. On the way, I extracted a solemn promise from Anne that 15 minutes of this stuff would be tops. I didn't want to talk to this mug or anybody else, and we'd really make it snappy, I said. Now these are the actual facts: We got there at five o'clock and it was 11:15 when we left."

Smitty recalled that although his father was pretty nervous, he was sober when they drove over to Henrietta's to meet this fellow who might help him. "I did not sit in on that meeting, of course, being a kid at the time, and Mother wanted Dad to open up in front of Bill. So I have no knowledge of what transpired there. However, I remember Bill came to stay at our house shortly afterward."

Describing his meeting with the man "who was to be my partner . . . the wonderful friend with whom I was never to have a hard word," Bill said, "Bob did not look much like a founder. He was shaking badly. Uneasily, he told us that he could stay only about 15 minutes.

"Though embarrassed, he brightened a little when I said I thought he needed a drink. After dinner, which he did not eat, Henrietta discreetly put us off in her little library. There Bob and I talked until 11 o'clock."

What actually happened between the two men? One of the shortest and most appealing versions came from Dr. Bob's old schoolmate Arba J. Irvin, who at least gave proper recognition to what was to become A.A.'s unofficial beverage—coffee—then selling at 15 cents a pound.

". . . And so they got together and started talking about helping each other and helping the men with similar difficulties. They went out into the city's lower edges, the city of Akron, and gathered together a group of drunks, and they started talking and drinking coffee. Bob's wife told me she had never made as much coffee as she did in the next two weeks. And they stayed there drinking coffee and starting this group of one helping the other, and that was the way A.A. developed."

This is true; but as we know, there was more to it than that. (There is such a thing as keeping it *too* simple.) A number of people had been chipping away at Bob for years. The Oxford Group had a "program." Henrietta had told him, "You must not touch one drop of alcohol." Obviously, Bill brought something new—himself.

What did he say to Dr. Bob that hadn't already been said? How important were the words? How important compared to the fact that it was one alcoholic talking to another? No one can say precisely. Indeed, Dr. Bob and Bill themselves placed slightly different emphases on the factors involved.

In "A.A. Comes of Age," written about 20 years later, after Bill had analyzed the event in the light of subsequent experience, he said that he "went very slowly on the fireworks of religious experience." First, he talked about his own case until Bob "got a good identification with me." Then, as Dr. William D. Silkworth had urged, Bill hammered home the physical aspects of the disease, "the verdict of inevitable annihilation." This, Bill felt, brought about in Dr. Bob an ego deflation that "triggered him into a new life."

Describing their talk as "a completely *mutual* thing," Bill said, "I had quit preaching. I knew that I needed this alcoholic as much as he needed me. *This was it.* And this mutual give-and-take is at the very heart of all of A.A.'s Twelfth Step work today."

In "Alcoholics Anonymous," published almost exactly four years after their first meeting, Dr. Bob noted that Bill "was a man . . . who had been cured by the very means I had been trying to employ, that is to say, the spiritual approach. He gave me information about the subject of alcoholism which was undoubtedly helpful.

"Of far more importance," he continued, *"was the fact that he was the first living human with whom I had ever talked who knew what he was talking about in regard to alcoholism from actual experience. In other words, he talked my language.* He knew all the answers, and certainly not because he had picked them up in his reading."

Whatever Bill said—and in the course of some five hours of conversation, he must have thrown in everything he ever knew or thought or guessed about alcoholism, and told the long version of his story to boot—Bob stopped drinking immediately.

Bill seemed to place more emphasis on what he was saying than on the fact that it was he himself saying it, while Bob indicated that, although it was helpful, he had heard most of it before. Important to him was the fact that *another alcoholic* was telling him. If William James, Carl Jung, and Dr. Silkworth, along with Frank Buchman and all the members of the Oxford Group, had been doing the talking, it would have been just another lecture.

Sue remembered that she kept expecting her parents home almost any minute that Sunday evening, but they didn't come until almost midnight. When they did return, her father seemed more at ease than he had been. Although he still wasn't in good shape, he apparently looked better all around.

"He was quite enthused about his talk with you," she told Bill. "I can remember that. He didn't go into it a whole lot, but I do remember Dad saying that you seemed to hit it off with him more because you both had the same thing. He realized that it wasn't just him. He told me that members of the Oxford Group just didn't have the same type of problem."

As Bill put it, "The spark was struck."

"Then," Bill recalled in a conversation with T. Henry Williams, "the group was formed here in the middle of your group."

"And it grew fast because you folks worked harder, I guess," T. Henry said.

"We had to," Bill said. "We were under awful compulsion. And we found that we had to do something for somebody or actually perish ourselves."

"Bill stayed in Akron," Henrietta said. "There was a neighbor of mine who had seen the change in my life brought about by the Oxford Group. And I called him and asked him to put Bill up at the country club for two weeks or so, just to keep him in town, because I knew Bill had no money left."

It was late May, and while Bill and Dr. Bob may have realized that something very special had happened between them, there is no evidence that they had any idea of its full significance. That is, neither of them said anything to this effect: "Well, we're co-founders of Alcoholics Anonymous, and we better get started writing the Twelve Steps."

Dr. Bob cited another point of identification, the association of both with the Oxford Group, "Bill in New York, for five months, and I in Akron, for two and a half years." But there was a significant difference: "Bill had acquired their idea of service. I had not."

This idea, which Bill brought and Dr. Bob never forgot, was put into action immediately. They started trying to help yet another drunk.

In a letter to Lois, Bill noted that he was writing from the office of "one of my new friends," Dr. Smith, who "had my trouble." He said together they were working to "change" a once-prominent surgeon who had developed into a "terrific rake and drunk." (Conceivably, this could have been the fellow Betty B. remembered—the doctor who wheeled patients into the operating room in the dead of night.)

Bill's letter was dated May 1935, and thus shows they had started carrying the message together at least within two weeks or so of their first meeting.

In this and subsequent letters to Lois, Bill made frequent if casual mention of the Smiths—that he had been there for meals and found the rest of the family to be "as nice as he is"—that he had to "buzz off to Dr. Smith's (Vermonter and alcoholic) for supper."

In one letter with a June date, Bill described Bob and Anne as "people 10 or 12 years older than ourselves" (Bill was then 39, while Bob was 55). "He was in danger of losing his practice," Bill said, "though he is apparently a very competent and mighty popular fellow. You will like them immensely."

In another letter, Bill mentioned that he was going to move into the Smiths' house. Anne, too, wrote to Lois, who reported this kindness to Bill in her next letter. (Bill didn't save letters then; Lois did.)

"Mrs. Smith is quite flattering," he responded. "You see, Bob had been in the group [the Oxford Group] and sort of backslid. They didn't have anyone who really understood alcoholics. And I was used to help him a lot, *I think*."

According to Bill, Anne Smith had decided that practical steps needed to be taken to protect her husband's newfound sobriety. She invited Bill to come live with them. "There, I might keep an eye on Dr. Bob and he on me," Bill said.

The invitation came at an opportune time. Bill was about broke, even though he had received some money from his partners in New York and was again hoping to come out ahead in the proxy fight that had first brought him to Akron.

"For the next three months, I lived with these two wonderful people," Bill said. "I shall always believe they gave me more than I ever brought them."

Each morning, there was a devotion, he recalled. After a long silence, in which they awaited inspiration and guidance, Anne would read from the Bible. "James was our favorite," he said. "Reading from her chair in the corner, she would softly conclude, 'Faith without works is dead.'"

This was a favorite quotation of Anne's, much as the Book of James was a favorite with early A.A.'s—so much so that "The James Club" was favored by some as a name for the Fellowship.

Sue also remembered the quiet time in the mornings— how they sat around reading from the Bible. Later, they also used *The Upper Room*, a Methodist publication that provided a daily inspirational message, interdenominational in its approach.

"Then somebody said a prayer," she recalled. "After that, we were supposed to say one ourselves. Then we'd be quiet. Finally, everybody would share what they got, or didn't get. This lasted for at least a half hour and sometimes went as long as an hour."

Young Smitty was aware of the early-morning prayers and quiet time, but he didn't attend. "I was too busy siphoning gas out of Dad's car so I could get to high school," he recalled.

"All of this would take place after breakfast, which with you around took place as early as six in the morning," Sue said in her talk with Bill. "You'd get down there in your bathrobe and scare the daylights out of all of us. You'd sit there draped around this drip coffeepot, then pour it around for everybody."

"I was more jittery then," Bill said. "Jittery as hell."

"I also remember the bottle on the kitchen shelf," Sue said. "To prove temptation wasn't there."

"Oh yes, I forgot about that," said Bill. "I was adamant on having liquor. I said we had to prove that you could live in the presence of liquor. So I got two big bottles and put them right on the sideboard. And that drove Anne about wild for a while."

"But I don't really remember you coming to the house until Dad went on the medical convention," Sue said.

Bill replied, "I had already started to live there, and he said one day, 'Well, what about my going down to Atlantic City for this convention?' "

This would have been the last week in May, when Dr. Bob had been sober about two weeks. The American Medical Association Convention began the first week of June, and he hadn't missed one in 20 years.

"Oh, no!" said Anne when Dr. Bob brought up the idea. For all her faith, she evidently had a practical side and some instinctive knowledge about alcoholic thinking. Bill, however, was more agreeable to the idea. To him, attending a convention was evidently like keeping liquor on the sideboard; he felt alcoholics had to live in the real world, with all its temptations and pitfalls.

Anne didn't want to go along with it, but she finally gave in.

Dr. Bob, who later recalled he had developed a thirst for Scotch as well as for knowledge, began drinking everything he could get as soon as he boarded the train to Atlantic City. On his arrival, he bought several quarts on his way to the hotel.

That was Sunday night. He stayed sober on Monday until after dinner, when he "drank all I dared in the bar, and then went to my room to finish the job."

On Tuesday, Bob started drinking in the morning and was well on his way by noon. "I did not want to disgrace myself," he said, "so I then checked out."

He headed for the train depot, buying more liquor en route. He remembered only that he had to wait a long time for the train. The next thing he knew, he was coming out of it in the Cuyahoga Falls home of his office nurse and her husband.

The blackout was certainly more than 24 hours long, because Bill and Anne had waited for five days from the time Bob left before they heard from the nurse. She (in response to Bob's call) had picked him up that morning at the Akron railroad station in what was described as "some confusion and disarray."

Bob was not fully aware of what was happening. "Bill came over and got me home and gave me a hooker or two of Scotch that night and a bottle of beer the next morning," he recalled.

As Bill and Sue remembered, however, there was a three-day sobering-up period after what was, incidentally, Dr. Bob's last A.M.A. Convention.

"Do you remember your mother and me going over to the home of his office nurse early in the morning to pick him up?" Bill asked Sue. "We brought him home, and he went to bed. I stayed with him up in that corner room, where there were two beds."

"I know he wasn't in too good shape," Sue said. "Then the dishes of tomatoes and Karo syrup came out."

"That was for the operation," Bill explained. Upon Dr. Bob's return, they had discovered that he was due to perform surgery three days later. "It was a worrisome thing, because if he was too drunk, he couldn't do it. And if he was too sober, he would be too jittery. So we had to load him up with this combination of tomato juice and sauerkraut and Karo corn syrup. The idea was to supply him with vitamins from the tomatoes and sauerkraut and energy from the corn syrup. That was a theory we had. We also gave him some beer to steady his nerves."

As Bill described it on another occasion, this typical tapering-off process took three days. There wasn't much sleep for anybody, but Bob cooperated.

"At four o'clock on the morning of the operation, he turned, looked at me, and said, 'I am going through with this,' " Bill recalled.

" 'You mean you are going through with the operation?'

" 'I have placed both operation and myself in God's hands. I'm going to do what it takes to get sober and stay that way.' . . .

"At nine o'clock, he shook miserably as we helped him into his clothes," Bill said. "We were panic-stricken. Could he ever do it? Were he too tight or too shaky, it would make little difference. His misguided scalpel might take the life of his patient."

On the way to City Hospital on the east side of town, Dr. Bob held out his hand from time to time to see whether the shakes had subsided. Just before they stopped, Bill, who also had his practical side, gave him a bottle of beer.

Bill and Anne went back to the house to wait. After many hours, Bob phoned to tell them that the operation had been successful. Still, he didn't return right after the call. Had he gone out to celebrate? Anne and Bill had no idea; they could only wait.

Finally, Dr. Bob came home. He had spent the hours after the operation making restitution to friends and acquaintances in Akron. The bottle of beer Bill gave him that morning was the last drink he ever had.

Although arguments have been and will be made for other significant occasions in A.A. history, it is generally agreed that Alcoholics Anonymous began there, in Akron, on that date: June 10, 1935.

VII. A.A. number three arrives

With the last drink under his belt and the idea of service in his heart, Dr. Bob was eager to join Bill in finding another drunk to "fix," as they put it in those days.

While Bill's release from the desire to drink had been immediate, Dr. Bob's was not. By his own account, the craving was almost always with him during his first two and a half years of sobriety—although he added, "At no time have I been anywhere near yielding."

One often hears that Dr. Bob never did get over the urge to drink. But his later reactions to thoughts of drinking indicated that the urge was neither constant nor violent. In 1948, he admitted that "I still think a double Scotch would taste awfully good. . . .

"But I have no legitimate reason to believe that the results would be any different," he said. When such an idea did occur, he took it as a sign that he hadn't been paying enough attention to the men in the ward at St. Thomas.

This confirms Bill's theory that his partner was so eager to help others because he found it the best way to stay sober. Dr. Bob held on to this discovery and developed it into the deep conviction shown in his last talk, saying that the Twelve Steps "when simmered down . . . resolve themselves into the words 'love' and 'service.' "

Simmered down—to the essence!

Nothing more was mentioned about the "terrific rake and drunk" they had been working on before Bob went to Atlantic City. However, the minister J. C. Wright sent Bill and Dr. Bob another prospect, who, if not a terrific rake, was a terrific drunk.

This was Eddie R., who lived down the block. Eddie had them enthusiastic one minute and despairing the next. They worked with him throughout the summer of 1935. From the stories told of him, Eddie could have kept an army sober. He was probably just what they needed.

Bill and Dr. Bob learned a great deal about the dos and don'ts of Twelfth Step work in trying to sober up Eddie, whom Bill described at the time as being "able to produce a major crisis of some sort about every other day."

In his letters to Lois, Bill said Eddie was an alcoholic atheist, and his recovery was bound to "create a great sensation. Bob Smith and I started to work on this chap a week ago Wednesday, got him sober. He and his wife made a surrender. He began witnessing to his creditors and was changing very rapidly.

"Sunday came," Bill wrote, "and for the first time, he ate heavily. Do you remember how nervous and depressed it used to make me when I sobered up and ate heavy food? In his case, the result was actual temporary depressive mania, and he rushed away to commit suicide, which he had attempted before, being pumped out just in time."

On this occasion, Eddie headed for the Cleveland docks.

But before jumping—taking a precaution not uncommon with alcoholics—he called the Smiths and informed them of his plans to end it all.

Bill told him to wait until they had a chance to talk. Then he and Bob "tore over to Cleveland in the middle of the night, got him here and to the hospital and commenced to give him the Towns [Hospital] treatment. That, plus more oxidizing, has been magical," Bill wrote Lois, "and is creating a great stir at the City Hospital, where the doctors are all agog, being unable to do anything with these cases." ("Oxidizing" was probably short for "Oxfordizing," but details on "the Towns treatment" are lacking at present. Bill's final drunk had sent him to Towns Hospital in New York City.)

"Meanwhile." Bill continued, "the effect on the group [the Oxford Group] is electric. Differences are being forgotten in this new wonder. Both he and his wife are profoundly changed and are sure to create a great stir in Akron."

A few days later, the "new wonder" was drunk again— eventually causing Bill to describe Eddie's situation as "sometimes so desperate that we have been at the point of putting him in an asylum."

That letter to Lois was followed by one mentioning "another brief but stormy affair with the R——s [Eddie and his wife], which resulted in a frightful explosion which kept us busy from Saturday afternoon until last night. But the smoke has cleared away, and all is very rosy now. Now that he is over the greatest possible bump, I am sure they are all in the clear," Bill said.

Young Smitty, who noted that Bill and his father were "*determined* to make a convert out of somebody at that time,"

Both nonalcoholics, T. Henry and Clarace Williams showed true concern for Dr. Bob and his companions in recovery.

recalled that our co-founders would lock Eddie up in a second-floor room of his house in an effort to keep him sober.

"One time, Eddie slid down the drain spout and was heading merrily up the street, Dad and Bill hot after him— Dad in his car and Bill running him down on foot," Smitty said. "Just before Bill gave out, Eddie did, too, and Bill cornered him and took him back to the house. Shortly after, Eddie lost his house, and he and his wife came to live with us."

Sue remembered the couple's arrival quite vividly, because they got her room, "She would come down in the morning, and she'd be all messed up," she recalled during a talk with Bill.

"He beat her up," Bill said. "I forgot about that. He was very nice to her in front of people, but when he'd get her alone, he'd beat her up and choke her."

This might have had something to do with the "frightful explosion" mentioned by Bill. Evidently, it happened because Eddie's wife had, in the Oxford Group tradition, openly confessed to and made amends for an indiscretion of which Eddie didn't approve. So the limitation in A.A.'s Ninth Step— "except when to do so would injure them or others"—didn't get in by mistake.

Smitty described Eddie as "a borderline mental case and depressive," as well as a confirmed alcoholic. "Folks would feed him baking soda, which would restore his sanity temporarily, and as soon as he got a meal in him, he'd go off his rocker again. They also tried sauerkraut, but that upset his ulcers."

The favorite story about Eddie—one Anne loved to tell—had to do with the time he chased her with a butcher knife. Elgie and John R. (who joined A.A. in April 1939) recalled hearing Anne's account of that interrupted lunch (tuna fish sandwiches and coffee) at the Smiths'. "Out of a clear blue sky, Eddie jumped up, grabbed a butcher knife, and chased Anne upstairs." In Anne's words, as Elgie remembered them:

"I didn't know what to do, so I got down on my knees and started praying. Eddie was gibbering about what he was going to do with that knife, and I just prayed and prayed. I started with the Lord's Prayer, then I kept thinking of different verses. I kept my voice low, in a monotone. I figured sooner or later it was going to bore him. Finally, he started to calm down, and Bill came up and got the knife. To this day, we can't figure out what happened, except Bob says he must have been allergic to tuna fish."

"After that, they thought maybe Eddie wasn't the right one to work on," said Elgie. "But years later, we went to Youngstown in the car, out to the country club where they were holding a big A.A. meeting, and the first thing Doc said was 'Holy Moses!' There was Eddie."

Eddie reappeared at Dr. Bob's funeral, in 1950, when Smitty said, "He came up and asked if I remembered him. He said he'd been dry, I believe, a year at the time and was over in the Youngstown, Ohio, group."

When Eddie had seven years' sobriety, Bill heard from him. Nell Wing, who was Bill's secretary and then became archivist at the A.A. General Service Office, remembers meeting Eddie and wondering how this serene, mild-mannered man could possibly have caused all that trouble.

It is an indication of their zeal that, while trying to deal with Eddie, Dr. Bob and Bill also decided to look for another alcoholic to work on at the same time.

"But where can we find any alcoholics?" Bill remembered asking.

"They always have a batch down at the Akron City Hospital," Bob said. "I'll call them up and see what they've got." He called Mrs. Hall, the admissions nurse, who was a friend of his, and explained that he and a man from New York had a "cure" for alcoholism and needed a prospect to try it out on.

As Bill later recalled, "The nurse knew Dr. Bob of old." She was the one who promptly asked whether he'd tried the new method on himself. "Yes," Dr. Bob replied, somewhat taken aback, "I sure have."

Mrs. Hall did have a prospect—"a dandy." He was a lawyer who had been in the hospital six times in the preceding four months. He went completely out of his mind when drinking, and he had just roughed up a couple of nurses. At the moment, he was strapped down tight. Somewhere during the conversation, she uttered those familiar words: "He's a grand chap when he's sober."

This was Bill D., who would become A.A. number three—"the man on the bed." And he was indeed a grand chap when sober. Akron-area members who now have 30 or 35 years' sobriety remember him as one of the most engaging people they ever knew.

"I thought I was a real big shot because I took Bill D. to meetings," said one Akron member, who noted that Bill, though influential in the area, was not an ambitious man in A.A. "He wasn't aggressive, just a good A.A. If you went to him for help, he would give you help. He would counsel with you. He never drove a car, but he went to meetings every night. He'd stand around with his thumbs in his vest like a Kentucky colonel. And he spoke so slow, you wanted to reach out and pull the words from his mouth. I loved to be around him. He put you in mind of a real 'Easy Does It' guy—Mr. Serenity."

Dr. Bob and Bill did not visit Bill D. right away. First, he was in no condition to see anyone. Second, they thought it a good idea to have a preliminary talk with his wife. And this became part of the way things were done in the early days: Discuss it first with the wife; find out what you could; then plan your approach. It should be noted, as well, that the

alcoholic himself didn't ask for help. He didn't have anything
to say about it.

Bill D.'s complete story is in the Big Book ("Alcoholics
Anonymous"). He recalled his own sense of hopelessness and
despair before the visit from Dr. Bob and Bill. There was the
identification with them, followed by surrendering his will to
God and making a moral inventory; then, he was told about
the first drink, the 24-hour program, and the fact that alcoholism was an incurable disease — all basics of our program
that have not changed to this day.

Bill D. also remembered how he was told to go out and
carry the message of recovery to someone else. One of the
things that really touched him was hearing Bill W. tell Mrs. D.
about a week later, "Henrietta, the Lord has been so wonderful to me, curing me of this terrible disease, that I just want to
keep talking about it and telling people."

Bill D. said to himself, "I think I have the answer.' " Bill
Wilson, he said, "was very, very grateful that he had been
released from this terrible thing, and he had given God the
credit for having done it, and he's so grateful about it he
wants to tell other people about it." To Bill D., that one sentence spoken by our co-founder became "sort of a golden text
for the A.A. program and for me."

Looking back in 1977, Henrietta D. described her husband as "a great alcoholic who, like other alcoholics, didn't
want to get drunk." She saw the whole event from another
perspective. She remembered telling her pastor, "You aren't
reaching him. I'm going to find someone who can if I have to
see everyone in Akron." And she prayed with the pastor of
another church that someone her husband could understand
would visit him in City Hospital, where he had been admitted
with "some kind of virus."

A day or two later, Mrs. Hall telephoned Henrietta D.
"There's a doctor here who has been on the staff for 25 years,

and he thinks he has found a way of helping a man with a drinking problem," she said. "He wants to know if you'll talk to him."

Henrietta agreed. "I went to the hospital, and Mrs. Hall put me in a room, where I waited. Dr. Bob came in. He was a big, rawboned fellow with a coarse voice. 'What kind of bird is this egg when he's sober?' he asked.

"I said, 'When he's sober, he's the grandest man in the world. But when he's drinking, he's the worst.'

" 'Yes, I know,' he said.

"He was gruff, but he had a big heart in him," Henrietta said. "He felt sorry for the wives, because he knew what he had put his wife through. I always felt that it never would have gone over so big if Dr. Bob hadn't said that they didn't want separate meetings, that husbands and wives had been separated long enough. Many years later, they had some closed meetings [for alcoholics only], but they didn't have any then.

"After he had talked to me a little bit, he said, 'There's another man here. He and I think we have found a way to help men with a drinking problem.'

"I thought he meant some kind of expensive cure, and I told him, 'We don't have any money. Our money is all gone.'

"He said, 'If you've got $50 to pay for a private room, whatever we do for your husband won't cost you a cent.'

"I said to Dr. Bob, 'Yes, I have that much.' This was another miracle, because two weeks before, we wouldn't have had *any* money. A man who had borrowed $150 had called when Bill was in the hospital and said he was ready to pay it off. It was a fortune to us, of course.

"Then I said to him [Dr. Bob], 'You're an answer to a prayer.'

"He said, 'No, I'm not an answer to a prayer. I'm trying to keep from drinking myseif.' Then he called the nurse and arranged to have my husband moved into a private room.

"When I went to see my husband, he was all upset about the private room," Henrietta continued. " 'Why did you do this?' he asked. 'You know we don't have the money to pay for it.'

"Then I told him what Dr. Bob said, that whatever he did for him wouldn't cost a cent.

" 'I never heard of anything like that,' my Bill said.

" 'I never did, either,' I said, 'but that's what he told me.'

"Then Dr. Bob went in and talked to my husband. Bill liked him an awful lot. Later that night, he returned with Bill Wilson, and they both talked to him. Then Dr. Bob put my husband on sauerkraut and tomatoes. That's all he was allowed to eat the whole time he was there. But he liked them both and didn't care.

"He was there about five days before they could make him say that he couldn't control his drinking and had to leave it up to God. Well, he believed in God, but he wanted to be his own man. They *made* him get down on his knees at the side of the bed right there in the hospital and pray and say that he would turn his life over to God.

"He came out of the hospital on the Fourth of July, 1935. I'll never forget it. I was out at the lakes with a friend of ours who had a cottage. Dr. Bob, Bill Wilson, Anne, and another young fellow they were trying to get sober, named Eddie R———, came out. (Eddie didn't get it at first, but later he did. I remember him speaking once. He said there were two firsts in A.A.,—the first one who accepted the program, and the first who refused it.) They all came out, and we had a picnic. And it *was* a picnic for me, let me tell you!

"About the second time Dr. Bob talked to me in the hospital, he said, 'The little woman wants to see you at the house.'

"I went over to a friend of mine who had a car and said, 'I'm supposed to go and see his wife, but I'm not going!'

" 'You're going,' she said. 'I'm taking you.'

"When Anne came to the door, I said, 'Are you Mrs. Smith?'

"And she said, 'Anne to you, my dear.' That broke the ice. I thought, 'Such rich people!' I couldn't compare with them, because we didn't have a cent. But I found out that they didn't, either. I remember going out there one Sunday, and there was Bill Wilson eating peas out of a can — not even warmed up.

"Anne was so sweet. Everybody loved her. There was never anything to make you feel she was better than anyone else. When she first talked to me about it, she said, 'Let's you and me stay in the background.'

"She talked to the wives a lot more than I did, because I never was a good talker. And I never was one to talk my troubles out. I kept them to myself. I went to work, but I did all I could in trying to help the others, telling them I had been through the same thing. I thought *my* husband was the worst, you know. And those women felt the same.

"Anne would prod the other wives to talk to new women. And she suggested we go around to their houses, too. I remember I went around to one lady's house. I'd never met her, but I told her who I was and said I wanted to help her. She was doing her laundry and didn't want to be bothered. So that threw a damper on me as far as going to their houses was concerned. She didn't understand what it would mean to her."

Evidently, Anne understood what it meant to Henrietta D., who remembered, "She would call me every single morning and ask me if I had had my quiet time. You were supposed to go by yourself with a pad and pencil and put down anything that came into your mind. Later in the day, it might come to you why. Probably for a year, she called me every single morning: 'Did you have your quiet time? Did you get anything special out of it?' She was wonderful!"

Anne Smith never stopped showing her love and concern for others in this way. Another woman, Peggy, recalled that in the year before Anne died, "there was seldom a morning when she didn't call. Even when they were leaving for Texas to see Smitty, she called bright and early and said, 'I missed you last night' (at the regular meeting of the King School Group). 'Where were you?'

"I said, 'I know you're leaving for Texas. I just didn't want to say goodbye.' I didn't realize I was speaking to her for the last time."

Henrietta D. also met Lois Wilson. "I don't remember how long it was before she came, but she came. I asked her, 'Do you think your husband is ever going to drink again?' She said, 'I *know* he isn't.'

"That meant so much to me," Henrietta said. "She *knew* he wasn't. She didn't just *think* it. She told me she knew from the first that Bill was never going to drink again.

"I came to know that, too, in a flash. I woke up in the middle of the night, and it seemed as though the whole room was light. I didn't see or hear anything, but it just came to me that Bill was never going to drink again. And he never did.

"Oh yes, my Bill became quite enthusiastic. He didn't have any time left for his own business. I told him, 'We don't have a lot, but if you give your time to this work, that's all I care about.' He loved it. It meant so much to him. He was always going someplace in Akron or out of town, wherever they wanted him to come. He liked people, and people liked him."

In the beginning, Henrietta D. had to work on Wednesday nights, when the meetings were held at T. Henry Williams's. But she said that the A.A. custom of refreshments after the meeting began right away, "with everybody talking to everybody, drinking coffee and smoking. . . .

"You say it's the same today? That's really nice.

"Anne calling me every day meant everything to me. I always remember the friendliness and kindness and closeness we all felt. Later, I could go anyplace in the whole United States and find a friend in A.A.

"I felt very sad when someone had a slip. We all prayed for him. I don't think anybody thought the *program* wasn't working. That was because Dr. Bob was so enthusiastic. And of course, Bill was there quite a bit. They were both so *sure*.

"You know, it never dawned on me until later how long Dr. Bob and Bill had been sober. If I'd known it was just a short while, I might not have been so sure it was going to work for my Bill." When Bill D. came out of the hospital, Dr. Bob had been sober only three weeks. "I thought they'd been sober for years. I think my husband thought so, too.

"It was all the Oxford Group then," she recalled. "I remember when I first heard 'Alcoholics Anonymous.' I thought, 'That's the awfulest name I ever heard.' But it stuck.

"We were all members," she said. "One day, Bill Wilson said to me, 'Now that your husband has given up his sins, how about you giving up yours?'

"I told him I didn't have any. 'I don't drink. I don't smoke. I don't go to the picture show or play cards on Sunday.'

" 'That's well and good,' he said, 'but how about self-pity and fear and worry?'

" 'Are those sins?' I asked.

" 'They sure are.'

" 'Well, if they are, I'm full of them, because I have all those,' I said.

"Dr. Bob didn't talk that much. I can't remember his ever leading a meeting. He talked to people privately. He was wonderful at getting surrenders. You know, at first, they made all these men surrender. Out at T. Henry Williams's where they met, Dr. Bob would take them upstairs and make them say that they would surrender themselves to God."

Henrietta D. was a matron in the Akron City Workhouse for 22 years. "When I found out my husband could quit drinking, I thought I could tell these girls how to do it, and they would. But they didn't. There were a lot of women there with alcohol problems.

"We had one nurse that came in," Henrietta recalled. "She had six days in the workhouse and six months ahead in jail. I called the judge and asked him if he couldn't let her stay in the workhouse for six months, because I knew somebody I thought could help her. So he did let her stay there.

"After I explained the program to her, I asked her if she would be interested in it, and she said she would. So I called a lady in A.A., and she came out several times, and the nurse accepted the program with much happiness. She was a lovely girl.

"Yes, I was trying to help," said Henrietta, who might well have been responsible for the first A.A. work in institutions. "I found it difficult missing a lot of things because of work. But I was always so happy to know it was growing. Is it true there are a million people in A.A. today? I hope it will be two million soon."

VIII. The first group forms, in Akron

As Dr. Bob and Bill began working with Bill D., Lois was becoming more and more impatient for Bill to return to New York, where there were also "plenty of drunks to work on." As she put it later, "I was nagging him."

Finally, Bill wrote and explained how important it was to him to stay longer. Not only did he want desperately to succeed in the business venture that had originally taken him to Akron, but he felt that he and Dr. Bob were really on to something in working with other alcoholics.

Lois was glad to learn how much had come from her husband's working with the drunks in Akron. At Bill's urging, followed by an invitation from Anne Smith, Lois took the bus out to Akron on her summer vacation from the Brooklyn department store where she was an interior decorator.

"I loved both Bob and Anne from the start," Lois said. "They welcomed me so warmly and took me right into the household.

"Bob and Bill were very busy at the time. They had just gotten Bill D—— into the program. So Anne and I spent a lot of time together. Anne was the person I related to as another wife of an alcoholic, even though we didn't talk too much about our problems or what was going on. She had a lot of wisdom and a wonderful insight into people. Not only wives and families came to her for advice, but many A.A. members did, too."

Lois described Dr. Bob as being full of humanity. "He definitely wanted to help people in trouble. And he was so excited and enthusiastic about this new thing he and Bill had.

"We grew very close together as families, and used to visit back and forth all the time. Bob and Anne used to come to see us every year. For a time, they were even thinking of buying a house here in Bedford Hills." (The Wilsons moved to that rural area of New York State in 1941.)

In 1978, Lois was still corresponding regularly with Sue Windows. And Smitty had recently stopped in for a short stay while he and his wife and youngest son were on an extended camping trip through the East.

Commenting on the special relationship Bill had with Dr. Bob, Lois said, "Bill had loads of friends, but not many real buddies. Only Mark Whalon in Vermont and Bob Smith. There was Ebby, of course, but with him it was more gratitude—and nostalgia." (Ebby T., Bill's friend in boyhood and drinking pal later, first got sober in the Oxford Group and took that message to Bill.)

"Bill realized, too, that he got things from Bob that he needed to complement his work. He always consulted with Bob. Bob might make suggestions, but he usually went along with Bill."

She recalled how Bob loved rakish, expensive cars and how he liked to drive fast. "It bothered Anne, but not me. I kind of like to drive fast, too," said Lois, at 86 (in 1978).

With Bill D., there were now three recoveries, and all three alcoholics felt that they had to carry the message or perish themselves. There were several failures before Ernie G. became the fourth member, in late July 1935.

Ernie was described as a wild, devil-may-care young fellow, 30 years old at the time. He had joined the Army when he was 14 and had done stints as a cowboy and then as an oilfield worker, drinking and brawling his way around the country.

After Ernie's return to Akron, there were lost jobs and a broken marriage. His parents were deeply religious people, who didn't know whether or not he wanted to stop drinking. He refused to have anything to do with the church.

However, Ernie finally agreed to listen to Dr. Bob and his two friends, who had together found a way to stay sober. He was put in City Hospital, where he was tapered off, as he recalled, "on three ounces of whiskey every three hours, plus some I had stashed away."

Talking with Bill Wilson in 1954, Ernie said that he was in the hospital six days before three men (Bob, Bill Wilson, and Bill D.) came to see him and "put this proposition to me as to whether I wanted any part of the program. I remember Doc emphasizing that it was an illness," Ernie recalled. "He got that across to each individual he worked with."

The young man agreed to give it a try. "I figured that if it worked for them, then there was a chance it might work for me."

They then told him, "Well, in that case, we'd like to have you make a surrender."

"What do you mean by a surrender?" Ernie asked.

"Well, you have to say a prayer."

"I'm not very well prepared to do that, because that's been a little out of my line," he replied.

Nevertheless, they agreed to help him. They said the

prayer and had him repeat it after them. "For some reason or other, I felt quite relieved after making this so-called surrender," Ernie said. "The surrender business was something that was in effect at the time and continued up to a few years later. I don't know when it was stopped. But I believe even today it was a good thing."

When Ernie got out of the hospital, Dr. Bob and Bill still had their hands full with Eddie R., Ernie recalled. "Eddie was full of either baking soda mixed with whiskey or just plain baking soda. It didn't make any difference, because he could get pretty wild on either of them.

"Sometimes, Anne would call me at work because Eddie was causing some sort of ruckus. But by the time I got there, he was as sweet as pie, and you wouldn't think he'd hurt a flea. Then as soon as I'd leave, he'd start acting up again.

"But I was sober, and they wanted to spend as much time with me as possible. I went to Doc's home, where Bill Wilson was staying, and spent a lot of time over there. Shortly after, I got a job selling cars. I didn't have any desire to drink and had a good release in that period."

Sue, especially, remembered Ernie's coming around the house and his helping with Eddie. She also remembered that Ernie was the producer of the first slip in A.A. After a year of sobriety, he started drinking and kept on for seven months.

Sue—who was married to Ernie in 1941, about five years after this—was heartbroken when he got drunk. He never really "jelled," as Doc put it. Following that first slip, he had periodic relapses, which got worse and worse until the time he died.

"They didn't quite know what to do with him," Sue said. "He even got to where he wanted to get paid for speaking at meetings. I never did find out what to do with him." The marriage ended in divorce, and Sue later married her first beau, Ray Windows.

In all fairness, she said, it should be noted that Ernie did help a lot of people during his dry interludes, and that he did once manage 11 years of sobriety, only to slip again.

Both Dr. Bob and Anne objected to Sue's marriage very strongly, not because of Ernie's alcoholism, but because of his slips. Nobody can say that their opposition was right or wrong—only that this was the way it was.

Though Bill said Dr. Bob was always even-tempered, one uncharacteristic incident was recalled by John R., who was still attending the King School Group in Akron every Wednesday night nearly 40 years after he first came to A.A., in 1939. "I remember one time he really got sore," John said. "We had a meeting, about a dozen of us there. Someone brought up Ernie's name. Doc jumped up, and I forget what he called him, but he called him *something*. 'No! No! No! Leave that guy right out of it.' I'll never forget that. Pretty soon, they [Sue and Ernie] were married. Doc didn't like Ernie! Well, Ernie didn't like Doc, either."

Ernie also recalled the entry of A.A. number five sometime in late August or early September 1935. This was Phil S., who probably met Bill Wilson just as Bill was about to go back to New York.

However, Phil didn't sober up until some weeks later. He was given the usual treatment at City Hospital for eight days, then sent out under close guard with Ernie in Doc's Pierce Arrow to look for his own car, which he had lost while drunk.

Phil excused himself "to get a milk shake." When he returned 15 minutes later, Ernie saw he was loaded to the gills. A few days after that, Phil was picked up and sentenced to 30 days in the workhouse.

Dr. Bob's daughter, Sue Windows, recalls vividly the days in her late teens when A.A. changed her family's life.

"He was upset that this should happen after all the sweetness and light," Ernie said. "And somewhat indignant because he was not a bum—other than walking barefoot in the street and being a little dirty.

"But Bill D—— had a talk with the judge, who agreed to release Phil only if he put himself in the hands of Dr. Bob for whatever period Doc thought would be best and would go wherever Doc thought he should go and get straightened out. But if he got drunk within the 30 days, they'd just lock him up again.

"Phil readily agreed to the deal, so we bundled him up and took him to a local drying-out spot, where we put him under lock and key."

After this, Phil stayed sober except for a slip two years later. So if Ernie was A.A.'s first young person—and first "slipper"—Phil S. was A.A.'s first court case. But that was one of the great things about joining up in those days. Practically everything you did was a first.

Smitty remembered how his father and Bill Wilson worked hard during that period to "formulate a little talk or scheme that would interest the other drunks."

Dr. Bob, noting that there were no Twelve Steps at the time and that "our stories didn't amount to anything to speak of," later said they were convinced that the answer to their problems was in the Good Book. "To some of us older ones, the parts that we found absolutely essential were the Sermon on the Mount, the 13th chapter of First Corinthians, and the Book of James," he said.

This was the beginning of A.A.'s "flying-blind period." They had the Bible, and they had the precepts of the Oxford Group. They also had their own instincts. They were working, or working out, the A.A. program—the Twelve Steps—without quite knowing how they were doing it.

As Dr. Bob recalled: "I didn't write the Twelve Steps. I

had nothing to do with the writing of them. But I think I probably had something to do with them indirectly. . . .

"There was hardly a night [during the three months of Bill's stay in the summer of 1935] that we didn't sit up until two and three o'clock, talking. It would be hard for me to conceive that, during these nightly discussions around our kitchen table, nothing was said that influenced the writing of the Twelve Steps.

"We already had the basic ideas, though not in terse and tangible form. We got them . . . as a result of our study of the Good Book. We *must* have had them. Since then, we have learned from experience that they are very important in maintaining sobriety. We *were* maintaining sobriety—therefore, we must have had them. . . .

"All this happened," Dr. Bob said, "at a time when everybody was broke, awfully broke. It was probably much easier for us to be successful when broke than it would have been if we'd had a checking account apiece. . . . I think now that it was providentially arranged."

In addition to Eddie, there were a couple of other alcoholics around in the summer and fall of 1935 who didn't jell. However, they still deserve to become a part of A.A. folklore.

There was a man we'll call "Victor," a former mayor of Akron, and a lady we'll call "Lil," who was the first woman to seek help.

Together, Victor and the lady known as Lil started out to write the "thirteenth step," long before the first twelve were ever thought of. What is more, they say it began in Dr. Bob's office—on his examination table—while he was at the City Club engaged in his sacrosanct Monday-night bridge game.

In any case, Victor decided it was time for him to go home—but Lil was loaded. So he called Ernie to explain the predicament. When Ernie arrived, he saw Lil grab a handful of little pills from Dr. Bob's cabinet.

"We started going around the examination table, and she was trying to get the pills in her mouth," Ernie recalled. "Then she made a dive for the window. I caught her halfway out. She was strong as a horse and used some profanity I never heard before or since.

"I got her quieted, and Doc came. We took her out to Ardmore Avenue and put her in a room in the basement. She stayed there two or three days, and then her people took her home. Of course, they were never too kind about it and thought we didn't handle her right. But we felt we had done all we could for her when she wasn't helping herself any."

They say Dr. Bob was leery of anything to do with women alcoholics for a long time thereafter, although he still tried to help as best he could with any who came along. And Bill Wilson, speaking with Sue Windows in the 1950's, recalled how they all were scandalized by the episode.

"As drunks, I don't know why we should have been," Bill said. "But we felt that the performance of some of those early people coming in would disrupt us entirely. —— ["Lil"], I guess, was absolutely the first woman we ever dealt with."

Bill thought Lil never made it, but Sue said that she straightened out after a few years, got married, and had children. Only it wasn't in the A.A. program that Lil recovered. That was a lesson, too: A.A. isn't the answer for everyone.

Ernie also recalled that Victor had ten quarts of rubbing alcohol in the house about the time of the World Series. It was, of all things, the remainder of the supply that had been used to give his mother rubdowns before she died.

As Ernie told it, Victor asked some gentleman loafers and knights of the road if they ever drank it. "It's better than champagne," one replied. Not thoroughly convinced, Victor gave them a pint and watched from behind the blinds as they drank it. It didn't seem to stiffen them up. In fact, they came back for more.

"Okay," Victor said, giving them another pint. "But this is the last one. If it's that good, it's just what I've been looking for." It lasted through the 1935 World Series between the Detroit Tigers and the Chicago Cubs, which went six games.

Ernie noted that Victor and Eddie R. were both examples of the ineffectiveness of wet-nursing, "which was given up in later years." And no wonder. They required full-time effort on the part of all members.

Ernie remembered, as well, one of the first unsolicited calls made by the early members in Akron. They went up to the man's house and had quite a talk with him. He had to listen and couldn't say much in return, because he was stretched out in bed.

"A day or two later, we went back, and his mother barred the door and refused to let us in, because we made him nervous. 'Besides, he doesn't have any whiskey trouble,' she said."

There were others. One unnamed drunk grabbed the wheel when Dr. Bob was driving, and almost wrecked the car. There was also an Indian waitress who was around for a time.

Smitty recalled how his father would dose the drunks with paraldehyde. "They'd lie there knocked out for 36 hours. Then one of them spilled some in the car, which reeked of the stuff until the day he sold it. The Pierce Arrow was referred to in the family as 'the Ark,' " Smitty said. "Dad, of course, was Noah."

In addition, Bill wrote to Lois about a Detroit man they had been working with that summer of 1935. "He is rather above middle age and typical of many I have seen in Towns," Bill said. "He is not so far advanced, but will get cracked in a couple of years more. Poor chap, he wants to keep it all a very dark secret, so we couldn't draw him out."

As Bill put it, "Scarce an evening passed that someone's home did not shelter a little gathering of men and women, happy in their release and constantly thinking how they might present their discovery to some newcomer." When there was a failure, "They made an effort to bring the man's family into a spiritual way of living [a foreshadowing if not a forerunner of Al-Anon], thus relieving much worry and suffering," he said.

"In addition to these casual get-togethers, it became customary to set apart one night a week for a meeting to be attended by anyone or everyone interested in a spiritual way of life," said Bill. This, of course, was Wednesday night at T. Henry Williams's.

"In those days, everybody had a nice, soft seat, because there weren't many of us," Ernie recalled in a conversation with Bill. "Clarace Williams never had to use more than a couple of straight chairs. There was you, Doc, Bill D——, me, and Phil S——. The rest were Oxford Groupers, what few showed up—13 or 14, all told."

In the beginning, the others would have included T. Henry and Clarace, Henrietta Seiberling, Anne Smith, and Henrietta D.

"The alcoholic squad," as some called it in later years, continued to meet at T. Henry's every Wednesday night from the summer of 1935 through late 1939, moving then to Dr. Bob's for a few weeks, and from there to King School in January 1940.

If, as Dr. Bob believed, the earliest members must have been working the Twelve Steps without knowing it, so was this the first group of Alcoholics Anonymous, though the members didn't know it.

Even then, however, there were undercurrents and a sense of separateness between the alcoholics and the other local Oxford Group members. "The guidance thing the groupers had never went down well with the drunks," Ernie said. "Maybe it wasn't explained thoroughly enough.

"It didn't strike me right from the beginning," he said. "It seemed to be getting a little too technical and detailed. Sometimes I felt like they were using a Ouija board. Me and some of the other alkies felt they put these things down on paper and it was their own personal idea for you. But out of respect for T. Henry, we didn't kick too much.

"On the other hand, we were taking them upstairs and getting them on their knees to surrender, which I felt was a very important part."

The surrender was more than important; it was a must. Bob E., who came into A.A. in February 1937, recalled that after five or six days in the hospital, "when you had indicated that you were serious, they told you to get down on your knees by the bed and say a prayer to God admitting you were powerless over alcohol and your life was unmanageable. Furthermore, you had to state that you believed in a Higher Power who would return you to sanity.

"There you can see the beginning of the Twelve Steps," he said. "We called that the surrender. They demanded it. You couldn't go to a meeting until you did it. If by accident you didn't make it in the hospital, you had to make it in the upstairs bedroom over at the Williamses' house."

Dorothy S. M. recalled the 1937 meetings when "the men would all disappear upstairs and all of us women would be nervous and worried about what was going on. After about half an hour or so, down would come the new man, shaking, white, serious, and grim. And all the people who were already in A.A. would come trooping down after him. They were pretty reluctant to talk about what had happened, but after a while, they would tell us they had had a *real* surrender.

"I often wonder how many people that come in now would survive an experience like that — a regular old-fashioned prayer meeting," said Dorothy, who was then married to an A.A. member, Clarence S., and later came into A.A. herself. (She died in 1971.) "The newcomers surrendered in the presence of all those other people." After the surrender, many of the steps—involving inventory, admission of character defects, and making restitution—were taken within a matter of days.

Dr. Bob, as we know, tackled what is now the Ninth Step of A.A. by consciously starting to make restitution to friends and acquaintances on the same day he took his last drink.

More than 40 years later, a number of "modern," A.A.-oriented treatment facilities were encouraging patients to go through the first five Steps of the A.A. program before they were released—a procedure not much different from what the first group was doing in 1935.

Hospitalization was another must in the early days. Dr. Bob himself was one of the few exceptions. Even prospects who were fairly well dried out when they asked for help were required to put themselves in private rooms at City Hospital for periods ranging from five to eight days. This approach was emphasized partly because Dr. Bob was a physician who was hospital-oriented and believed alcoholism to be a disease. The advantage of having the alcoholic alone in a room as a captive audience also had something to do with it. These patients were allowed only a Bible as reading material. Generally, their only visitors were recovered alcoholics.

This was so much a part of the treatment that Warren C., who came to A.A. in Cleveland in July 1939, recalled that there was considerable debate about whether he should be admitted to the Fellowship, since he had *not* been hospitalized.

So when an A.A. mentions now that they didn't rush the Steps or have all this hospitalization when he came into the program, he's talking about the old days—not the *old* old days.

What was this hospital treatment like? Betty B., the student nurse, witnessed an early example of it, taking place in what she remembered to be the summer or fall of 1935.

"I was doing 3:00 to 11:00 on a posh, private-room floor," she recalled. "This was a place not usually assigned to student nurses. . . .

"I was passing the elevator when its door clanked open, . . . and I was startled to see Dr. Bob shove a dirty, unkempt, unshaven, and obviously intoxicated man out into the hallway. I'm sure my surprise showed. This type of patient was never seen on M3. He obviously belonged two floors below in the charity ward.

"But Dr. Bob, steadying the lurching figure by the scruff of the neck, peered at me over his horn-rimmed glasses and said, 'Now listen to me, woman! I want you to do *exactly* what I tell you to do. *Exactly!* Forget all those things they've been teaching about admitting patients. I don't care what your charge nurse tells you. Don't undress him. Don't give him an admission bath. Forget about the urine specimen. Don't do anything— do you understand? Nothing! I don't care if he wets the bed or pukes all over it. Don't change it. I don't care if he lies on the floor. Leave him there. Just one thing: He's gonna want a drink—I mean whiskey. Tell him he can have all he wants, just as long as he drinks an ounce of paraldehyde before he has the whiskey. Remember, one ounce of each— paraldehyde, then whiskey.

" 'And remember, woman, forget you're a nurse. I'll write the orders so you won't get in trouble. Put him in 306. They know about it downstairs. I'll be around tomorrow morning.' With that, he strode down the corridor, his wild socks, as usual, showing below the cuffs of his blue serge trousers.

"The offbeat patient did just as Dr. Bob predicted. He started to yell for a drink in a very short time. He got the paraldehyde and whiskey, then curled up on the floor, started to snore, and was incontinent of bladder.

"Three hours later, the procedure was repeated, and just

before I went off duty, I looked in on him. He had somehow gotten into bed but waved me away, saying, 'I'm not gonna drink any more of that damned white stuff!'

"And he didn't. I was told to stay out of the room unless he lit his light. But each day, I'd look in, and there was always someone at his bedside, sometimes several people, including women. Then one day, he walked into the utility room where I was rinsing out syringes. Surely, this wasn't the same man! He was clear-eyed, shaved, and smiling. Not only that, he was courteous and obviously well educated.

"The most peculiar thing about this man, however, was the fact that he talked about his drinking problem. He didn't seem unhappy, either. He said now he knew he was going to get better. He had hope! He told me, too, that he was a lawyer and had been born in the South. . . .

"I don't know to this day any more about the patient, but I do know that I had the rare opportunity to see my beloved Dr. Bob in action—carrying that miraculous message." The message was carried to Betty herself some 35 years later.

In addition to hospitalization and surrender, there were undoubtedly other musts, even though Dr. Bob and Bill weren't quite sure what they were. But since it was an experimental program, and they were interested in what worked— the pragmatic approach noted by William James — procedures were changed or modified as they went along.

"You see, back in those days we were groping in the dark," Dr. Bob said. "We knew practically nothing of alcoholism."

Bob understood that the spirit of service was of primary importance for his own recovery, but he soon discovered that it had to be backed up by some knowledge as well. He remembered, for instance, talking for five or six hours to one man who was lying in a hospital bed. "I don't know how he ever stood me," he said. "We must have hidden his clothes.

"Anyway, it came to me that I probably didn't know too much about what I was saying. We are stewards of what we have, and that includes our time. I was not giving a good account of my stewardship of time when it took me six hours to say something to this man I could have said in an hour— *if* I had known what I was talking about."

Medical textbooks weren't very helpful, either, Bob said. "Usually, the information consisted of some queer treatment for D.T.'s, if a patient had gone that far. If he hadn't, you prescribed a few bromides and gave the fellow a good lecture."

Commenting on their own sauerkraut-tomatoes-and-syrup "treatment," Dr. Bob said, "Of course, we discovered later that dietary restrictions had very little to do with maintaining sobriety."

He thus made it sound as though he had given up easily and gracefully on this special supplementary diet, but Ernie, recalling that Bill and Doc were anxious to try anything that might dull the craving for whiskey, indicated that it took a while.

"I can see Doc now with the tomatoes, sauerkraut, a can of Karo syrup, and a big spoon," he said while reminiscing with Bill Wilson. "The men got to where it almost gagged them, taking it straight. He did back down finally on the sauerkraut, but he kept up the tomatoes and corn syrup for years."

Both Sue and Smitty had vivid memories of how things changed after their father met Bill and the two started out to help other alcoholics get sober.

"Things were pretty rough before he stopped drinking," said Sue. "But after that, things were extra nice. Mother was a lot less anxious about Dad, and I think he was a lot more satisfied with himself. Things got better as far as finances were concerned, and we all got along better, too. The whole family had good laughs, and it was really a happy time. Things didn't always stay that way, due to boyfriends and growing up, but as I look back, it was great."

As Sue recalled many years later, she had two things to do every Wednesday night before her folks returned from the meeting at T. Henry's. The first was to make coffee for them and whoever might be coming home with them. The second was to get rid of Ray Windows, the schooldays beau who eventually became her second husband.

"I remember how they stayed up late every night talking," said Sue. "It was good for me, too, because I had always been shy around people and it helped me out a lot in that way. They were strangers one minute, and then they were coming over to the house every night—or even living with us."

"Gradually, I noticed that Dad was staying sober," Smitty said. "This, of course, was in 1935, the depths of the Depression, and nobody had any money. But they had a lot of time, which apparently has been very beneficial.

"As the group picked up a little momentum," Smitty continued, "there began to be more and more people gathering around the kitchen table with their talks and little meetings in the morning. The coffee consumption, I remember, rose to nine pounds a week.

"Some of the earlier people I remember: Ernie G——, who became my brother-in-law, Bill D——, George D——, Walter B——, Henry P——, who is still dry with A.A. to the best of my knowledge, and Tom L——.

"In the meantime," Smitty recalled, "our homelife was much happier, and Dad began to prosper a little bit in his practice, although he was not wealthy by any means. But he was beginning to gain back some respect from the brothers" (in the medical profession).

"He took his work as a doctor very seriously, although he

had a wonderful sense of humor and kidded with anyone who would listen to him. However, he was dead serious when he entered the hospital to do any kind of medical work.

"I never had a chance to know him well during the time he was drinking, but he livened up so much and had such a wonderful time after. It was a phenomenal change as far as my relationship with him was concerned.

"During this period, Dad was enjoying good health. He had always been an extremely active, healthy person, and he had more steam at that age than anyone I ever knew.

"Mother, of course, was tickled to death, and she was trying to live the principles to help him. They became a wonderful pair—very considerate and devoted to each other.

"As the movement continued to grow, Bill and Lois were often visitors at our home, and we loved to have them. Dad and Mother, along with Sue and me, also visited them at their house on Clinton Street in Brooklyn, New York.

"Dad often told me that, although he and Bill saw things from different angles, they never had an argument and their two minds seemed to mesh in developing an intelligent program which they could present to alcoholics."

ix. Twelfth Step approaches evolve

When Bill left Akron in late August 1935, there were four members—possibly five counting Phil, who might have been in the process of drying out.

From that fall to spring, Bill helped Hank P. and Fitz M., among others, get sober in New York. He made a short visit to Akron in April 1936, writing Lois that he had spent the weekend and was "so happy about everything there. Bob and Anne and Henrietta [Seiberling] have been working so hard with those men and with really wonderful success. There were very joyous get-togethers at Bob's, Henrietta's, and the Williamses' by turns."

In September 1936, there was another visit, with Bill's arrival "a signal for a house party, which was very touching," he wrote. "Anne and Bob and Henrietta have done a great job. There were several new faces since spring."

In February 1937, another count was taken, and there were seven additional members in Akron, for a total of 12.

Half of these had or would have some sort of slip, and at least one would never be really successful in the A.A. program thereafter. For most, however, the slip was the convincer. (If we take Dr. Bob's last drink as the founding date of A.A., incidentally, his Atlantic City sojourn does not count as a slip. He, however, referred to it as a slip.)

There were dozens of others who were exposed to the program up to February 1937. Some were successful for a time, then drifted away. Some came back. Others died. Some, like "Lil," may have found another way.

Over this period, Dr. Bob and the early members worked out with new prospects a procedure that was very rigid at first but became more and more flexible and open as the months and years passed.

First, there was the interview with the wife, which was continued into the early 1940's. One early member recalled how Dr. Bob asked his wife, "Does your husband want to stop drinking, or is he merely uncomfortable? Has he come to the end of the road?"

Then Dr. Bob told the man himself, "If you are perfectly sure you want to quit drinking for good, if you are serious about it, if you don't merely wish to get well so you can take up drinking again at some future date, you can be relieved."

"In Cleveland or Akron, you couldn't just walk into A.A. the way you can today," said Cleveland's Clarence S., one of those early members. "You had to be sponsored. The wife would call, and I would go to see her first. I told her my story. I wanted to find out several things about the prospect and his relationship with her. Is he a chronic or a periodic? Then I would know how to approach him, figure out how to reach him. I might set some kind of trap for him. I had a lot of whammy working."

"We didn't know anything about a program of 'attraction,' " said Warren C., speaking of the hectic days of twelfth-stepping in Cleveland in the fall of 1939. "We called the wife, or we would go and see her. We'd get all the background we could on this person—where he worked, what kind of job he had. We might even talk to his boss, because his boss was concerned about his drinking. When we went and sat down with this fellow, we knew all about him.

"In most instances, they wanted to do something about it when you talked with them," said Warren. "We had great enthusiasm in those days, a dedication that sold this program. We transmitted the way we felt about it to the fellow. By the time we were through, most of them at least wanted to try it.

"But not all of them," he added. "I have been kicked out of some of the finest homes in this man's town. 'What? Me an alcoholic? Get the hell out of here!' "

Following this preliminary questioning, the new prospect would be hospitalized and "defogged." Looking back, some members recalled being tapered off on whiskey. Others didn't remember much of anything (because they had been too "fogged," most likely), while the condition of some had not called for special treatment, though they were still hospitalized.

When the newcomer was well enough, all of the members in town visited him every day—three or four in the beginning, 20 or more a few years later. There was a sharing of experience, in the hope that the prospect would "identify." At the same time, Dr. Bob explained the medical facts in plain, everyday language. Then the patient was told that the decision was up to him.

If the newcomer agreed to go along, he was required to admit that he was powerless over alcohol and then to surrender his will to God—in the presence of one or more of the other members. While the emphasis on this was very strong, the earliest A.A.'s agree that Bob presented God to them as a God of love who was interested in their individual lives.

Paul S., who, after a bit of trouble, was to become one of the most active and influential of the early Akron A.A.'s, first met Dr. Bob in January 1936 and saw him then as a gruff and forbidding sort of person.

"I had the impression that he knew what I was thinking, and later learned that he did," Paul said in a conversation with Bill Wilson. "He didn't trust me for some months. He knew I was kidding him.

"Dr. Smith formed the habit of stopping at our house for coffee after office hours on Tuesdays and Thursdays," said Paul. "At first, his topic was honesty, and after several trips, he suggested that I stop kidding myself. Then our topic was changed to faith—faith in God.

"We had much prayer together in those days and began quietly to read Scripture and discuss a practical approach to its application in our lives," he said.

Just about a year later, in February 1937, Paul S. tried to get his brother interested in the program. "I explained to my sister that I couldn't afford to be seen with people like that," said Dick S. "But I would certainly pay Paul's dues if it would keep him from drinking."

J. D. H., who came into A.A. in September 1936, recalled that he was taken care of by the "nine or ten who preceded me." J. D. had met Dr. Bob and heard of his "screwball idea about the drink problem. He was a Vermonter and I was a Southerner, and to me, he had that professional Northern type of attitude—gruff and blunt. But later, after he told me his story, I knew it was just his manner of speaking.

"He was great on slang. He used to call me 'Abercrombie.' Why, I don't know. He'd call up and say, 'Bring your frail over,' meaning my wife. He had a peculiar vocabulary, but a wonderful one. He was an educated man, but some of his slang you didn't hear the ordinary person use."

Smitty noted, however, that while his father used a great

deal of slang, he didn't swear—"not even when he hit his thumb with a hammer. 'Godfrey mighty!' was the strongest thing I ever heard him say."

Although J. D. also had heard about the "cure," it was his wife who sought help for him, as was true in most cases then; the husband didn't either know or have anything to say about it. She called Dr. Bob's home. It was a Monday when he was playing bridge at the City Club, so Smitty and Bill Wilson, who was visiting, came over and picked her up, then took her to see Dr. Bob.

"It was the first time in her life that she had ever gone out with two strange men, not knowing where they were going," J. D. said. "But she was willing to do anything to help me with this drinking situation."

The next day, his wife gave him something to drink and got him to agree to see Dr. Bob on Wednesday. But he had to be completely sober by then.

"We went to see Doc at his office, and he told me of his drinking days," J. D. recalled. "Then we drove to his house on Ardmore, where I met Ernie, Joe D——, Harold G——, and Paul S——. Then they rode me around town practically all day without any lunch, telling me about keeping dry. But no one would tell me *how*."

J. D., one of the few who weren't hospitalized, was invited to attend the meeting at T. Henry's that night. "I met seven other men there who had a drinking problem, together with Dr. Bob and Bill Wilson. They all told their stories, and I decided there might be hope for me.

"I sat under a bridge lamp, with the rest of the crowd facing me. My wife told me I sat there with a silly grin on my face like Calvin Coolidge for the whole night. But I was embarrassed, you know, among strangers. After the meeting, Bill talked to me for about 30 minutes, and the other boys also came up and talked. Then we had coffee in the kitchen.

"The next day, I called some of the fellows, and that night, two of them called at my home. It seems as though we just lived together when I first came into the group—me and Paul S—— and Harold G——. We would go from house to house during the day and wind up one place every night —Bob Smith's."

J. D. wasn't allowed to do anything or to say anything when they called on new prospects. "I was listening and learning and being taught," he recalled.

Finally, he was allowed to talk to a prospect—after everyone else had seen the man. "We used to have almost a set story," J. D. recalled. "And we'd finagle around and wonder who was the best guy to talk to a new man. We wanted to hit him with the right guy at the right psychological time, and we had to tell him about the spiritual part of our program.

"Doc would hit first with the medical facts. He described the slip I had as a relapse, just the same as a diabetic going on a candy binge, for instance. He also emphasized that it was a *fatal* illness and that the only way a man could recover from it—or rather, not die from it—was not to take a drink to start with. That was the basis of the whole thing. In turn, we were pounding it into each other. After this, we got to the spiritual part."

A number of members who joined from then through the 1940's recalled that Dr. Bob used the analogy of the sugar diabetic in explaining alcoholism to new prospects, while others recalled his describing it as an allergy.

"When I asked Dr. Bob how he evolved his thinking on alcoholism," said one member, "he replied, 'If you're allergic to strawberries, you don't eat them, do you? Well, an alky is the same way. He's allergic to alcohol. His body just won't handle it. That's what I'm trying to get over to these guys— that they're actually drinking poison, because their systems just won't tolerate it.' And he said, 'Once you get sensitized to anything, there is no way you're going to handle it from then on.' "

J. D. noted, "We would discuss new prospects, and also how we might help others who were already in the group and might be on the verge of a slip. We tried to anticipate those. For instance, Bob told me one night we should go down and see this fellow who was swearing a lot, had missed a meeting or two, and was just about ripe for a slip.

"We talked about how to get more members and how to handle them. Then we talked about the mistakes we had made in telling our stories. We didn't hesitate to criticize each other. We suggested certain words to leave out and certain words to add in order to make a more effective talk. It made a bunch of amateur psychologists and after-dinner speakers out of us."

During this period, J. D. recalled, he saw Dr. Bob every day of the week, either at his office or in his home. "I was over there four or five times a week in the daytime, and then I'd wind up there at night.

"I've gone to their home on a morning, opened it up, and gone in," J. D. said. "No one up. I'd just go ahead and start the pot of coffee going. Somebody would holler out, 'Who's down there?'—thinking maybe it would be a drunk who had stayed overnight. Anne never knew who would be on her davenport when she got up in the morning.

"She was a sweet, motherly type of woman you couldn't help but love. She didn't care very much for style. If she wanted to go anywhere, she went whether she had a new dress or she didn't. She'd pick up a hat whether it was five years old or ten years old, put it on, and go. I've heard her say she only had one pair of stockings.

"One thing I'm grateful for," J. D. said. "Dr. Bob and Anne had planned to go to Vermont two days before I came into the group. But Anne woke up in the middle of the night and said she felt they shouldn't go—that they would be needed here."

A similar story was told by Dorothy S. M. (whose first husband was Clarence S.). She said that Anne had a "deep sense of believing in her guidance. When she got an idea that something was going to happen or something was right, there wasn't anything that was ever going to sway her," Dorothy said.

"I was down spending the night with her, and we were all going to a picnic on Sunday. On Saturday night, Anne announced firmly that she wasn't going. Something told her it wasn't right. Sure enough, along about five o'clock in the morning, there was a call from Detroit about a man they wanted to send down.

"So we waited for little Arch T——. He stayed with the Smiths for almost a year, because he was too frail, too broke to get a job. Later, he was the beginning of the Detroit group. So that was one instance where Anne's guidance really worked."

Archie T. said, in later years, "I had been taken in off the streets and nursed back to life by Anne Smith. I was not only penniless and jobless, but too ill to get out of the house during the day and hunt for work. So great was Anne's love and so endless her patience with me, so understanding her handling of me, that ten months later, I left a new man, perhaps imbued with just a few grains of that love.

"Their love for each other and for their two children was of such a nature that it permeated the house, and if one lived in that house and were willing, that same love was bound to get under one's skin. In the ten months I lived in their home," Archie said, "young Bob and Susie treated me exactly as another member of the family. Neither of those kids ever, for so much as a single instant, did anything or said anything to make me feel 'out of the family.'

"Anne let me feel my way along without interference, let

me figure things out for myself, knowing, with a wisdom not granted to many, that in that way I would learn and apply in my daily life what I had learned."

For many years, Archie found it very difficult even to tell the story to anyone. Finally, on his tenth anniversary, in 1948, back home in Detroit, he was introducing Anne to 1,500 people when he realized that he must share the story with the others. Archie's anniversary was also the occasion of Dr. Bob's last major talk, from which this book has quoted extensively.

"When I arrived in Akron, I was in pretty tough shape, completely spent physically, mentally, and emotionally," Archie said.

"He was so run-down, there wasn't much left," agreed Smitty. "We thought he was kind of simple."

Archie remembered thinking, "How am I going to get out and earn a living? What do the Smiths think of me, just sitting around doing nothing? Can I gather enough pep to look as if I am gong back to Detroit, and then, once away from them, commit suicide?

"Not a word to anybody of what I was thinking. I was always a self-contained bird. Anne read my thoughts, however. Out of a clear sky, she said, 'Archie, Bob and I want you to know that as long as we have a home, that home will be yours, too.' I do not know what I said or did at that juncture, but I do know that all the weight of depression and fear vanished. Seldom has greater comfort been extended to anyone in such simple words."

Bob E. remembered that he, too, spent a lot of time with Anne. "She had a quiet, soft way of making you feel at home. I shared a good many of my life problems with her. She read the Bible and counseled with me.

"She tried to keep things simple, too. I told her about being nervous and demoralized. She gave me a couple of phrases to say whenever I got downhearted or confused or frustrated. One I remember is: 'God is love.' And I used it consistently."

Bob E. had met Paul S. at a lunch counter early in 1937. Paul, who had been out of City Hospital six months at the time, "had a new homburg and a pack of Lucky Strikes," Bob recalled.

"If you want to know more about why I'm dressed up and in good shape, come to my office tomorrow, and I'll tell you," Paul said.

"The thing was all a mystery," Bob said. "When people came to see me later in the hospital, they didn't tell me how to stay sober. They just told me stories for seven days about how they drank.

"I did show up at Paul's office, and he told me about this program of the alcoholic squad of the Oxford Group. Then he took me out to see Dr. Bob, who was at home with a cold. He was lying on a couch, covered with a blanket.

"He looked at me. I was only 32, and I was shaking so bad, I couldn't hold anything. I remember how I tried to hide my hands. 'You're pretty young,' he said. 'I don't know if you can make it.' Then he said, 'I haven't got any time or strength to waste on this unless you're serious about it.'

"After that, he told me I was headed for one of three things—death, an asylum, or the penitentiary—if I didn't stop drinking. He told that right off the bat to anyone he ever talked to. And you had to make up your mind right then and there whether you were serious or not.

"Dr. Bob said there wasn't any question about my being an alcoholic, that I needed help or I wouldn't be there. He said I was chemically constituted different from the average individual, that I was allergic to alcohol. He stayed away from the spiritual angle. It was put to me on the basis of the fellowship, and what he later called moral psychology.

"He talked to me for three hours, and convinced me to

go to the hospital and give it a try. I told him I didn't have any money, but he said it could be taken care of. 'You go in.' Apparently, they put it on the cuff. Later, A.A. got out of City Hospital because of money problems. But I paid my bill when I got work. I felt I was morally responsible.

"I enjoyed those men coming to see me. Dr. Bob came at least once a day. The last thing I did at the hospital was make a surrender, which I think was very important. You had to be on your knees with another person, praying and sharing out loud. You know, in the first draft of the Twelve Steps, people were to be on their knees when they surrendered. But the other drunks made Bill take it out."

Once released from the hospital, Bob E. maintained daily contact with other members. "Wednesday was the formal meeting, but we met every night," he said. "We were scared stiff. We'd lost everything and were afraid of drinking. Nothing had worked before, and we weren't always so sure that this would."

The day usually started off at Dr. Smith's house in the morning, Bob recalled. "He was trying to work his way back into the hospital at that time, and his practice didn't amount to much. The coffeepot was always on, and somebody was there at all times.

"Doc was just like we were. Later, as he got under more pressure, you could notice that he withdrew more within himself. But then, he was one of the boys and so free with his conversation. When he would come into the hospital, he'd say, 'Roll over. I'm just as tired as you are.' And he'd light a fag and he'd say, 'Well, here's another nail in my coffin.' 'Coffin nails,' he called them.

"Dr. Bob was a prominent man in Akron. Everybody knew him. When he stopped drinking, people asked, 'What's this not-drinking-liquor club you've got over there?' 'A Christian fellowship,' he'd reply. That's because we started meetings with a prayer and ended them that way. The first casualty I remember was Bill J——. He was a salesman and went to Cincinnati. He had sense enough to call. We all chipped in, and we sent Harold G—— down after him. It must have cost us ten or 20 dollars. That was a lot of money then. He found Bill potted in the hotel.

"But money wasn't important," Bob E. said. "I remember I complained that I didn't have a job, and Paul said, 'You do have a job. Your job is staying sober and working at this program. That's a full-time job by itself.' "

Bill V. H., who came into the program in September 1937, recalled that his first impression of Dr. Bob was in the hospital. "I just lay there and enjoyed the conversation. He'd come every day. He said, 'Of myself I am nothing.' I try to have some humility such as I saw in him and Annie. Their doorlatch was always open, and there was always a large pot of coffee back there in their small kitchen. And it was really potent, as any will remember who enjoyed it."

One of the wives hardest to convince was Annabelle G.—probably because her husband, Wally, had brought home an A.A. member he had met in a bar. This was Paul S., who had "busted out" in early 1936. Paul told her that if she wanted Wally to stop drinking, she should talk to Dr. Smith.

Naturally, she was somewhat skeptical. Then her own doctor, who had an office in Dr. Bob's building, told her, "There's a Dr. Smith down on one of the lower floors who seems to have a way with people who drink too much." They went down to see him, but he wasn't in.

Finally, the minister J. C. Wright got a woman to talk to Annabelle and then made an appointment for her with Dr. Bob. This was more than a year later, in the summer of 1937. "I went down and talked to Dr. Smith for about two hours, and still I was very doubtful," Annabelle recalled. " 'Do you think there is any hope for Wally?' I asked.

"He banged on the desk and said, 'After all I have told you, you still have doubts?'

"And I said, 'I certainly do. You don't know my Wally!'

" 'Would it convince you if I call about 15 or 20 men and have them all here in half an hour, men who have the same trouble your husband has? Would that convince you?'

" 'No, it would not,' I said.

" 'Well, try and get him here Saturday,' Dr. Bob said.

" 'I'll see that he gets here.'

" 'I don't want you to see that he gets here. I want him to come under his own power, not drinking. And I want him to *want* to come.'

"Later, Doc called me and said, 'Well, the big boy was in to see me, and I think he was interested. But don't be surprised if he comes home tight. I gave him plenty to think about, but I'm going on vacation. If he thinks it over and wants to be helped, we can put him in the hospital when I come back.'

"Wally kept drinking until Dr. Bob came back, two weeks later. Then Wally went into the hospital. He looked different when he came out, and I thought maybe this was it.

"In the meantime, Dr. Bob called Maybelle L—— [Tom's wife] and told her, 'Get ahold of that dame [Annabelle], or her husband will be drunk before he's been out of the hospital two hours.' So you can see what I was like," said Annabelle.

"She called me and asked me to come over. I was canning peaches and couldn't be interrupted. She said, 'What is more important, peaches or your husband?'

" 'Well, if you must know, the peaches,' I replied. But I went over anyway. And I hadn't been there more than a few minutes before Doc and Anne came in.

"I couldn't let go," said Annabelle. "Maybelle took me upstairs, and I poured my heart out to her. 'Why don't you just surrender him to God?' she said. 'Let go and let God.'

"That night, I couldn't sleep, and all of a sudden I said

out loud, 'All right, God, I can't do anything. Maybe You can. You can take over.' I felt such peace, I went right to sleep.

"Then Anne Smith took me under her wing. She told me a lot and called me up every day. I saw Wally was taking an interest; he was different. So I decided I would find out what it was all about myself. I started to study, and you know, it has done me every bit as much good as it has done Wally.

"We went to meetings, and these people were all friendly. They called each other by their first names and would go around and take care of the new people as they came in. The women would get together, and we'd talk and open up our hearts with all we had kept inside us for so long."

Annabelle recalled that sometimes the women would have separate discussions over at T. Henry's, but not too often. And sometimes they would get together over at the Smiths'.

Reminiscing with Bill Wilson about those days, Annabelle also noted that she and Wally had read a great deal about the Oxford Group meetings being held at the Mayflower Hotel, and it wasn't until later that they realized the meeting at T. Henry's was "sort of a clandestine lodge of the Oxford Group."

"That's right," replied Bill. "Some of the groupers did snoot the Williamses pretty badly about having all those alcoholics."

x. The co-founders face money problems

Word of Akron's "not-drinking-liquor club" had already spread to nearby towns, such as Kent and Canton, and it was probably early 1937 when a few prospects started drifting down from Cleveland. In the beginning, it was in twos and threes. (By 1939, there were two carloads.)

Bob E. remembered that Jane S. was making the 35-mile trip to the meeting at T. Henry's in 1937, about the same time he started. Colorful and vivacious, with a fine sense of humor, Jane is said to be the first woman in the area to have attained any length of sobriety—meaning a few months.

Oldtimers long remembered her story of being left unattended by her husband to supervise the wallpapering of a room. Trouble was, she and the paperhanger started drinking. Each time he began to hang a roll of paper, one or the other of them would walk into it. When her husband came home that evening, both Jane and the paperhanger had passed out, surrounded by empty bottles (as her husband told her later) and all bound up in shredded paper and paste.

In November of that year, Bill Wilson went on a business trip that enabled him to make a stopover in Akron. Bob E. remembered meeting him then for the first time. "You'd just got a new suit of clothes," he said to Bill later. "I don't know what you'd been wearing before, but it must have been a hit-or-miss affair, because Doc made a lot of it. I can't remember whether you had your violin with you then or not, but you would manage to get one if you didn't bring it."

Bill's writings record the day he sat in the living room with Doc, counting recoveries. "A hard core of very grim, last-gasp cases had by then been sober a couple of years," he said. "All told, we figured that upwards of 40 alcoholics were staying bone dry."

Dr. Bob and Bill realized a "chain reaction" had started, and "Conceivably it could one day circle the whole world . . . We actually wept for joy," Bill said, "and Bob and Anne and I bowed our heads in silent thanks."

Up to then, prospects had come to the founders from other cities. Now, the question was whether every alcoholic had to come to Akron or New York to get sober. Was it possible to reach distant alcoholics? Was it possible for the Fellowship to grow "rapidly and soundly"?

This was when Bill began to think of setting up a chain of profit-making hospitals, of raising money, of subsidizing missionaries, and of writing a book of experiences that would carry the message of recovery to other cities and other countries.

Loyally, Dr. Bob sided with Bill on the need for a book, but he was "frankly dubious" about the hospitals, paid missionaries, and fund-raising. He wondered what these complications might do to A.A.'s spirit of service with no strings attached. It was he who suggested that they talk it over with other members in Akron. "Despite his doubts, Dr. Bob strongly backed me up, especially about the need for a book," Bill said.

A strong minority felt they would lose the goodwill of alcoholics, who would think A.A. was a racket if it ever went into the hospital business. These members believed that the basis of the program was free service, with no cost or obligation. They also thought the Fellowship should shun publicity. One member remarked humbly that the Twelve Apostles hadn't needed literature.

It was a long, hard-fought session. But together, Bill and Bob persuaded a bare majority of 18 A.A.'s gathered at T. Henry's to accept the whole package.

Bill returned home, where the New York members received his ideas somewhat more enthusiastically. He started to try to raise the millions that would be needed.

Later, of course, Bill expressed his thanks to that "powerful minority" in Akron. "Their contention that going into big business and hiring paid missionaries would destroy us turned out to be correct," he said. "On the other hand, had the ultraconservatives prevailed, and had we done nothing, A.A. might have got nowhere at all."

Bill eventually saw that this meeting in Akron had resulted in the first real expression of A.A.'s group conscience—instrument of the "ultimate authority"—to which neither he nor anyone else was as yet fully attuned. He cited the incident to illustrate why a strong minority should always be heeded, and concluded that the answer would usually be found in the middle—between the promoters and the conservatives.

A great many questions concerning A.A. structure and policy were to come up in future years. Where did Dr. Bob stand? He certainly was not a superpromoter, but he wasn't an ultraconservative, either.

One of the problems in looking at Dr. Bob and his view of change in A.A. structure is that he is inevitably compared to

Bill. And in relation to Bill, he *was* conservative, but so were many, many other members. Where the organization of A.A. was concerned, Bill saw further ahead than most, and it took the majority a few years to catch up to his thinking. But if Bill was a visionary and ahead of others, Dr. Bob might have been more in touch with what was—the here and now. As has been said by many who knew them both, they balanced each other out.

Bob was likely at first to express caution and prudence—to exert a quiet "censorship"—when Bill expounded some radical new approach. Quite often, Bob made suggestions. And quite often, Bill modified his ideas to fit in with Dr. Bob's. They moved toward, rather than away from, each other—a tendency that we take to be the A.A. way. Between these two men, there was a willingness to agree and act together when it came to doing the right thing for the Fellowship they both loved.

Both were complex individuals—yet able to express profound ideas in a simple way—and there are probably more reasons than we can ever fathom for this ability they had to work together. Love certainly had something to do with it. Loyalty was another ingredient as far as Bob was concerned. It has been said that he found it hard to refuse Bill—his sponsor—anything. Each wanted to agree with the other and was therefore flexible. There was also a good deal of practical thinking involved. As "co-founders," both were shrewd enough to know that they had to be in agreement before anything could get done in the Fellowship.

A.A. structure aside, it might also be noted that Dr. Bob was not entirely conservative when it came to the A.A. program. First, the whole notion of one alcoholic's helping another was considered revolutionary at the time. Second, he and Bill modified what was at first a very rigid approach as they went along. Third, Dr. Bob continued through the years to look for new ideas and experimented with new ways to carry the message.

As early as 1938, for instance, Bill noted in a report to the Alcoholic Foundation (A.A.'s board of trustees, established in 1938 and now called the General Service Board) that Dr. Bob had arranged to take several alcoholic patients out of the state asylum at Massilon, Ohio. "All but one are doing well," he said. And in a letter two years later, Dr. Bob reported on "the boys from Toledo State Hospital (nut factory), which institution seems to have adopted us lately." Bob continued this "institutional" work at least through the early 1940's — perhaps until it was taken up at a group level.

As far as Dr. Bob, the man, is concerned, there is a probability that many people took his conservative appearance to mean a conservative nature. His youthful rebellion against authority, however, does not suggest innate conservativism. In adult years, he took Smitty and Sue to a number of different church services so they could make up their own minds. It was ironic that a doctor should have included a Christian Science church in the search. He was an M.D. and surgeon, yet he once took Smitty, who was suffering from an allergy, to a homeopath, who treated the illness with minute doses of the substance that had caused the allergy in the first place. Bob was open to the possibility of spiritual healing as well.

Later, he proved equally open-minded about the need for changes within himself, to correct character defects that, in his view, he had developed as an only child. These included impatience with himself and others — he wanted what he wanted right now—and an inclination to be intolerant and think only of himself. We have only to look at his record of service to A.A. and its members in order to see the changes in those areas.

"Dealing with all those alcoholics, he heard and saw a lot of different viewpoints," said Smitty. "He learned to adjust."

Though Dr. Bob was never political, Smitty did note that there was one famous office-holder whose very name was enough to evoke a howl of pain and outrage from his father. But Dr. Bob was a Vermonter, after all. And, as was said in those days after the 1936 election results, "As goes Maine, so goes Vermont."

Friends saw Dr. Bob as becoming more openly gracious and softer as the years passed. The Dr. Bob of the late 1940's was not the same man who met Bill Wilson in 1935. He was a man in process—growing throughout the rest of his life in the very program of recovery he did so much to help develop.

If one is not convinced regarding Dr. Bob's nonconforming, nonconservative nature, there is the story of the early A.A. who called on Clarence S. He thought he had stumbled into the first hippie hangout. Clarence was operating the phonograph; Bill Wilson was reclining on the floor playing his violin; and Dr. Bob was shuffling to the tune of "Japanese Sandman," which he loved. Dr. Bob once said that all he ever wanted was "to have curly hair, to tap-dance, to play the piano."

That is hardly a portrait of a "rigid" personality. So it may not be surprising that Dr. Bob's initial doubts about the ambitious new projects were so quickly overcome. Once the idea of a hospital to be run by the Fellowship was approved, Dr. Bob and other members began looking around for an old house that could be converted into a hospital for drunks. As Dick S. later put it, they were sure they "could pick one up in which new men could be inoculated with the A.A. germ."

Though it never came to pass, it was an idea that was to intrigue Dr. Bob for a few years. His practice was still very poor, and he was already giving most of his time to A.A. work. His house was mortgaged, and he was in debt. A salaried position in an alcoholic hospital would have offered him a way out of this financial predicament. And it would have been okay, because he had the approval of the group in Akron.

"I know we got into it one day about money," Elgie R. (John's wife) said, recalling a conversation in the late 1930's when Doc was talking about charging for his services to alcoholics.

" 'You can't do that,' I said.

" 'Why not?'

" 'These people have been conned all over. If you put money into it, it will never work. It's a God-given program, and if you put money into it, you're through.'

"Then there was a time somebody wanted to give them a house or something," Elgie recalled. "I couldn't figure it out, so I said no."

Temptations rarely come only once, to be vanquished and disappear. Whether the attraction is that of money or alcohol, it is likely to surface again and again over the years. Still, there is no evidence to be found, either on or off the record, that Dr. Bob ever charged one cent for his work with alcoholics. Every member interviewed was asked a direct question on this matter, and each replied that there was no charge whatsoever for Dr. Bob's services. Even the physical examination necessary for admittance to some hospitals was provided by another doctor on the staff.

While Dr. Bob was investigating possibilities for a hospital in Akron, Bill Wilson and other members in New York were trying to raise the money they would need. They were making plans for a foundation to accomplish this purpose (and others), since their unaided efforts were largely unsuccessful. But Bill did get to see John D. Rockefeller Jr., who dispatched Frank Amos out to Akron to investigate what was going on.

Mr. Amos, who was soon to become one of A.A.'s first nonalcoholic trustees, did a thorough job of investigating what he referred to as the "self-styled Alcoholic Group of Akron, Ohio." He called on Dr. Bob and attended meetings.

He questioned members and nonmembers, including professional associates of Dr. Bob. He also looked at the vacant
house that the A.A.'s wanted to convert into a hospital.

In his report to Mr. Rockefeller in February 1938, Mr.
Amos said that he had checked up on Dr. Smith as follows:

"Dr. G. A. Ferguson, one of Ohio's foremost eye special-
ists, told me Dr. Smith was a brilliant and skillful surgeon. He
said there were no better in his line within his knowledge. He
stated, however, that for years Smith's drinking had grown
worse, that he, Ferguson, had at different times carted him
home drunk, as had other doctor friends. As a result, his
medical brothers and his patients had about lost confidence in
him, solely because of his drunkenness.

"Nearly three years ago, he [Dr. Ferguson] said, Smith
had stopped drinking, and ever since had been regaining the
confidence of all. He was still today, said Ferguson, just as
skillful a surgeon and as highly regarded by the profession as
he was in his earlier days.

"Ferguson had learned of the work Smith was doing with
alcoholics. Said he didn't fully understand it, but that it
worked. He was for it, and had unbounded admiration for
Smith both professionally and in this work.

"He stated further that Smith was called upon to give so
much of his time, free, to this work with alcoholics that it was
very difficult for him to handle enough professional business
to make a decent living. He thought it was vital for Smith to
continue this work, but that he needed help so he could better
organize it personally and improve his practice."

The next person mentioned in the Amos report was "Dr.
Howard S——, general practitioner at Cuyahoga Falls, aged
about 35. S—— had been an alcoholic and had been cured by
Smith and his friends' activities and the Christian technique
prescribed. S—— said that Smith stood at the top of his
profession. He said Smith was the keystone of the alcoholic

reform movement there, and that something must be done to help him so he could regain more of his remunerative practice and still give much of his time to this work. At present, his work with alcoholics was taking an average of ten hours a day. S—— thought Smith should head a small hospital for this purpose."

The report continued: "Judge Benner—formerly probate judge and for 40 years chairman of the board of the Akron City Hospital. Benner is credited with having put this hospital in the position of being one of the finest in the Midwest.

"Benner said that only physicians of the highest standing were permitted on their staff, and that Smith stood at the top professionally. Benner said further that he knew all about Smith's alcoholic troubles; had seen him come out of them and was with him 100 percent in his fine work. His board, he said, was proud to give Smith fullest privileges in handling alcoholics at City Hospital. He didn't claim to understand the method, but whatever it was, he said it worked and he was for it."

Frank Amos also reported on Henrietta Seiberling's "unstinted admiration for Dr. Smith and his entire group who have followed him," as well as that of the T. Henry Williamses, "who had become so impressed with the work of Smith and his associates that they turn over their home to them twice weekly for religious and social gatherings."

Mr. Amos said that the alcoholic group comprised "some 50 men and, I believe, two women former alcoholics—all considered practically incurable by physicians—who have been reformed and so far have remained teetotalers."

In meeting with a number of the men, their wives, and "in some cases, their mothers," Mr. Amos heard varying stories, "many of them almost miraculous." He noted, however, that when it came to recovery, they were all remarkably alike in "the technique used and the system followed." He described the "Program" as follows:

"1. An alcoholic must realize that he is an alcoholic, incurable from a medical viewpoint, and that he must never again drink anything with alcohol in it.

"2. He must surrender himself absolutely to God, realizing that in himself there is no hope.

"3. Not only must he want to stop drinking permanently, he must remove from his life other sins such as hatred, adultery, and others which frequently accompany alcoholism. Unless he will do this absolutely, Smith and his associates refuse to work with him.

"4. He must have devotions every morning—a 'quiet time' of prayer and some reading from the Bible and other religious literature. Unless this is faithfully followed, there is grave danger of backsliding.

"5. He must be willing to help other alcoholics get straightened out. This throws up a protective barrier and strengthens his own willpower and convictions.

"6. It is important, but not vital, that he meet frequently with other reformed alcoholics and form both a social and a religious comradeship.

"7. Important, but not vital, that he attend some religious service at least once weekly."

Mr. Amos said, "All the above is being carried out faithfully by the Akron group, and not a day passes when there is not one or more new victims to work on, with Smith as their leader by common consent."

Stressing Dr. Bob's importance in the work at Akron, Frank Amos went on to note that even though there were other able men in the group, they all looked to Dr. Bob for leadership.

"There are a few from Cleveland," he said, "but they have not yet found a leader there. Nonalcoholics, Christian ministers, Oxford Groupers, Christian Scientists, and others have tried, and failed. Apparently, with most cases, it takes a former alcoholic to turn the trick with an alcoholic—and a fine physician of excellent standing, himself formerly an alcoholic and possessed of natural leadership qualities, has proven ideal."

Mr. Amos quoted Paul S. as saying, "Most of us have our jobs and can make a good living. I am an insurance man and can go out aggressively for business. Smith, as a reputable and ethical physician, can't be an ambulance chaser or advertise himself. All he can do is meet regularly with physicians and keep up his professional contacts, since from that source he, as a rectal surgeon, must get most of his surgical patients.

"At present, his income is so low that he can't keep an office secretary and finds it difficult to meet his necessary home expenses. Either we must help him, or he must give up most of this alcoholic work."

Mr. Amos said that Paul felt it "would be criminal," at that point, to lose Smith as their leader. "Mr. [T. Henry] Williams, with whom I discussed the same matter, stating that I was speaking for four Christian laymen who were interested, expressed practically the same ideas as [Paul] S——," he said.

Mr. Amos suggested that Mr. Rockefeller confidentially arrange for a monthly remuneration for Dr. Smith for a period of at least two years, until the whole proposition could get well under way and perhaps become absolutely self-supporting in all respects.

He continued, "Dr. Smith has a wife—a lovely, cultured lady who supports him to the limit in this work—and a son and daughter around the ages of 18 and 20. His modest

Always a car buff, Dr. Bob had to settle for an elderly model in early years when most A.A.'s were broke.

home is mortgaged, and he has not been able to keep it in proper repair.

"He needs a competent secretary, not only to receive his calls when not in the office (his office hours are from 2:00 to 4:00 p.m.), but one who is thoroughly sympathetic with this work and who could handle a lot of assignments and details with other reformed alcoholics in routing them to see patients, etc., which Smith himself has to do now.

"Mrs. Smith has her hands full with the home and with her work with wives of alcoholics, also with an occasional woman alcoholic who turns up. Smith says that men can rarely work satisfactorily with women alcoholics. The sex problem makes it difficult. He, as a physician, can and has helped, but his wife and other wives must handle most of this, for which there is a growing need.

"Such a secretary would cost about $1,200 a year," Mr. Amos said, noting that "Smith needs to keep a good car—he now drives an Oldsmobile of somewhat ancient vintage—to afford swift, safe, prompt transportation. He needs better office facilities, not only for his regular paying patients, but to better handle these ex-alcoholics who come to him daily for inspiration and instruction. Altogether, I think a sum of around $5,000 a year for two years should be made available to help make up for his loss of practice, to pay a secretary, and to meet expenses which he cannot possibly handle under present circumstances. I am sold on attempting this at once."

As a kind of postscript, he added: "For reasons which I can explain verbally, not much local financial support can be secured at present. I believe within two years much, if not all, needed support can be secured."

All told, Frank Amos suggested that Mr. Rockefeller donate $50,000 to the movement. But one of Mr. Rockefeller's advisers, Mr. Albert Scott, chairman of the board of trustees of New York's Riverside Church, made the same point as the

minority of members in Akron: that money, property, and
professionalism might "spoil this thing."

Mr. Rockefeller therefore decided against the $50,000,
but he did agree to put up $5,000 for the personal use of Bill
and Dr. Bob. Of this, $3,000 went to pay off Bob's mortgage.
The rest was parceled out to the two co-founders equally at
$30 a week.

In another report made later that year, Amos noted the
movement leaders' strong conviction that "commercialization
of this movement must at all hazards be avoided."

Furthermore, he said, they believed that "early publicity
would be ruinous—because it would result in the few present workers' being swamped with requests from relatives and
friends and from alcoholics themselves. As a consequence,
the whole movement probably would bog down.

"Alcoholics who were reasonably normal mentally and in
other ways, and who genuinely wanted to be cured of their
alcoholism, were the type with whom they had achieved their
greatest success," Mr. Amos said. "On the other hand, alcoholics who were mentally defective, or who were definitely
psychopathic, had proven very difficult problems, and so far,
the percentage of cures had been very low in these cases."

He also stated that members did not want the movement
connected directly or indirectly with any religious movement
or cult; they stressed the point that they had no connection
whatever with any so-called orthodox religious denomina-
tion, or with the Oxford Movement. (Obviously, Amos meant
the Oxford Group; the older, Anglican movement played no
part in A.A. history.) It was also emphasized that they were in
no way practicing medicine but were cooperating with physicians and psychiatrists.

Of the 110 members then in the program, 70 were in the
Akron-Cleveland area, the report said, noting that "in many
respects, their meetings have taken on the form of the meet-

ings described in the Gospels of the early Christians during the first century."

There are several interesting implications in the report:

1. It indicated that the movement in Akron was separating from the Oxford Group as early as 1938. However, this thinking could have been more wishful than real, since Frank Amos might have considered it desirable to present the alcoholic group as nonaffiliated, for purposes of obtaining money from Mr. Rockefeller.

2. The A.A. members of that time did not consider meetings necessary to maintain sobriety. They were simply "desirable." Morning devotion and "quiet time," however, were musts.

3. Members saw that the difficulty in working with women was primarily because of sexual problems. It was considered safer for the nonalcoholic wives to work with them.

4. City Hospital's cooperation in extending "the fullest privileges" to Dr. Bob was on some kind of official basis; he was by no means sneaking patients in just with the help of the admissions nurse.

5. Some members were afraid of publicity, because it might bring in too many prospects too fast.

(It might also be noted that many terms now considered by A.A.'s to be misleading were then used, not only by non-A.A.'s discussing the movement, but sometimes by members themselves: "cure," "ex-alcoholic," "reformed alcoholic.")

XI. Early meetings and Big Book controversies

Whether similar to those of early Christians or not, the meetings at T. Henry's house every Wednesday night were approaching their peak — attended by the alcoholic squad, wives, and other family members, as well as by good friends like Henrietta Seiberling. Some alcoholics, but probably not all, considered themselves members of the Oxford Group during this period. Others might have considered themselves Baptists, Christian Scientists, or Roman Catholics.

As T. Henry described it, a typical meeting in 1938-39 went like this:

"First, there was a set-up meeting on Monday. This was made up of those who had a part in the group and felt a responsibility. We would think about who was going to come and how they might be affected. There were certain new people, just out of the hospital, for instance. We would wonder whose story would mean the most to them and who was the best to lead the meeting. We sat down and sought guid-

ance and direction as to what to put together for the meeting.

"We would ask people to take a certain part and be willing to give testimony, keeping the new person in mind. Usually, the person who led the Wednesday meeting took something from *The Upper Room* [the Methodist periodical mentioned earlier] or some other literature as a subject. Sometimes, they selected a theme such as 'My Utmost Effort' or 'My Highest Goal.' There would be a quiet time. Then different people would tell something out of their own experience.

"After the meeting," T. Henry continued, "we might take the new man upstairs, and a group of men would ask him to surrender his life to God and start in to really live up to the four absolutes and also to go out and help the other men who needed it.

"This was in the form of a prayer group. Several of the boys would pray together, and the new man would make his own prayer, asking God to take alcohol out of his life, and when he was through, he would say, 'Thank You, God, for taking it out of my life.' During the prayer, he usually made a declaration of his willingness to turn his life over to God."

Clarence S. (from Cleveland) remembered that it was the "most surrendered" people who set up the meeting on Wednesday nights. There were those who were only "surrendered" (usually the alcoholics, who were a minority), compared to those who were "more surrendered" or even better, "most surrendered" (both of the latter usually nonalcoholics). In any case, Clarence thought it "amazing" that so many of the "more and most surrendered" would write down the same name on their pads for leader of the meeting.

"The leader would open with a prayer, then read Scrip-

In this house, the hospitality of T. Henry and Clarace Williams was extended to "the alcoholic squad."

ture," Clarence recalled. "Then he would spend 20 to 30 minutes giving witness—that is, telling about his past life. Then it
would open for witness from the floor. And it would get
pretty emotional. I thought one of the women was a madam
and that another was one of her girls, the way they sobbed
and cried about their sinful lives."

Clarence also recalled one Oxford Grouper holding up
his pipe and saying dramatically, "This is my worst sin."

" 'Oh yeah?' I thought. 'Well, that pipe will never take you
to the gutter.' "

J. D. H. (the Southerner who joined the Akron group in
1936) remembered one woman who "used to get on my
nerves with her constant chatter. One day, I called her into T.
Henry's study and said, 'I don't like you for some reason or
other.' (In those days, you were supposed to 'check' people.)
'You interrupt and talk too much. I'm getting a lot of resentment here, and I don't like it, and I'm afraid I'll get drunk
over it.'

"She laughed and said something. Then we sat down and
had a very pleasant visit. And I lost all resentment."

J. D., who apparently had his problems with "the spiritual
part" of the alcoholics' program, told Bill Wilson how Ernie G.
and Paul S. were at his house one day trying to explain it to
him, when Ernie said, "Why, Jesus Christ is sitting right on
the arm of that chair by you. Damn it, He wants to help you if
you just reach out your hand."

"Well, I did chuckle for a few minutes," J. D. said. "Then I
got to thinking about it—'Maybe the guy is right.' And I began to give this thing a great deal of spiritual thought after
that. You know how crudely Ernie talked. But I would listen
to him trying to explain it to me a lot quicker than I would a
polished man like T. Henry. Isn't that peculiar?"

Wally G. (whose sobriety overcame wife Annabelle's original doubts) noted that not too much was said about alcohol-

ism or drinking in the testimonials. "That was conversation the alcoholics had among themselves. T. Henry was apt to have a number of Oxford Group guests who were visiting. Their witnessing would have nothing to do with alcohol.

"You would be surprised how little talk there was of drinking experience even among ourselves," Wally said. "That was usually kept for the interviews with new prospects in the hospital. We were more interested in our everyday life than we were in reminiscing about drinking."

Wally also noted that almost everyone in the room made some sort of witness. "For one thing, Dr. Bob urged us to say something as quickly as we could at the meeting, with the general idea that if you did make a statement, you were then likely to stay with it.

"After the meeting closed with the Lord's Prayer, all the men beat it to the kitchen for coffee, and most of the women sat around talking to each other," said Wally. "Usually, the social part of the evening lasted from an hour to an hour and a half. But it wasn't until we started going to Kessler's Donut Shop that it became a real social hour."

Bill V. H. (one of the Akron newcomers of 1937) noted how T. Henry and Clarace "did all they could to make us feel comfortable." But Bill was not too strong on the surrender, "because it was throwing the spiritual right at the new person. It was too hard. We were supposed to share all our sins besides alcohol with the new man and encourage him to do the same, but few actually did it."

By 1939, the emphasis on surrender had changed to such a degree that Ernie G. the second (a later arrival—not the Ernie G. who became Dr. Bob's son-in-law) attended several meetings before he and his wife, Ruth, made theirs.

"We were supposed to get there early," Ernie said. "I went up to the bedroom with the two I picked, T. Henry and Tom L——. They told me that if I had anything on my mind, to throw it out. 'It will never leave this room.' I said there was nothing really bothering me, and they said, 'Let's pray about it.' The three of us knelt down, and each one of us gave up a little prayer. I had something to surrender, but I wasn't about to tell them all of my escapades or anything like that. I never have, since I've been in A.A. I have never, never gotten up at a meeting and gone into a drunkalog. I never expect to."

"I never missed a meeting at the Williamses'," said Bob E. "We all looked forward to the Wednesday nights. That was the night of the week."

As he remembered it, Dr. Bob and T. Henry "teamed" the meeting; T. Henry took care of the prayers with which the meeting was opened and closed. "There were only a half dozen in the Oxford Group," he said. "We [the alcoholics] had more than that. Sometimes, we'd go downstairs and have our meeting, and the Oxford Group would have theirs in the sitting room."

"I looked forward to the meetings down in Akron more than I ever did to any dates when I was young," recalled Dorothy S. M., then Clarence's wife. "We went down there for a year and a half, missing only two, because the weather was absolutely impossible. Every week, we would run around and pick up people. Finally, we were going down with eight people in two cars."

Clarence S. was one of those who came from Cleveland at the beginning of 1938 to be "fixed" by Dr. Bob. His wife, who later became very close to Anne and Dr. Bob, had talked to a number of ministers and doctors before her sister Virginia in New York, who was a patient of Bill Wilson's brother-in-law, Dr. Leonard V. Strong, told her about Dr. Bob. One of these ministers, incidentally, was Dilworth Lupton, who was later to have a great deal to do with the rapid growth of A.A. in Cleveland.

"I called Dr. Smith, and I still remember my words and

how gruff his voice was," Dorothy recalled in a 1954 conversation with Bill. "He scared me to death. I said, 'Is this the Dr. Smith who helps drunks?' When he said yes, I wept, and said that my husband was an alcoholic.

"Right away, he wanted to know how old Clarence was. 'Thirty-four,' I said. 'Impossible,' he replied. 'He hasn't suffered enough. There's never been anyone that young come into the Fellowship and recover.' "

This could have been one of Dr. Bob's tactics at the time—to suggest that a newcomer wasn't ready because of being too young, or being a woman, or not having suffered enough. Prospects were thus forced to "prove" that they were indeed ready and willing to accept the program.

Upon hearing Clarence's age, Dr. Bob very likely thought of the first Ernie G., who was also under 35 and had not stayed sober.

"Dr. Bob was about to hang up on me," Dorothy continued, "But then he relented and said there was one man in Cleveland who might be able to help Clarence. And he gave me Lloyd T——'s address.

"I went over to see Lloyd. He talked to me, but they were very secretive in those days. He didn't tell me what the solution was. I did know that it was tied up with the Oxford Group," said Dorothy, who described herself as being bitter and skeptical at the time. "I decided that I would pretend to go along with it if Clarence took to it."

So she bought her husband a bus ticket to Akron. There, Clarence made arrangements to go to the hospital, where he stayed for a week. He remembered Paul S. coming in and eating his breakfast, then coming in and eating his lunch. "I couldn't eat," said Clarence.

"Doc Smith came in later and took over. He sat on the edge of my bed and said, 'Well, what do you think of all this?' Then he paused and looked at me doubtfully. 'I don't know if you're ready yet. You're kind of young.' I was down to 135 pounds, no job, no clothes, and no money. I didn't know how much more ready I could be," recalled Clarence. "Still, I had to convince them I was ready.

"Then he asked, 'Do you believe in God, young fella?' (He always called me 'young fella.' When he called me Clarence, I knew I was in trouble.)

" 'What does that have to do with it?'

" 'Everything,' he said.

" 'I guess I do.'

" 'Guess, nothing! Either you do or you don't.'

" 'Yes, I do.'

" 'That's fine,' Dr. Bob replied. 'Now we're getting someplace. All right, get out of bed and on your knees. We're going to pray.'

" 'I don't know how to pray.'

" 'I guess you don't, but that's all right. Just follow what I say, and that will do for now.'

"I did what I was ordered to do," Clarence said. "There was no suggestion."

(Dr. Bob was always positive about his faith, Clarence said. If someone asked him a question about the program, his usual response was: "What does it say in the Good Book?" Suppose he was asked, "What's all this 'First Things First'?" Dr. Bob would be ready with the appropriate quotation: " 'Seek ye first the kingdom of God and His righteousness, and all these things shall be added unto you.' ")

As Dorothy recalled, "Clarence went directly to the meeting at T. Henry's from the hospital. I hadn't seen him during that time. Lloyd's mother took me down.

"Even in those days, they were picking out one person to talk to," she interjected. "The sponsorship thing was beginning, and they really sponsored you, too. We had callers all the time, and Lloyd never gave up on dropping in to see us.

"Walking up the path to that door was one of the hardest things I've ever done," she continued. "I didn't want to meet a bunch of drunks, and I didn't want to meet their wives.

"I walked in there, and all these people came up to me. One of the very first was Anne Smith. Somebody introduced her to me as Mrs. Smith, and she said, 'Call me Anne.' Well, that did it. I could hardly even talk. It seemed to break the shell that I had been so careful to build up all those years.

"By now, I thought Clarence was just about the lowest of the low, stealing money out of my purse for drinks. I thought nobody could have told me there was anything decent about him. Bill V—— H—— came up to me and said, 'I want to meet you. We think that Clarence is a pretty wonderful person, and we want to see if you're good enough for him.' Well, that helped me more than you can imagine. Me good enough for that drunk!

"I'll never forget it. There were about 50 people there. The living room was packed, and it was a big living room. I think Paul S—— talked, because he impressed me with that light he had.

"But the thing that impressed me most was the joy that was there. Everybody seemed happy, and all these women I thought I hadn't wanted to meet—I just thought, 'If I could only be like them. If I could only have friends like this.' Life began for me that night. I knew it right then and there.

"I remember Henrietta D—— talking about faith. The words were like a hammer, striking away all the fears when she said, 'God had a plan.'

"I was never so exhilarated in all my life. I went home from that meeting, and for the first time in years, I got down on my knees. And I said, 'God, if you have a plan for me, I want that. I don't want any of my own plans.'

"Another thing that they did noved me so," said Dorothy. "They handed out little address books with everybody's name in it. Very few people, of course, had phones then. We were all too poor. But the ones who had phone numbers, there they were. And when they said, 'Drop in on us—anytime,' they meant it. I knew they did."

As shown by Anne's daily calls to Henrietta D., which "meant everything to me," the telephone played an important role in A.A. from the very beginning.

Alex M., who came into A.A. in 1939, recalled, "Bob E—— made up the little address books [as did Elgie R. and others afterward], and every one of us got one. They'd say, 'Put a nickel in that telephone and call before you take a drink. If they don't answer, call somebody else.' "

John S., who joined A.A. in January 1940, thought his A.A. friend Wade was nuts. "He'd pick up the phone and say, 'How are you? . . . All right. How's your pigeon?' And that was the end of the conversation. I though he had telephonitis. But he was just keeping in touch."

(Incidentally, the word "pigeon"—as applied to an A.A. newcomer or prospect—was probably coined by Dr. Bob himself. "He used that word," said Smitty, and one A.A. recalled that Doc would often announce at a meeting, "There's a pigeon in Room so-and-so who needs some attention.' " Or he might refer to the patient as "a cookie.")

Contacts by phone or face-to-face were needed. "The only trouble was that Wednesday nights were too far apart," Dorothy said. "I could see Clarence was getting nervous. So I'd say, 'Well, let's go down and see Henrietta and Bill D——.' And we'd just pick up and go down to see them. They might be sitting down to dinner or whatever it was, but they would welcome us in. And we knew we were welcome.

"We felt the same privilege with Bob and Anne. You remember how poor they were. Sometimes, they were having bread and milk for dinner. Well, there was always some more bread and more milk for us. And Anne would serve it just as graciously as though it had been a complete turkey dinner.

"You know that sentence in the Big Book, that we were people saved from shipwreck. That was it, really. We had that closeness. This was the pioneering group, and you weren't absolutely sure it would work, so you couldn't possibly overdo it. You couldn't take anything for granted. And the friendship. None of us had friends before. We had lost all our friends."

While there was nothing regularly scheduled for the rest of the week, "We always planned for something on Saturday night," said T. Henry, "a party here, or somewhere else, with plenty of food and lots of coffee. That was the night people needed it."

"Annabelle and Wally G—— had a lot of get-togethers," said Henrietta D., "and so did Mother G—— [whose son was Ernie the first]," Henrietta tended to minimize her own effort in helping others. ("She was always there and always available," said one member.) "And of course, as we got a little more money ourselves, we'd have parties at our house.

"We had covered-dish suppers and picnics, and later we had a few dances," Henrietta said. "Every year, there was a New Year's party at the Y. But for a long time, we just had coffee and tea and crackers. It was funny. Everybody was so happy to be together."

J. D. H. recalled that "Ernie's mother used to throw a party every two weeks during this period. She'd make the doughnuts, and though everybody was broke, we all bought something. It was nothing unusual to see 25 or 30 people over there drinking coffee and eating doughnuts.

"I've been at those parties when there were calls from Cleveland from people who wanted to come down," he said. "Two men would hop in a car, go to Cleveland, and bring the man down to Akron."

"We'd sit and talk," said Mrs. M., Alex's wife, remembering A.A. of the late 1930's. "And we used to have a lot of fun. Oh, those were the good old days. And we're old enough to be sentimental about them. Sometimes, I feel kind of sorry for the people today, because they don't have what we had then. They have so much of everything else that they don't have *time* to have what we had."

A.A. members, and then groups in Akron, began giving parties regularly, including an annual one on Mother's Day to celebrate the meeting of Dr. Bob and Bill Wilson. Ed B., another early Akron member, remembered that the New Year's Eve dance became traditional, "with everybody gathering around Dr. Bob at midnight. He'd say a few words, and they'd have the Lord's Prayer. It was kind of small, and we kept together that way. Now, it's so big we can't find a place large enough."

Daily contact was also emphasized. Ernie G. the second would drive around making business calls, then stop in at an A.A. place for a cup of coffee, maybe make another call, and then stop into another A.A. place and have another cup of coffee. Then, maybe someone would invite a group in for the evening. A lot of them even had breakfast together every morning.

"We had an intense loyalty to each other," said J. D. "We would meet each other on payday to make sure nothing happened. When I had a slip after four months, I felt as though I had let down the most wonderful fellows on earth."

J. D. was involved in another A.A. first during this period. The newspaper on which he worked sold out in May 1938, and he moved to Evansville, Indiana, about as far from Akron as if he had moved to Philadelphia.

"I left an established group and had to start alone," he said. "The question was whether I could stay dry by myself. The thing to do was get a group started. I worked for about eight months before I even got a prospect.

"I went to four or five preachers, and they couldn't help. I even went to some bartenders. Finally, a minister told me about a chap he thought was an alcoholic. The fellow's wife dragged him over to my house by his ears. I was willing to consider him an alcoholic, but I found out later that he wasn't.

"I worked on other prospects. Then I heard of a doctor. About this time, the book ["Alcoholics Anonymous"] came out, and I took it to him to read. He smiled and was courteous. He read the book about halfway through. Then he told me he thought it was all very fine, but he wasn't having any trouble.

"Well, on Thanksgiving Day, 1940, I heard that the doctor was in jail and wanted to see me. I had gone there more than two years without being able to help anybody. But working at it helped me stay sober. Mother G —— wrote me regularly.

"The doctor was sitting there in jail as if he owned the joint. 'I think there may be something in what you said,' he told me. 'I want to know more.'

"A friend and I scraped up $75 to pay his expenses to Akron. Since he was a doctor, I wanted him to meet Dr. Bob. Well, he came back to Evansville, and he had a list of prospects a yard long that he already knew.

"We worked night and day there for about three months and got 12 or 14 people. And from that little group, it started. After two years, we had four groups."

Bob H.—who eventually became general manager of the A.A. General Service Office in New York—was in the Army and stationed near Evansville in 1942. He remembered going to a meeting there, although he didn't remember J. D.

'I received a letter from Bobbie B—— [a worker at A.A. headquarters in New York], who told me a group had formed in Evansville," Bob H. said. "The meeting was in a school, and we had to squeeze into little chairs. I had fancied myself an agnostic not too long before this time, and I remember a guy saying, 'Brother J——, would you care to give us a testimonial?' It kind of shook me up."

This shows, not only how emphasis differed from one area to another, but how groups were beginning to adopt customs that gave them a distinctly local flavor. Years later, Eastern A.A.'s would be just as "shook up" when Los Angeles members responded to their identification at a meeting with a loud "Hi, Joe!"

Ed B. recalled that Dr. Bob, always the accomplished storyteller, had a tale to fit every occasion, including this topic of local variations. "You know," Ed said, "you go to another part of the country, and they operate in a different way, and you come back and say, 'If I had to go by their kind of A.A., I could never stay sober.' Well, that happened to an Akron member when Dr. Bob was alive," said Ed. "I remember Dr. Bob told the fellow the story of this American who was putting flowers on a friend's grave while a Chinese man was putting food on his friend's grave. The American thought that was funny. 'When do you expect your friend to come up and eat that food?' he asks. And the Chinese guy says, 'When your friend comes up to smell those flowers.' That was to show we all have our way, and sometimes one way of doing things makes just as much sense as another."

Morning quiet time continued to be an important part of the recovery program in 1938-39, as did the spiritual reading from which the early members derived a good deal of their inspiration.

"Here in Los Angeles, they now emphasize meetings," said Duke P., who used to live in Toledo and was one of the pioneering members there. "I guess that's because there are so many of them. When I started, they stressed morning quiet time, daily reading, and daily contact. They also told me I had to do something about my alcoholism every day." Duke remembered taking a poll of "slippers" in the early 1940's and finding that they had all stopped having their morning quiet time. "Now, after 38 years, Katie and I still have our quiet time and morning reading," he said.

The Bible was stressed as reading material, of course. Many remember that "The Sermon on the Mount," by Emmet Fox, was also very popular. "That was required reading for everybody," said Dorothy S. M. "As soon as men in the hospital could begin to focus their eyes, they got a copy of 'Sermon on the Mount.'

"Then there was that little nickel book *The Upper Room*," she recalled. "They figured we could afford a nickel for spiritual reading. They impressed on us that we had to read that absolutely every morning. There wasn't any well-equipped bathroom in A.A. that didn't have a copy And if you didn't see It opened to the right day, you immediately began to suspect them."

Bob F. of Akron recalled that another popular book at the time was "The Greatest Thing in the World," by Drummond. This, along with *The Upper Room*, was furnished to the members by Mother G.

Though there was a good deal of reading material around at this time, there was definitely a need for literature directed specifically to the alcoholic. And of all the projects that Bill and Dr. Bob had discussed—hospitals, paid missionaries, etc.—the furthest advanced was the book, which was begun in May 1938.

The first two chapters were completed by June 1938, when Bill sent Bob a letter asking, "What would you think about the formation of a charitable organization called, say, Alcoholics Anonymous?"

At one time, this name was suggested just to indicate the authorship of the book: "One Hundred Men," by Alcoholics

Anonymous. Among other proposed titles were "A Way Out,"
"Haven," and "Comes the Dawn." But Alcoholics Anonymous
was already in some limited use as a name for the Fellowship;
references to it may be found as early as 1937.

In the same letter, Bill suggested that Anne have a chapter in the book to herself. "My feeling," said Bill, "is that Anne
should do the one portraying the wife." Her modesty—her
inclination toward staying in the background—may have
been the reason that she did not write it.

Lois did not write the chapter, either; she wasn't asked.
When she suggested that she do so, Bill said, "Oh, no. It
should be in the same style as the book."

Recently, Lois said, "I've always been hurt by it, and I still
don't know why Bill didn't ask me, although I never brought
it up again."

Bill himself wrote the chapter that came to be called "To
Wives," and Marie B., the wife of a member from Cleveland,
wrote a personal account for the story section of the first
edition.

Bob E. recalled that Bill began sending the rough drafts
to Akron. "We didn't show them to too many people," he said.
"I was one of the chosen few." He recalled going over the
drafts with Doc in his living room. "We were very serious
about it, and awed by the realization that it was beginning to
take form," he said.

As Dorothy remembered it, however, Bill would write the
chapters, have them reviewed by the New York A.A.'s, then
send them on to Akron. "We would read them in the Akron
meeting. Then we would send back any comments and cor-
rections."

There is a discrepancy here, as there is regarding very
many things that happened in these early years. "It was like
we were all witnesses to an accident," said one member. "It was
the same accident, but we all saw it from different angles."

Perhaps Dr. Bob showed the early chapters to only a few members, and then to more of them as the book progressed. Or he might have had it read first by the "chosen few," then passed it on to the others.

"I'll never forget the time the fifth chapter came out," Dorothy recalled. "*Our* fifth chapter. I was staying all night with the Smiths, and Anne and I sat up, and we read the thing until four in the morning. And we thought, 'Now, this is it. This is really going to bring people in.' "

Bill was coming through on his end, but getting the stories written in Akron proved difficult. And these stories were vital, because most of the recoveries had taken place there.

One problem was that some members wanted no part of the book. They felt it was a commercial venture—which it was, in part. It was meant primarily to publicize the movement, but also to provide income for Bill and Doc and funds for the establishment of an office through which alcoholics in distant places could be reached and helped to recover.

John and Elgie R. recalled one guy who claimed he got drunk because of the book (interesting reaction—if only because the chief purpose of the book was to get people sober). "He got it into his head that Doc and Bill were going to make a fortune, and he wanted his share. Nobody paid any attention, and he got so mad he went off and got drunk.

" 'It's a racket all the way through,' he'd say. 'Those guys are just a couple of Vermonters. They know each other. When Bill first came to Akron, he knew he was going to meet Bob.' "

Dorothy S. M. remembered a fellow who was going to write his story and then said it was all a fraud. He withdrew the story and then put it in again. "This was one example of the really serious contention we were going through," she recalled. "For a time, we thought the whole Akron group might break up over the book."

Just the same, Bill Wilson maintained that in Akron there

was better support for the book and for the Twelve Steps, which it introduced, than there was in New York, where "hot debate" centered on the manuscript. In this case, Bill might have been assuming that his part of the stove was warmer.

"There was so much controversy, and quite a bit of nagging to get the stories written," Dorothy recalled. "Time kept drawing closer, and still the stories weren't in.

"About this time, Bob Smith came to the house and told us he had found a bum down on the Akron skid row who had been a famous newspaperman. Now he was selling hair oil and panhandling in between.

"This was Jim S——," Dorothy said. "Bob put him in the hospital and said if we could straighten him out, he would be able to help us get the stories written.

"Jim did sober up, and helped all the Akron and Cleveland men with their stories. He kept after them to get the stories on paper, and sat over them until they did. He made rewrites, but he was always careful to keep the flavor," she said.

"Jim was a real lone wolf—tall and skinny, and he didn't look well," recalled Sue Windows. "He went down pretty far before he came in. I was going to business college and I needed the practice, so I typed some of the Akron stories. The funny thing is, I never read the Big Book until three years ago [1975]. People started asking me to go to meetings, so I thought I might as well know what I was talking about. More A.A.'s have contacted me lately because I am Dad's daughter. They want to know about the early days. I never dreamed it would grow like this."

If the alcoholics in Akron had their problems with the Big Book, members of the Oxford Group had even more. There was the impression that it was commercial, for one thing. Another reason they were disappointed was that there was no mention of the Oxford Group in the book. Furthermore, the Twelve Steps had replaced the four absolutes, which were not mentioned, either.

Various reasons have been given for the lack of references to the Oxford Group. One was that A.A. had to avoid giving the appearance of being affiliated with any religious or spiritual group. As Bill stated in a conversation with T. Henry, "A number of Catholics were coming into A.A. at the time, and we couldn't give them [the Oxford Group] the credit they deserved." Differences in method and approach were also cited.

There was one more reason, which never came out publicly: Frank Buchman, founder and leader of the Oxford Group, was not only trying to influence political and business affairs on an international level, but was regarded by some as being in sympathy with Hitler, following a widely publicized interview with Buchman in 1936.

The separation between A.A. and the Oxford Group had already taken place in New York, late in 1937, but the group's lack of regard for the book led to increased friction in Akron, where A.A. and the O.G. were still quite close, despite growing problems.

As Bill once put it: "In Akron, they [the local A.A. members] were the Oxford Group, or at least many thought they were, until the book came out in 1939. Not only it, but the Fellowship, was named 'Alcoholics Anonymous.' We had consciously withdrawn from the Oxford Group, in fact, definitely here in New York at a much earlier time, and although the older people in Cleveland or in Akron realized that it wasn't any longer an Oxford Group, we carried the label as long as the meetings went on at T. Henry Williams's house."

XII. Cleveland A.A.'s leave the Oxford Group

In some ways, it is possible to see early 1939 as a happier, simpler time as far as the A.A.'s of Akron were concerned, and many do remember it that way. The earliest struggles were over; there was a book; and the members, sticking closer together in warm love and comradeship than many families, knew they could stay sober in the program.

There was only one meeting—the highlight of everybody's week. In between, there were coffee and conversation daily, a party on Saturday night, and a new drunk or two to visit the City Hospital. A.A. was growing, but not yet fast enough to make anyone uncomfortable.

Actually, the situation was not idyllic. There was a real problem with the Oxford Group.

As Bob E. put it, "We started with just a few fellows horning in on an Oxford Group meeting. We increased in numbers and noise until we took the place over. Instead of being the alcoholic squad of the Oxford Group, we were the main body, and we had the most to say, and we were kind of running the thing.

"But we were limited. We couldn't question the guidance. We used to sit around in a circle when we first started there, because there were so few of us. T. Henry and Clarace, Florence Main, and Hen Seiberling called the shots. They were the leaders.

"They had us in silence, listening for guidance, half the time. It made the drunks very restless. We couldn't stand that. We got the jitters. As we increased in numbers and influence, the silence was almost cut out. They [the nonalcoholics] could see their fundamentals were not being adhered to.

"We were Oxford Groupers until we physically moved out. There was a lot of talk about wearing out T. Henry's carpet — there were so many fellows coming in, it was an imposition. But that wasn't it, even though he had to set up about 30 chairs toward the last, and we did need more space."

That, of course, explains a good deal. Most alcoholics accepted *some* part of the Oxford Group program and rejected other parts. And the group's insistence that a member had to take the whole thing in a lump did not go down too well with the alcoholics.

Bill noted that the Oxford Group's practice of "checking" (one member's judging the authenticity of divine guidance that another claimed to have received) gave alcoholics the feeling that the O.G. leaders were ganging up on them. He also cited a technique of making people feel unwanted or uncomfortable until they agreed with some particular O.G. point of view.

As Bill put it, drunks "would not take pressure in any form, except from John Barleycorn himself. . . . They would not stand for the rather aggressive evangelism of the Oxford Group. And they would not accept the principle of 'team guidance' for their own personal lives."

If the alcoholics did not feel quite comfortable with the Oxford Groupers, neither did the groupers feel entirely at ease with the alcoholics.

Some groupers might have regarded this association with drunks as a kind of social work, since much of the "guidance" they received and transmitted seemed to be for the alcoholic squad rather than for themselves. Later, this became known as "taking someone else's inventory," a practice at which even A.A.'s can be expert.

Other Oxford Groupers felt that participation by alcoholics lowered their own prestige, and they let T. Henry, Clarace, and Henrietta know this. They were, after all, supposed to be concentrating on community leaders—the elite. And most alcoholics were far from being community leaders. Some Oxfordites even suggested that the alcoholics be screened so that only the most socially acceptable would be allowed in.

A number of Akron alcoholics who came into the program in 1939 were more plainspoken on the matter than Bob or Bill ever could have been. "They didn't want us" was perhaps the kindest comment made about the majority of nonalcoholic Oxford Groupers, who had their own meetings and did not associate with the alcoholic squad. "They didn't want the peons," said John R. (Elgie's husband). "They wanted the people with money. With the exception of T. Henry. He didn't give a damn who you were. He was a great guy."

As mentioned earlier, Frank Buchman was never quite comfortable with this most famous spin-off of his Oxford Group. And as far as he and other leading Oxfordites were concerned, a split was considered desirable for a number of other reasons as well.

For one thing, A.A.'s as a group were inclined to confine their approach to other alcoholics only—what we now regard as "our primary purpose." Dr. Buchman, on the other hand, thought alcoholism was only part of what was wrong with the world—a symptom, perhaps.

In addition, the alcoholics were becoming more insistent on anonymity at the public level — a principle that clashed with Buchman's program of advertising the "change" in people's directions as a way of attracting others to his organization.

Furthermore, the Oxford Group was beginning to have trouble at the local level. There had been splits and controversy in Akron along social, church, and company lines. When the rubber baron's son (whose "change" had, incidentally, been very highly publicized) took a dive back into the bottle, many church people became rather patronizing toward the Oxford Group. The group had also involved itself in solving or refereeing questions of business ethics among the big rubber companies. This wasn't viewed with much favor by the industrialists in town. After all, changing people was one thing—changing business was another.

Henrietta Seiberling believed that A.A. should not be involved in raising money, that this was a means the devil would use to destroy A.A., and she argued the point with Bill and Dr. Bob. At the same time, she felt the A.A.'s were not placing enough emphasis on God.

"In the early days," she recalled, "Bill said to me, 'Henrietta, I don't think we should talk so much about religion or God.' I said to him, 'Well, we're not out to please the alcoholics. They have been pleasing themselves all these years. We are out to please God. And if you don't talk about what God does and your faith and your guidance, then you might as well be the Rotary Club or something like that, because God is your only source of power.' Finally, he agreed."

Bill *may* have agreed, and many others as well. Still, there were quite a few A.A.'s who hadn't changed or surrendered to that extent. They were doing all they could to comprehend

the First Step and weren't quite ready to face the others. And their concept of a Higher Power was different from that of the groupers, who were not prepared to accept light bulbs and Third Avenue buses as examples of "God as I understand Him." Years later, Henrietta was disappointed in the A.A. talks she heard at a big meeting, saying, "You would have thought they were giving you a description of a psychiatrist's work on them. There was no spirituality or talk of what God had done in their lives."

This, too, was an attitude that represented a fundamental difference between the A.A.'s and the Oxford Groupers. A.A.'s were more and more inclined to allow newer members to arrive at a concept of a Higher Power in their own time and manner.

Considering all these factors, as well as comments from Bill and others, Dr. Bob very likely was aware, not only that a break was about to occur, but that it was overdue. However, he was a prudent man when it came to making changes. He might have been willing to wait and let the inevitable happen.

Another thing: One of Dr. Bob's strongest characteristics was loyalty—not only to Bill, but to Henrietta Seiberling and T. Henry and Clarace Williams. These three had done so much to help him before he stopped drinking, and then—in the face of criticism from members of their own Oxford Group—had given so much support to him and the early members in the crucial years that followed.

So when the first break in Ohio came, it came in Cleveland, rather than in Akron. And the immediate reasons were almost entirely different from those underlying factors mentioned earlier. Furthermore, it was seen by a few to be almost

"Changes" in A.A. upset Henrietta Seiberling, whose home had been the site of Dr. Bob's first meeting with Bill.

as much a break from the Akron A.A.'s as it was from the Oxford Group.

By early 1939, Clarence S. had developed into a spark-plug for the Cleveland A.A. contingent. He and Dorothy were bringing men down every week to the meeting at T. Henry's. Many of them were Catholic. Clarence remembered telling them that the Oxford Group meetings wouldn't inter-fere with their religion. "However, the testimony given by members at the meetings seemed like open confession to them, and this was something they were not allowed to prac-tice," according to Clarence. "Furthermore, the idea of receiv-ing guidance didn't sit well. And to top it off, they [the Ox-ford Groupers] were using the wrong Bible. As a result, I received a lot of flak on the way home," Clarence said.

Dorothy (then his wife) pointed out that the growth of the Cleveland contingent was in itself an important reason for the split. "We had been discussing having Cleveland meetings for quite some time," she said. "I think we had about 13 peo-ple, and it was not only an effort getting everybody down to Akron, but we felt it was putting a big load on Bob with the hospitalization. He was getting very busy in Akron."

Dorothy, too, cited the problem for Catholic members. However, not all Catholic members felt there was a problem. It should also be noted that some Protestant churchmen looked askance at the Oxford Group. Soon after Clarence got sober, Dorothy returned to see the Reverend Dilworth Lup-ton, the noted Unitarian minister who had previously told her about his lack of success in helping alcoholics.

"I said, 'We have a solution,' and I told him about Clarence and the meetings. I asked him to attend one. I said, 'There are going to be a lot of other women sitting here in your study just as I did. I would like you to know that there really is some hope.'

"Well, I was disappointed, because he wouldn't come. He

said that inasmuch as A.A. was mixed up with the Oxford Group, it was bound to fail; that any movement as tremendous as this should never be mixed up with a religious organization. How right he was!"

There are several versions of how the split occurred, to say nothing of the whys and wherefores: who was right and who was wrong; who had resentments and who didn't; and who wasn't speaking to whom for how many years.

Most of the people involved in this situation are now dead. And many of those who survive were then so new in the program that they really didn't have any idea of the undercurrents and machinations. They were just happy to be sober and not yet ready to attend what an A.A. group would today call its business meetings.

In any case, Clarence remembered telling Dr. Bob about the problem the Catholic fellows were having with the Oxford Group methods.

"We're not keeping the Catholics out — the church is keeping them out," he reported Dr. Bob as replying. "We can't do anything about it."

"Yes, we can," Clarence said.

"What do you have in mind?"

"To start a group without all this rigmarole that's offensive to other people. We have a book now, the Steps, the absolutes. Anyone can live by that program. We can start our own meetings."

"We can't abandon these people," Doc replied. "We owe our lives to them."

"So what?" Clarence replied. "I owe my life to them, too. But what about all these others?"

"We can't do anything about them," Doc said.

"Oh yes, we can."

"Like what?"

"You'll see," concluded Clarence.

"At this time," said Clarence, "Al [sometimes known as "Abby"] G—— was in Akron City Hospital all smoked up with paraldehyde and all the other things Doc gave them. I had gone out to see him with Bill Wilson. Then Bill and my wife Dorothy drove him down to the hospital. Al was a patent lawyer and had a big house in Cleveland, so I asked his wife if we could have meetings there. I didn't ask Al."

Dorothy remembered that it took four hours to get Al down to Akron, because he wanted to stop in every bar along the way. "I'll never forget seeing him disappear down the end of the corridor with the nurse," she said. "He turned around and waved to us dramatically and said, 'If this works, I'll never forget this day, or you two.'

"Abby was well educated, and what was interesting to me was that the person in Akron who made the most impression on him was a man who hadn't gone beyond the fourth grade. Anyway, when he came out of the hospital, he said he would like to open his home for Cleveland meetings."

Clarence said, "I made the announcement at the Oxford Group that this was the last time the Cleveland bunch was down as a contingent — that we were starting a group in Cleveland that would only be open to alcoholics and their families. Also that we were taking the name from the book 'Alcoholics Anonymous.'

"The roof came off the house. 'Clarence, you can't do this!' someone said.

" 'It's done.'

" 'We've got to talk about this!'

" 'It's too late,' I said.

"The meeting was set for the following week [May 11, 1939]," Clarence said. "I made the mistake of telling these people the address. They invaded the house and tried to break up our meeting. One fellow was going to whip me. All in the spirit of pure Christian love! But we stood our ground."

Dorothy's recollections differed slightly. "We didn't have any name," she said, "but we let everybody know it was definitely not an Oxford Group. Just alcoholics."

"Anne and Bob, of course, felt that they, too, should fall away from the domination of the Oxford Group," she added. "But they felt, in loyalty to T. Henry and Clarace, that it was going to be a very difficult thing.

"As a matter of fact," Dorothy said, "at one of our very first meetings, all the strict Oxford Group contingent came up from Akron and was very bitter and voluble. They felt we were being extremely disloyal to everyone in doing this. It was quite a step to pull away from Akron."

Al G. recalled entering the hospital on April 17. Before he got out, Dr. Bob came to see him and asked whether he intended to follow the program. "Dr. Bob then pulled up his chair with one of his knees touching mine, and said, 'Will you pray with me for your success?' " Al recalled. "He said a beautiful prayer. Many times in my efforts with A.A. candidates, I feel kind of guilty because I haven't done the same thing."

That night, Al went to the meeting at T. Henry's. "I attended several of these meetings before I discovered that not all the people there were alcoholics," he said. But in spite of his being Catholic, his reaction to the meetings was good.

"We went to Akron for several weeks," he said, "before it was finally decided to undertake the organization of the Cleveland group. Toward the middle of May 1939, the first meeting was held in this room. At that meeting, there were a number of Akron people and all the Cleveland people.

"When we began to have meetings, there was considerable debate as to what we would call the group. Various names were suggested. No others seemed to be fitting, so we began to refer to ourselves as Alcoholics Anonymous."

Whatever conversation Doc may have had with Clarence before the Cleveland group started, he gave it his full support from the beginning, as did many other Akron A.A. members.

"Dr. Bob was at all of these early meetings, which took place at our house," Al said in a letter to Bill.

When John R. was asked whether he remembered any hard feelings on Doc's part, he said, "Well, my goodness, Doc and Anne and my wife [Elgie] and I went up there to meetings—the first meetings they had.

"I remember we went up there one night, and coming back—Doc was a boy at heart, you know—he turned off the highway and started down through the River Road. And I said, 'What are you going down this way for?' It was snowing, see. I said, 'We're gonna get stuck down here somewhere.'

" 'Oh no, we're not,' he said. And he started up Portage Path Hill. We got up three-quarters of the way and had to back down. He just laughed. He must have thought he could make it. Yeah, Doc was a great guy. I remember he was around 60 then, and my, he *was* a boy, yes sir."

It is difficult to assess Dr. Bob's exact position in the matter of the Cleveland split. Some observers settled it by putting him in the middle: "The only thing that kept them [the local A.A.'s] on an even keel was the sound wisdom of Dr. Bob. How he kept his sanity seemed a miracle. There he was in the middle of a bunch of unstable people, not yet dry behind the ears."

Perhaps Dr. Bob just turned it over. According to a quote attributed to him at the time: "There's no use worrying about these things. As long as people have faith and believe, this [A.A.] will go on."

A truth important to A.A.'s future had been demonstrated in Cleveland: For whatever reason, one A.A. group *could* break away from another — without necessarily endangering the old group or the new. As anonymous members have put it at unrecorded times: "All you need to start a new group in A.A. is a resentment and a coffeepot."

At that time, Clarence and Dorothy were maintaining a warm and active correspondence with New York—that is, with Bill Wilson, Hank P., and Ruth Hock, the nonalcoholic secretary of what was later to become the A.A. General Service Office.

On June 4, 1939, a few weeks after the Cleveland group began its meetings, Clarence wrote Hank P.: "Bill J—— and I and Clarace Williams and etc., etc. had a knock-down-drag-out affair a couple of weeks ago, and they have chosen to leave us alone and confine their activities elsewhere. We lost the activities of three or four rummies, but I guess it had to be that way.

"As I analyze it," Clarence said, "the main trouble was, the Oxford Group wants the bows, also the fact that I was the one who took the initiative to get our Cleveland gang started. Bill J—— got Lloyd T—— and Charlie J—— and Rollie H ——." These four were evidently part of the Cleveland contingent. Rollie was a baseball player, sober only a few weeks or days at the time.

"There is nothing to disturb Bill or you or anyone else here now, and we really expect to do a lot of work," Clarence continued. "Most of the people (15 or 16) are intensely interested and are out working and doing something about it.

"Our policy will be mainly this," he wrote. "Not too much stress on spiritual business at meetings. Have discussions *after* meetings of any business or questions arising. Plenty of fellowship all the time.

"Leaders of meetings have been chosen so far by seniority in the bunch," he said. "Cooperation in visiting at the hospital so as not to gang up on a patient, but rather one or at the most two fellows to see him at a time. We have an ideal hospital setup and have an alcoholic physician in attendance. Doc Smith came up and talked to the superintendent of the hospital and the resident physician last week, and they are very sympathetic and enthusiastic. We have had one patient through the mill there already, and expect two or three more this coming week.

"We intend to stress the hospitalization of all cases possible. In fact, we are trying to make it almost 100 percent. The man who lines up the new patient assumes the responsibility for him, for visitors, dollars, etc. After he is defogged, we feel him out, then give him the book and lots of conversation. Our book certainly has been a tremendous help. We also contact the family when he is in the hospital and give them conversation and the book. We have the experience of New York and Akron before us to guide us, and we feel that we are now on a very good footing. Hope you and Bill can get out this way soon and meet our gang and give us some of your experience and wisdom."

Bob and Anne had taken a trip to New York in June. "Bob and Anne and Little Bob arrived to spend two or three days," reads a June 23 notation in Lois's diary. Undoubtedly, Bob and Bill discussed the Cleveland matter, among other things, but all Lois said was: "Drove over to Montclair [New Jersey] with Bob and Anne Smith. Good meeting. Twenty-six present." By this time, of course, groups outside New York had formed in the East.

Dorothy recalled that Warren C. came into the Cleveland group the following month (July 1939). "He was one of our best workers at the time. He was absolutely broke, but one of the proud people who wouldn't even take a dime for carfare. He'd wait until his son came home from caddying to get some money from his tips," she said.

"I didn't have the price of hospitalization when I came in," recalled Warren, whose son the caddy celebrated his own 25th A.A. anniversary in 1977. "I was a noble experiment, the first one who went through the program in Cleveland without hospitalization. There were some people who didn't want me in the program unless I did go to the hospital, but [Clarence] S—— fought that one.

"After Clarence talked to me at my home, others would come over and talk to me. They wouldn't let you in a meeting just by one guy talking to you, as they do now. They felt you should know something about what you were going to hear and the purpose of the program.

"Then Clarence made me go to the home of one of the newer members every night for three months, and they had nine or ten people talking to me. Then I had to read the Big Book before I went to my first meeting. As a result, I think I had a better understanding of what they were trying to do.

"When I went to Al G——'s home, it was a mixture of Oxford Group plus those who came in new like myself. In November of 1939, the first all-A.A. group was formed in the city of Cleveland—the old Borton Group. That was the first group where the Oxford Group people and the A.A.'s weren't mixed.

"We still continued to go down to Akron—a half dozen of us in the car," Warren said.

"At the same time, there were probably half a dozen Akron people who came up to Cleveland—Doc Smith, the S—— boys [Paul and Dick], Bill D—— [A.A. number three], and so forth. Not every week, but once in a while. We sort of supported each other in the beginning."

This mutual support was indicated in a letter from Dr. Bob to Bill in September 1939, in which he noted that he had "attended a meeting of the Cleveland gang, as I do once or twice a month, and enjoyed a wonderful gathering. Think they have about 38 in their bunch now—refer to men only. Our meetings still have 75 or 80 every week, including both men and women."

"In addition to going to the meeting at Al's and to Akron, nine or ten of us would run into each other every night,"

Warren C. said. "We would unfold our problems and troubles of the day and get the fortification we needed for the new day that was coming up.

"Of course, in this part of the country, Dr. Bob is our man," Warren said. "That is a result of knowing him and being in contact with him as we were. He'd make Twelfth Step calls with you, and he talked to all the people who went to the hospital. He had that look about him, and he transmitted that feeling, too. I mean, you sort of worshiped him."

xiii. The movement spreads in the Midwest

Dr. Bob apparently did not involve himself deeply in A.A.'s break with the Oxford Group in Akron, for other reasons in addition to those already mentioned.

First, this seems to have been a period when Dr. Bob was in desperate straits financially. And he was being called upon to give more and more of his own time to the increasing number of new prospects flocking to Akron to be "fixed."

When Dorothy S. M. spoke of the Smiths' having bread and milk for dinner, she wasn't overstating the case. Dr. Bob had then been sober about four years. Others who had come in and sobered up later were working at salaried jobs. He was not.

As Jack Alexander was to write in his *Saturday Evening Post* article of March 1, 1941, "Dr. Armstrong [the name used to preserve Dr. Bob's anonymity in print] is still struggling to patch up his practice. The going is hard. He is in debt because of his contributions to the movement and the time he devotes gratis to alcoholics. Being a pivotal man in the group, he is unable to turn down the requests for help which flood his office."

In the spring of 1939, Dr. Bob was about to turn 60—an age when other men were ready to settle back and begin to enjoy the fruits of their life's work. Evidently, his situation was beginning to bother him a great deal.

In a letter to Frank Amos in May 1939, Dr. Bob said he realized that "some of the boys are in quite deplorable condition financially, which happens to be my condition also."

The summer passed, and there was a letter to Bill in which he wrote: "I just cannot drift along living on hopes, because, after all, I have three people dependent on me. I am really anxious to help put this thing on the map as a national movement, if such is possible.

"Able to borrow from Mother $1,200 to take off some of the pressure, but that cannot be repeated. I think the uncertainty is perhaps the thing that distresses me most of anything.

"Some efforts to raise some jack, but results will be slow . . . two or seven in hospital at all times. I get pretty tired with too much of it continuously."

Bill, who was also in terrible financial shape, responded with a letter in which he informed Dr. Bob that they were working with a money-raising organization and pushing for results, but that, in the meantime, he was approaching the Guggenheim Foundation in hopes of gaining a fellowship for Bob. Bill enclosed a letter he had written on Bob's behalf:

"At Akron, Ohio, there is a physician, Dr. Robert H. Smith, who has been responsible during the past four years

In an era of hard times and nickel magazines, an article by Jack Alexander spread the A.A. message nationwide.

for the recovery of at least 100 chronic alcoholics of types hitherto regarded by the medical profession as hopeless. . . .

"For more than four years, without charge to sufferers, without fanfare and almost without funds, Dr. Smith has carried on work among alcoholics in the Akron-Cleveland area. In this human laboratory, he has proved that any alcoholic, not too mentally defective, can recover if he so desires. The possible recovery among such cases has suddenly been lifted from almost nil to at least 50 percent, which, quite aside from its social implications, is a medical result of the first magnitude. Though, as a means of our recovery, we all engage in the work, Dr. Smith has had more experience and has obtained better results than anyone else.

"Because of his great amount of voluntary alcoholic work, the doctor has been unable to rebuild his surgical practice. If he continues alcoholic work at the present pace, he may lose the remainder of his practice and probably his home. Obviously, he should continue. But how?"

Bill proceeded to answer his own question by suggesting that the gentlemen of the Guggenheim Foundation give Bob $3,000 to continue his work for a year, part of which he would need for expenses.

Later, Bill was to receive a letter from the foundation stating that no evidence had been found to indicate Dr. Bob's qualification for a Guggenheim fellowship, which could be granted only "upon evidence of demonstrated capacity for original research or creative works in the arts."

Bill then wrote to an A.A. friend employed by Ford Motor Company, voicing his hope that a place could be found for Bob on the staff of the Ford Hospital. "I feel that in time Dr. Smith will be known as the Louis Pasteur of alcoholism," Bill said. "It seems strange that we cannot lay our hands on funds to help him out."

Hospital and treatment problems that resulted from

steadily increasing A.A. activity must also have had a draining effect on Dr. Bob's time and energy—and put increased pressure on him as well—from May through December 1939. As he had written Bill, there were then two to seven people in the hospital at all times, compared with one or two only a few months earlier.

Some of this increase could be credited to publicity. An article appeared in *Liberty* Magazine that fall. Ernie G. the second remembered being with Doc when it came out. "Doc said, 'Let's go down to the drugstore and get the *Liberty*.' We drove down and came home and read it. You never saw such an elated person in your life."

"We all were," said Ernie's wife, Ruth. "Anne especially. She said, 'You know, it looks like we might be getting a little bit respectable.' There was an aura that afternoon, a feeling of complete oneness that this great thing had come into the world."

"There were a lot of inquiries came in from that," said Ernie. "I read somewhere that 300 or 400 letters came in almost overnight."

There was also a steadily increasing number of inquiries resulting from favorable reviews of the book "Alcoholics Anonymous" in newspapers and religious publications throughout the country. By the fall of 1939, the book was selling 60 copies a week.

At this time, Dr. Bob wrote and *may* have signed an article on A.A. and the Big Book that appeared in the August 1939 issue of a magazine called *Faith*. He alerted Ruth Hock (in the New York office) to its publication, and later reported he had received inquiries from 12 other doctors as a result.

"I rushed right out and bought a copy of this month's *Faith*, and it was quite a thrill," Ruth replied. "If my opinion is worth anything—bravo! That's the way I like to see it set out—honest, straightforward, and unembroidered."

Further on, she continued: "With constant pounding like the New York *Times* review, your contribution in *Faith*, the medical articles, etc., we'll make constant, steady progress, I'm sure."

The possibility that Dr. Bob signed this article means that he may have been among the first to break his anonymity at the public level — before there were any A.A. Traditions. When queried in 1978, Ruth vaguely remembered the article and thought Dr.Bob did sign it.

At the same time, the New York office was referring to Bob all inquiries from other doctors throughout the country, as well as from problem drinkers who lived anywhere near Akron.

There was also the cumulative effect of more and more eager A.A. members carrying the message of recovery to those who still suffered. What was happening in Cleveland was happening on a smaller scale in other Midwest cities such as Toledo, Detroit, and Chicago—as well as in the East. In the beginning, however, they had no hospital setups in those cities. Thus, men who had been sobered up in Akron and had returned home to spread the word were in turn sending all their new prospects to be "fixed" by Dr. Bob.

While none of these effects were explosive, they were certainly steady. In addition to putting a heavy load on Doc, they put too much strain on the facilities at City Hospital, which was still being used to some extent as late as Easter week, 1941, according to Duke P.

Perhaps it had been all right with the hospital administration and staff when only one or two drunks were being treated at a time. But half a dozen at once was too much. There was a change of administration, and doctors grumbled about not having beds for patients who were "really sick." Then there was the matter of money. As Bob E. put it in later years, "We owed so much money to City Hospital, we were never able to pay it back." A combination of space and money problems was probably the chief factor in the lessening of what had been at least four full years of cooperation between Dr. Bob and the City Hospital administration. That is, the administration did know and approve of Dr. Bob's treatment of alcoholics, in a period when most hospitals would admit them only under some other diagnosis.

As Dr. Bob was already using other hospitals and sanitariums such as Green Cross, Fair Oaks Villa, and People's Hospital (now Akron General Medical Center) for treatment of alcoholics, the situation was not catastrophic by any means.

According to John and Elgie R., Wally and Annabelle G. began taking drunks into their home on a regular basis around the same time. This, of course, was an extension of what they and other members, starting with Anne and Lois, had been doing on impulse since the beginning.

As Annabelle recalled in a conversation with Bill Wilson: "I had an uncle who was drinking and was then hospitalized. He was still in bad condition, so I brought him home. I was trying to build up his health at first. Then, each day, we would have quiet time, and I would talk and read to him. I kept him nine weeks, and he went home entirely different."

That was in 1938, and "home" was some 100 miles away in Sandusky, Ohio, where Annabelle's uncle "helped 25 or 30 men" thereafter.

"A short time later, Doc brought a couple of men from Chicago, Jack G—— and Dick R——," Annabelle continued. "Then it was one after another. They'd come and go. They needed time to recuperate and get exposed to the group.

"We had about 62 over a period of two years. Ty M—— was here," she said. (Ty's wife, Kay, was the woman who took the A.A. book to Los Angeles in the late fall of 1939.) "I figure three out of four made it. Tom and Clarence took care of quite a few.

"I wanted so badly to help these people," said Annabelle. "I could almost see and live inside of them, understand what they were going through. I got so I could tell by their expressions, the way they talked, and their attitude, just how they were reacting. It was a wonderful experience, and it helped me more than it helped them. They had to have good food, so we charged $12 a week after a while. But we were in the hole every time—especially with the telephone bills. If I wasn't there, they'd call long-distance."

Bill Wilson remembered a time when four drunks, still shaking and not knowing what it was about, were staying with Wally and Annabelle. "They would start out in the morning reading from *The Upper Room* and say the prayers," he recalled. "Annabelle, of course, mothered them all and stuck by them, and they generally stayed there a week. If they could, they would pay. If they couldn't, Annabelle took them in anyway."

Bill found it odd that Wally and Annabelle G. helped sober up a lot of people and Lois and Anne didn't have that many successes. "A few people sobered up in later years, but never while they were living in our house," Bill said. "And we had a good 20 of them.

"At the G——s', they did, and I don't know why. Maybe they just hit the right cases. There certainly wasn't any difference in the treatment. I think there may have been times when we attributed it to their morning hour of meditation," Bill said. "I sort of always felt that something was lost from A.A. when we stopped emphasizing the morning meditation." (Bill and Lois themselves, however, continued this practice together until his death, in 1971.)

Apparently, there were slight differences in approach between New York and Akron A.A. during this period. But there was also cooperation; it was all one Fellowship.

"People would read the book and then write New York,"

Elgie R. said. "Then they'd get referrals to come to Akron. They'd stay a week up at Wally's, and then maybe they'd go somewhere else and get a room and hang around for a while until they got everything they wanted to know.

"There was no nurse, just Doc. People would come and talk to them, and some people would take them out to see other members. It was a person-to-person system, and it worked.

"That was when things began to move fast," Elgie said. "People would go, and there'd be more coming. Then it began to grow everywhere, because we'd say, 'Now go back where you came from, and *do* something.' They'd go away, and you'd not hear anything from them. And maybe five years later, they'd come back. They'd never had a drink and were doing fine. You couldn't tell."

Thus, A.A. began to spread gradually from Akron to other cities in northern Ohio and elsewhere in the Midwest, with members beginning to meet in little groups of two or three. The same thing was happening simultaneously out of New York to cities on the East Coast, such as Washington, Boston, Baltimore, and Philadelphia. Often, both A.A. centers helped get things started in the same town.

Among the earliest of the pioneers to go home from Akron was Earl T. of Chicago. Recalling the afternoon he spent with Dr. Bob in his office, Earl said, "He very carefully helped me through my moral inventory, suggesting many, many bad personality traits and character defects. When this was finished, he asked me if I would like to have these defects removed.

"Without much thought, I said, 'Yes, I would.' And then he asked me to get down on my knees at the desk with him, and we both prayed audibly to have these defects of character removed."

Earl returned to Chicago in 1937. "It took a year before I

could find anyone to work with, and two years without the book before we had six people," he said. "I would go to Akron every two months for a meeting in order to maintain my sobriety and work with others.

"I would tell Dr. Bob that I had talked to a couple of people I thought should sober up, but nothing seemed to happen—that they would tell me, 'Well, that's wonderful. If I ever need that, I'll let you know.' Dr. Bob told me that when the time was right and I was right, it would work out providentially, which it did."

Earl managed to help one man get sober. Then, another recovered alcoholic returned to Chicago from Akron in 1938. A year later, two doctors began guiding alcoholic patients to the small A.A. group.

These alcoholics included two women. One was Sylvia K., a glamorous divorcee with $700 a month alimony. Later, Dorothy S. M. explained how A.A. reached Sylvia in 1939.

"My whole family just went overboard on A.A.," Dorothy said. "After Clarence got sober, my sister Caroline, a nurse who had been married to Hank P—— [an A.A. of the New York area, active in the office there], went to Chicago with a Multilith copy of the Big Book and took it to a doctor she knew. He was impressed and said, 'I have just the person—a woman patient of mine.' "

Caroline called Dorothy to say she was bringing a woman to Akron for A.A. According to Dorothy, Dr. Bob threw up his hands and said, "We have never had a woman and will not work on a woman." But by that time, Caroline was on her way with Sylvia K.

Sylvia arrived, and stayed two weeks with Dorothy and Clarence. "Dr. Bob talked to her, and he corralled the A.A. men, who were only too willing to talk to her after they saw her," said Dorothy.

In the meantime, Sylvia started taking little white pills,

which she said were saccharin. No one could understand why she was so rubber-legged, and a nurse had to be flown in to take care of her. After talking to Bob, Sylvia decided to live in Akron. This caused great consternation, since her presence threatened to disrupt the whole group. But someone told her it would mean a great deal more if she could go back and help in Chicago.

This appealed to Sylvia, so the members put her and her nurse on the train. Sylvia headed for the dining car and got drunk. She sobered up, however, when she got to Chicago and got in touch with Earl.

He wrote to New York in September 1939 that the A.A.'s in Chicago were organizing a group and would have regular meetings. "There are eight of us—with three new prospects who will go to Akron in the near future," he said. "Sylvia back in Evanston and anxious to help with the work here. Whether she has it yet is a question, but we will continue to work with her."

A few weeks later, Earl wrote Bill that they had four doctors and a hospital very much interested in working with them. "At the present time, we have ten rummies—three women and seven men—and five nonalkies in the group," he said, "all working hard on the eight new prospects that we have at the present writing. Several of these have come through you from the *Liberty* article."

It is interesting to note that while Chicago had three women out of perhaps a dozen members, there were none to speak of in Akron or Cleveland. Sylvia and one other woman, who came in at the same time as her husband, stayed sober from then on.

Helped by her nonalcoholic secretary, Grace Cultice, Sylvia set up a phone service in her home. At the time of the *Saturday Evening Post* article, in 1941, they rented a one-room office in the Loop, and Grace directed a stream of prospects to A.A. This was one of A.A.'s first organized local service centers. Many groups within several hundred miles trace their origin to the work of the Chicago Central Office—including Green Bay, Madison, and Milwaukee, Wisconsin, and Minneapolis, Minnesota.

When Archie T. arrived in Akron in 1938 to stay with Dr. Bob and Anne, he was sure he was never going back to Detroit, where his personal reputation and financial credit were zero. Six months later, he knew that he did have to go back to the town where he had made a mess of things, to "face them and then carry the A.A. message to any who might want it."

He gave credit for this change of heart to Anne Smith, and cited it as another example of her wise understanding and patience, since she always waited for Archie "to search out the answers for myself," he recalled, "and then for me to pursue the path that these answers indicated."

This time, the path led back to Detroit. Archie was still sick, frail, and frightened when he returned. He made amends where he could, and made a living by delivering dry cleaning out of a jalopy to the back doors of fashionable one-time friends in Grosse Pointe. With the help of nonalcoholic Sarah Klein, he started a basement A.A. group.

In October 1939, Archie managed to get a six-minute radio interview about his recovery in A.A. It was heard in a number of Midwest cities and certainly represented a first for the area. A year later, Dorothy wrote: "Archie's assurance and confidence are a miracle."

There was also an outreach program, of sorts. Early in 1939, Jack D., one of Bill Wilson's New York pigeons, who had sobered up and gone home to Cleveland, went to Youngstown to see an old buddy. This was Norman Y., who was totally blind from bootleg liquor and had lost his wife, family, and job.

"I was living in the basement of an apartment building,

and I had a mattress on the floor," Norman said in 1977. "I knew I was an alcoholic, but it took two hours before Jack could get me to admit I was powerless over alcohol. Then he said, 'Let's pray about it.'

"Once, his salary was $150,000 a year, and there he is sitting on the mattress with his arms around me," Norman said. " 'Dear God, here we are, two alcoholics, and we want to change our way of living so we won't be bothered by alcohol anymore. With Your help, we know we can make it.'

"That was my introduction to A.A. There were no meetings around. I stayed dry, and all I said was 'Thank You,' every hour on the hour. When I was dry eight weeks, they had four people get together over in Youngstown. They'd been dried up in Cleveland Hospital and Pittsburgh Hospital—two men and two women. They talked a little bit about the Oxford Group, a little bit about Dr. Bob and Bill. They were using the Lord's Prayer.

"They all had jobs," Norman said. "Later, one of the men came up to me and said, 'Let me tell you something, you blind old bat. You got no more intention of staying sober than the man in the moon. The only reason you come here is to get acquainted with these people so you can beg. The thing for you to do is stay the hell away.'

"That was my first A.A. meeting. I went back to that mattress and I lay down and I said, 'I'm gonna get drunk and go out and kill that bastard. I'll kill his wife, then I'll kill him. No, I won't. I'll kill the whole damn A.A.'

"Then something said to me, 'You go, and go there regular. And don't take any material help from any of them.'"

He never did—not for jobs, nor trips to speak at meetings, nor anything else. In fact, when Norman finally got a job, in 1940, helping other blind people, he started to put aside ten percent of his salary to pay for speaking trips, contributions at meetings, and other A.A. expenses.

"I got to the King School meeting in 1940—when I first met Dr. Bob," Norman said. "'How did you get here?' Dr. Bob asked me.

"'I came by bus.'

"'We'll get you back,' he said.

"'No, I'll go back the way I came.'

"'You're too damned independent,' he told me.

"He was real outgoing, but so forceful," said Norman, who, after five years, got his wife and family back. "I couldn't see him, and that made me a little shy and backward. We just didn't register with our personalities at first.

"Bill [Wilson] was soft—quiet," Norman said. "I felt calm and peaceful sitting in a room where Bill was. But inside him, he was the promoter. And Dr. Bob would say, 'Don't sell it. Give it to them.'

"Bob was wonderful. He kept it down to earth, I'll tell you. Later, I'd tell him stories about my job, and he'd laugh and laugh. His wife—she wanted to adopt me like her child. Dr. Bob would sit around and listen, but she'd do the talking."

xiv. A.A. and St.Thomas Hospital

Neither Dr. Bob nor Sister Ignatia ever recorded the exact time they started talking about treating alcoholics at St. Thomas Hospital. Their conversations on the subject stretched out over a considerable period, with Dr. Bob getting more serious as the situation deteriorated at City Hospital.

"We often discussed the problem of alcoholism and the tragedies caused by excessive drinking," according to Sister Ignatia, who said she could never understand why she must turn away one drunk on the verge of the D.T.'s and admit another with a bashed-in head. Both were sick and needed help.

She recalled that all they could do for the man nearing D.T.'s was call the police, because otherwise he might get into an accident. In fact, she was able to name five men who had been in "terrific accidents" and had later come into A.A. This included two of the earliest members, Bill V. H. and Dick S.

"I believe that Doctor must have had this in mind for

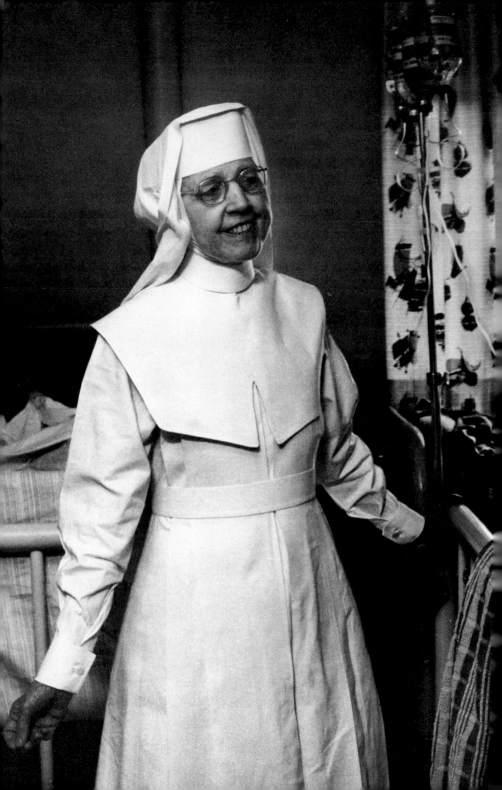

some time," Sister Ignatia said. "There was an accident once where an intoxicated driver was the cause of three or four machines' colliding. They took some patients to City and some to our place, and it seems to me I said to Doctor, 'Isn't it a pity someone can't do something for these people before they get into a wreck like this?'

"He said, 'Well, we've tried to do something for these fellows. We've been kind of working on something. Haven't got very far, but we're trying.' I don't recall exactly, except that it was a combination of medical and spiritual.

"Then one day, to my great surprise, Dr. Bob told me about his own drinking problem," Sister Ignatia said. "I could hardly believe it, as I had never seen Doctor under the influence. He told me about his contact with the Oxford Group and how, after attending meetings, he found himself with the Bible in one hand and a glass in the other. He related his providential meeting with Bill and gave me the résumé of all that had been accomplished between the years of 1935 and 1938."

She remembered still more clearly the day when Dr. Bob came to St. Thomas after being told in no uncertain terms by another hospital "to seek refuge for his jittering patients else-where," as Sister Ignatia put it. "I had never seen Doctor in a depressed mood before that memorable day. I thought he was ill, but I soon learned the cause of his discouragement.

"Dr. Bob explained his problem, but I was fearful to admit an alcoholic," said Sister Ignatia. "Just a short time before, I had admitted an alcoholic on my own, put him on general medical services, and asked him to promise me that he wouldn't make any noise or give any trouble. The next morn-

Once wary of alcoholics, Sister Ignatia learned how they could be helped, and she became a loving friend of A.A.

ing, the night supervisor told me in unmistakable terms that
the next time I admitted a D.T., I had better be prepared to
stay up all night and run around the corridors after him.

"Naturally, I was pretty well intimidated after that and
when Doctor proposed my admitting this patient, I was a little
shaky inside. But he assured me he would see that the patient
didn't cause any trouble, so I consented to try it.

"I was rather proud of myself the next morning, because
I hadn't heard any serious report from the night supervisor.
Then Doctor came down and said, 'Sister, would you mind
putting my patient in a private room? There will be some men
here to visit with him, and they'd like to talk privately.'

"I said, 'Doctor, we do not have any beds, much less private rooms, but I will do what I can.' I looked around to see
who was going home. Finally, I happened to think of the
room where we used to prepare the patients' flowers. I wasn't
even sure that a bed would go through the door, but it did,
thank God. So we pushed it in, and there the patient was,
perfectly satisfied—because these men came and talked with
him and made him forget himself.

"We were quite amazed at the men who came," said Sister
Ignatia. "I had an idea probably they'd all be rather . . . well, I
don't know what I was expecting. But they were a fine lot of
men. I couldn't believe that they were alcoholics. I checked
with them later, and they all said yes, they were alcoholics.
There must have been four or five. They sort of timed their
visits so they would not all be there at the same time.

"I was pretty well governed by whatever Doctor said as to
the length of the stay and type of treatment."

This was in August 1939. Dr. Bob could never remember
just what the policy of St. Thomas was at the time, nor did he
recall ever having asked. But between that day and the time
he died, 4,800 alcoholics were admitted into St. Thomas under his care.

Dr. Bob and Sister Ignatia began to work more and more closely through the fall of 1939 in getting drunks into St. Thomas for treatment. One thing worried her, however: Alcoholics Anonymous seemed to be closely connected with the Oxford Group.

"At the time, I feared we might become involved with a religious sect of some kind," Sister Ignatia recalled. She then asked Father Vincent Haas, a newly ordained priest, to investigate the meetings for her.

They had met only a few days earlier, when Sister asked him to talk to a drunk with a pregnant wife. He tried; but after an hour, the man asked, "Have you ever been drunk for a week?"

"No. As a matter of fact, I don't drink," the young priest replied.

"Then you don't know what you're talking about," the man said. "Come back when you've been drinking a week."

Soon after, Sister Ignatia asked Father Haas whether he knew anything about alcoholism. "I wish I did," he replied. Then she asked him to check out A.A. "She couldn't go out, being a sister," he recalled.

Fortunately, the group had moved to King School by this time, and Father Haas was favorably impressed. He told Sister Ignatia that if A.A. continued on the course it was then following, it would become one of the great movements of the age in the conquest of alcoholism.

Following this report, Sister Ignatia and Dr. Bob began to set up "a definite program for the care of alcoholic patients." They obtained the approval of the monsignor of the Akron Catholic deanery and the Reverend Mother Clementine, who was administrator of St. Thomas.

"There was a time when alcoholics were a great trial to us," the Reverend Mother said later. "We worried lest they jump out of a window to get into other serious trouble. Today, under this treatment, things have changed. Evidently, Dr. Smith knows how to take care of these patients."

In the meantime, Sister Ignatia had found another task for Father Haas. "The chaplain at the hospital didn't want to hear the confessions of alcoholic patients, because he didn't think they truly repented," he recalled. "Sister Ignatia would sneak me into a quiet, secluded place so I could hear them. She had a tremendous love of God and of people. She was a mother, sister, and friend to many."

Sister Ignatia was then assigned the task of providing a permanent hospital plan for treatment of alcoholics in cooperation with Dr. Bob. Like the Akron A.A. group itself, the St. Thomas program was to provide a pattern for many other hospitals in cities throughout the country, if not the world.

"We coasted along slowly and cautiously at first," Sister Ignatia said, "trying to arrange accommodations so patients would have privacy and A.A. visitors might talk with them. Soon, we learned that they did better with other patients in two- or four-bed rooms. The group therapy helps one forget himself in helping others. He soon learns that it is more blessed to give than to receive, and that it is a privilege to help others. The individual is kept so busy assisting others that he does not have time to think of a drink."

As the number of alcoholics being admitted for treatment increased over the years, accommodations were enlarged to an eight-bed ward. At one end, there was a small lounge and kitchenette equipped with comfortable chairs, sofa, and coffee bar. The corridor served as a larger lounge, where sponsors could visit patients.

The visits developed into a continuous discussion of A.A. with the patients from noon until ten o'clock at night. One member who had been active at St. Thomas in the 1940's said there was an average of at least 15 visitors a day. So at the end of a five-day period, the prospective A.A. had met from 60 to as many as 100 visitors, a few of whom at least would click.

Patients were allowed only A.A. visitors, and there were no repeaters among the patients. The latter custom eliminated the problem of a newcomer's being given a disheartening view of the program by someone who had tried once and failed. There were other advantages for the alcoholic patient—a physical checkup, regular diet and sleeping habits, and doctors on call for emergencies.

"We learned from experience that the program is defeated in institutions where the majority of inmates are repeaters," Sister said. "It creates an atmosphere of pessimism and discouragement."

That situation has changed, however. One oldtimer in the Akron area said in 1977, "It used to be you could only get into the A.A. ward once. Now, it's once a week. In those days, if Sister caught you with a newspaper, it was your . . . well, she got mad. And if you complained that you didn't have anything to read, she'd say you didn't come here to read, you came here to get well."

Joe P. (the Akron A.A. who was Dr. Bob's fellow Dartmouth alumnus) said that the general thinking among local A.A.'s in the early 1940's was similar: If you had something wrong with you, that's what you talked about; you didn't talk about sports or politics.

"We had a group of nine people who went up [to the hospital] every day," Joe said. "We felt that when you were up there, you were the sickest you would ever be, and you owed it to yourself to get well. Second, you kind of owed it to the people who took their time to visit, to at least pay close attention to them.

"Dr. Bob felt if you were taking it seriously, you would make every effort to use all things that were available," said Joe. "And he was a little bit perturbed when you didn't. I think he was responsible for having only one admission to the A.A. ward. The other day, I ran into a guy I put in the hospital eight times, and he's still back where he was."

"It's different today," agreed Dan K., another Akron A.A. "When I was [a patient] at St. Thomas, I saw a man crying. 'What's he crying for?' I asked a nurse.

" 'He's crying for Franklin,' she said.

" 'Franklin who?'

" 'Franklin Roosevelt.'

"The President died, and I didn't know it! They did bring in the *Plain Dealer* on the day Harry Truman was inaugurated, so we could see the headlines.

"Dr. Bob gave basic talks at the hospital—what A.A. is about," said Dan. "He always emphasized 'Easy Does It' and 'First Things First.' We called the ward the basic-training grounds for Alcoholics Anonymous.

"Bob said there was the hard way and the easy way. The hard way was just by going to meetings. In five days at St. Thomas, you would hear as many talks as you would hear in six months outside.

"People came to St. Thomas from all over," Dan said. "Once, they had an exhibition with a map of the world. There were red strings from different countries leading to St. Thomas. 'You mean they bring alcoholics here from all over the world?' one woman asked. 'I think we already got enough in Akron. We don't need any more.' "

Nonetheless, they still tell the story about the fellow who was flown in for the "cure" in a private plane. "Please pray for me," he begged Sister Ignatia.

"I will indeed," she said. "But pray for yourself as well. There's nothing God likes to hear more than a strange voice."

Many a recovery began in the alcoholic ward at St. Thomas, under the care of Dr. Bob and Sister Ignatia.

In later years, the A.A. ward opened into the gallery of the chapel, which patients could visit at any time in hospital attire. "What could be more conducive to the regeneration of the whole person spiritually, mentally, and morally than five to seven days spent in an institution where the spiritual atmosphere prevails?" Sister Ignatia said.

She naturally put more emphasis on the spiritual than many others. However, she felt that Dr. Bob shared her views on this emphasis. "There was one thing that always irritated Doctor," she said. "Some people who were on the program for a length of time would come up to him and say, 'I don't get the spiritual angle.' I heard him say time and again, 'There is no spiritual angle. It's a spiritual program.'

"I feel all these people run away from God," Sister Ignatia said. "I tell them, 'We are all God's children. He loves us, or we wouldn't be here. Now, if we will start from where we are and begin to bend our knees instead of our elbows and ask for His help . . .'"

While Sister Ignatia stressed prayer, she knew how to get her point across with different people. They tell the story of Morris, a Jewish member whose sponsor was an Irish cop. Morris felt a bit out of place at St. Thomas. As one Akron A.A. remembered it: "When the others went into the chapel to pray, Sister Ignatia came in to him and said, 'Morris, why don't you kneel down by the side of the bed and pray to God as *you* understand Him?' After that, she was a saint as far as Morris and his wife were concerned."

Though Sister Ignatia was frail and in physical pain a good deal of the time, her sense of humor never failed. On one occasion, a former patient returned to tell her, "Sister, this is the tenth anniversary of my sobriety."

"That's wonderful," she said. "But don't forget, should you ever need our services again, we still have your size in pajamas."

Sister Ignatia gave each of her newly released patients a Sacred Heart medallion, which she asked them to return before they took the first drink. She would occasionally give out St. Christopher medals as well, but she would tell the recipient not to drive too fast. "He gets out after 50 miles an hour," she warned.

Sister Ignatia remembered Dr. Bob as "the essence of professional dignity. He had a fine sense of humor and an exceptional vocabulary. With a little humorous phrase or slang expression, he would bring into the conversation an air of finality which left no room for criticism or comment. He had no time for idle chatter and would always make his point quite clear in as few words as possible.

"Dr. Bob took a personal interest in all the ward activities," Sister Ignatia recalled. "He visited the patients daily without salary until his health failed.

"He screened most of the patients himself in the early days, either before or after they were admitted. After making rounds in the morning, he would sometimes say to me, 'Sister, that monkey up there doesn't want the program.' I would then give him a pathetic tale about the man's wife and little family and how his job was in jeopardy if he didn't straighten out. Doctor would shake his head and say, 'Sister, he just isn't ready.' Doctor was always right.

"I learned from experience that it was a waste of time to force anyone to accept the program," said Sister Ignatia. "Many of these patients were a great source of worry to me. They would come with their complaints, imaginary or otherwise. I didn't like to bother Doctor too much, so I would call Anne. Anne's advice was of great value to me. Her calm, soothing tone and sympathetic understanding were a source of encouragement. She always found the correct answer. In her diplomatic way, she would present the problem to the doctor, then telephone me and advise.

"I didn't realize that Doctor suffered so much, but he told me in later days that often he would be scrubbing and he'd overhear other doctors saying, 'You have to be a drunk to get a bed in this place.' He said he would go right on scrubbing and pretend he didn't hear. He suffered from these things, but I think later things changed a great deal.

"I had plenty of difficulty myself. I would overhear remarks from doctors and even nurses to the effect that it was hard to get beds around the hospital unless you were an alcoholic. But I would be blind and deaf and dumb."

Sister Ignatia made a point of helping her charges through their Fourth Step self-inventories, and told them how to take care of resentments and anger. She believed in the Ninth Step, making restitution, which she felt, even as she reminisced back in the 1950's, was not stressed as much as in the early days. "I can recall when some of those first men would come back to me after making their restitution," she said. "One told me, 'Do you know, I have the finest feeling. I feel that they are my best friends.' "

Sister Ignatia always made it a point to see what she could do to reconcile the family. "If it's the husband, I have the wife come in the day before he leaves. She'll say, 'I just don't want to see him. I'm finished with him.'

"Then I ask if she'll just come and see me. She doesn't have to see her husband. I tell her, 'Now, you've traveled a long way with this man. Wouldn't it be worthwhile taking one more chance on this program? This is not only a sobering-up process. We wouldn't use valuable hospital space if we were in the business just to sober people up. The thing that is so heartening to us is that so many who come through here get the program and never have any more trouble. Now, won't you, on the strength of that, just give him one more chance? If you can do this, if you can pull the curtain on the past and start off again, I assure you we'll return to you the man you married in the first place.' After I finish talking to her, I say, 'Of course, you don't want to see him.' She will usually say, 'Well, perhaps he doesn't want to see me.' 'Well, I'll see. Just wait here a moment. It's up to both of you. I'm not getting into any domestic troubles.'

"So I get him in the corner and say, 'You know who I have in the office? Your wife. But of course you don't want to see her, I suppose.' He says, 'Well, I'm ashamed to talk to her.' 'Well, would you like to see her? Maybe she would if I talked to her.'

"I get the two of them together. I go in with him, and as soon as the ice is broken and I see that they are beginning to get together and talk, I say I have to go out to answer the phone or something, and leave them."

When Anne died, in 1949, Sister Ignatia wrote Bob a letter in which she recalled some of the experiences they had all had together.

On Christmas Eve, Bob replied with a characteristically short but quite eloquent note. "My dear Sister," he said, "it is most fortunate for me that I have been blessed with the friendship of one so staunch and true as yourself. You have demonstrated in so many ways your love, loyalty, and kindness that I cannot even begin to thank you adequately. In a lifetime, one may meet some one or two wonderful characters like yourself. So, for my rare privilege of knowing you, I feel most humbly grateful. May God's blessing be ever on you. With a great deal of love, Dr. Bob Smith."

Dr. Bob made his last visit to the ward about then, perhaps on Christmas Day, 1949. On that day, Sister played the organ for him and showed him the beautiful new chimes, which in themselves told how the criticism of ten years before had changed to complete cooperation.

In 1952, Sister Ignatia was transferred from St. Thomas to administer the alcoholic ward at St. Vincent's Charity Hospital in Cleveland. At her suggestion, it was dedicated as Rosary Hall Solarium. The initials R. H. S. carved in flowing script over the door "just happened" to be the same as those of Dr. Robert Holbrook Smith.

In the course of her life, Sister Ignatia was involved in the treatment of many thousands of alcoholics. Through it all, she not only picked up an education about alcoholism, but acquired the lingo that went with it—not too different from Dr. Bob's own.

A Cleveland newspaper feature reported Sister Ignatia's telling new patients in the 1950's, "Some of you lads, no doubt, started out on top-shelf whiskey—maybe you even finished there. But I bet there's many a one of you who has sampled bay rum, 'open switch' [sherry and rubbing alcohol], or 'derail' [antifreeze strained through rye bread]. Some of you probably sat for days in some stupid barroom, half drunk, without money or credit, praying that a 'livey' would drop in the joint."

When Sister Ignatia died, in April 1966, she was eulogized as a charming, radiant little woman with no other aspiration than to be a humble, dedicated, and anonymous Sister of Charity.

"She was unconscious of greatness and fame," the priest said. "The more she tried to conceal her holiness, the more it became apparent to all men."

Perhaps Bill said it as well when Sister Ignatia told him she wanted her name kept out of the second Jack Alexander article in the *Saturday Evening Post.* "To be anonymous, Sister, you'll have to take a little drink," Bill said.

Sister Ignatia's favorite quote was the divine paradox posed by the Apostle to the Gentiles: "But the foolish things of the world hath God chosen that He may confound the wise, and the weak things of the world hath God chosen that He may confound the strong, and the base things of the world and the things that are contemptible hath God chosen, and the things that are not, that He might bring to nought things that are; that no flesh should glory in His sight."

xv. Sudden growth in Cleveland

A.A. members in Cleveland were doing all they could to carry the message, but, Dorothy S. M. said, "It was just trial and error, and a great deal of it error. We weren't going to let anybody stay drunk. I remember how we chased one man around. He would stay sober for a little while and then get drunk and disappear. But we looked for him all over Ohio, getting him out of jail and dragging him back.

"I felt that nobody in Cleveland should be drunk—or anywhere in the world—as long as there was an A.A. So I was pounding the streets trying to show different bookstores the A.A. book. I went down to the public library and tried to get orders. Nobody would even listen to me, and they looked at me like I was Salvation Nell."

Dorothy wrote Ruth Hock at the New York office, in October 1939: "Doc Smith told me last night that God did have one or two other agents besides me, and that He could put the world to bed and hang out the sun without me. I love

Doc for remarks like that. I slowed down—mentally, anyway."

Regarding Dr. Bob, Ruth wrote Dorothy: "Queer that having met him only once, I feel he is one of the best friends I ever had." In later years, Ruth (married by then to an A.A. member from southern Ohio) recalled that Dr. Bob seemed to have a great sympathy and interest in you—that he also had a twinkle and loved to tease the young people.

"Yeah, he did have a twinkle," agreed Smitty, Dr. Bob's son. "And he had a tremendous magnetism for women. He was extremely courtly and flattered them. They knew it and they loved it."

Another physician was among the alcoholics who drew the earnest attentions of Cleveland A.A.'s. Clarence's letter to Hank P. when the first group was formed there noted that "the boys have lined up the doctor and are watching him like hawks to try and keep him straight until the dangerous time is past." He was referring to Dr. Harry N., who had then been sober only a few weeks and was to devote a great deal of his time thereafter to new members who were hospitalized.

A.A. was able to get beds in Cleveland's Deaconess Hospital through the efforts of Edna McD., who was married to one of the members. According to Al G. (the lawyer at whose home early Cleveland meetings were held), Edna was a county visiting nurse whose job brought her into contact with the administrative organizations of all the hospitals in the county.

She felt that Dr. Kitterer of Deaconess, an ordained minister as well as a trained institutional administrator, was the most likely to understand alcoholics' need for a spiritual program such as A.A.'s. She found him sympathetic.

Hoping to secure beds for alcoholics at Deaconess, with visiting privileges for A.A.'s, Dr. Bob and Dr. Harry N. "hastened to see him Dr. Kitterer liked the idea," Al said. "But he had to go to bat with the board of trustees. He sold them, but the medical staff was quite critical. We entered our first patient (a bartender) at the end of May 1939.

"We put candidates in the hospital without any forethought as to how the bills would be paid," Al recalled. "By 1940, we owed some $1,200 to $1,400. Eventually, we raised funds to retire the debt over two or three years."

Dr. N. did not charge for his services; but some years later, another doctor member took on this work, and the groups decided that a nominal fee of $10 for him should be added to each patient's bill. "This led to the usual argument about professionalism, which was debated often and furiously," said Al.

"St. Vincent's Charity Hospital, later to become home of Rosary Hall, followed Deaconess in 1940 by taking patients in single rooms, and eventually Sister Victorine established a ward there," Al said.

Apart from the work with hospital patients, there were other significant developments in Cleveland. In October 1939, Dorothy S. informed the New York office that a committee of seven—five men and two women—was functioning in the Cleveland area. In addition to being the first central committee, this is said to be the first example of rotation in A.A., since one man and one woman dropped off each month to be replaced by the next in line according to seniority.

Bill Wilson gave Al G., the first chairman, credit for setting up the principle of rotation in A.A., either in the fall of 1939 or upon the later establishment of a more formalized central committee. "Up to that time, all of our affairs had been in charge of the ultra-oldtimers, and we naturally supposed it would always be that way," said Bill. But Al was older (in years) than most other A.A.'s, had family affairs to keep him busy, and so was ready to pass along responsibilities.

"We met once a month, and then we decided to open an office," Clarence said in later years. "Up to then, we had a post office box and telephone." He said the committee had been organized to coordinate efforts regarding hospitalization and sponsorship.

"It's really functioning," Dorothy noted in her letter to the New York office. "They appoint leaders, discuss tendencies, and arrange social affairs, and they are thinking of a masked dance for Halloween," she said.

Whether they had time for the dance is questionable, for Clarence was planning bigger things. Somehow—accounts vary—he had come across a reporter for the Cleveland *Plain Dealer* and persuaded him to write a series of articles about A.A., which appeared in the latter part of October 1939.

Warren C. (the member who had been broke but proud when he joined the Cleveland group) said of Clarence, "I think he, more than anybody else— at least, around here— foresaw the great possibilities of the growth of A.A. He was raring to go. Well, so was I, for that matter. He wanted it to grow, and he wanted it to become all A.A. And I think Doc was supportive. He could see the possibilities of working this program face-to-face, man-to-man.

"Clarence sneaked a *Plain Dealer* reporter into one of the meetings. He posed as an alcoholic. He wasn't really. He was a writer," Warren said.

But Dorothy recalled, "Clarence got hold of a reporter. I'm sure he was an alcoholic. He came to the meeting at Al G——'s."

In "A.A. Comes of Age," Bill refers to Elrick B. Davis as "a feature writer of deep understanding."

According to Clarence, *someone* brought Davis to the meetings. "I convinced him to write a series on A.A. and told him he might catch fire if he did a good job. He had been probated to the nuthouse and was on the way down."

So you pay your money and you take your choice. Or, looked at another way, this discrepancy might be one explanation for the general A.A. opinion that it is up to the individual to identify himself or herself as an alcoholic: Even A.A. members don't always agree.

Whatever his status, the articles Davis wrote set off an unprecedented wave of growth for A.A. in the Cleveland area. The five-part series, according to Bill, "ushered in a new period for Alcoholics Anonymous—the mass production of sobriety."

As if anticipating the breaking wave, Bill had written Dr. Bob in September, following publication of the article about A.A. in *Liberty* Magazine: "We are growing at an alarming rate, although I have no further fear of large numbers." A few weeks later, he reported that "the press of newcomers and inquiries was so great that we have to swing more to the take-it-or-leave-it attitude, which, curiously enough, produces better results than trying to be all things at all times at all places to all men."

The *Plain Dealer* articles furnished as good a description of A.A. as one could find at the time, and except for the differences in words and phrasings, would not have been very much out of date 40 years later.

In the first article, Davis told, for instance, how "every Thursday evening, 40 to 50 members meet for a social evening. Nearly every Saturday evening, they and their families meet for a social evening during which they buck each other up.

"Requests for help," he wrote, "would be forwarded to a Cleveland banker [probably a bank teller, Bill J.] who is head of the local fellowship, or to a big-league ballplayer [Rollie H.] who is recruiting officer of the Akron fellowship."

Davis also noted that "although a good many of the Akron chapter find help in the practices of the Oxford Group, there are several Catholics and Jews in Cleveland." He stressed that A.A. differed from churches in that members could choose their own concepts of "God as you understand Him."

At the same time, Dorothy S., armed with a copy of the Big Book, had gone back to see the Reverend Dilworth Lupton. "I felt that now we had fallen away from Akron, now there was no Oxford Group [connection], Dr. Lupton should be interested. So I went back to him and said we were no longer an Oxford Group and asked him to please come to a meeting.

"He read it [the Big Book], and he said that he would definitely come to one of our meetings. He did, and he was so impressed that he said, 'Dorothy, you go back to the *Plain Dealer* and you tell them that I'm going to preach on A.A.'

"That was for publicity. He was one of the really big Protestant ministers in Cleveland, and what he said was good copy," said Dorothy.

As reported in the November 27, 1939, issue of the *Plain Dealer*, Dr. Lupton preached a sermon called "Mr. X and Alcoholics Anonymous." Mr. X was Clarence, and the sermon was later turned into a pamphlet that served the Cleveland area for many years.

In his sermon, Dr. Lupton noted that there was room in A.A. for all creeds, through the concept of God as "a Power greater than ourselves." Such an attitude "displays nothing short of genius," he said.

Clarence had anticipated the result of the publicity to some extent, for he wrote Ruth Hock in the New York office that he was going to forward all inquiries from the articles, so she could "send out letters with books, just as you did for the *Liberty* article.

"No doubt you shall receive some inquiries direct, as the address is noted in the first article," Clarence said. "Use the inquiries, and then send them to us for personal contact if they want it. Send all the inquiries in this section to me, and any around Akron to Doc Smith, and he will handle them. The *Plain Dealer* expects quite a number of inquiries from these five articles. We also have some other publicity in the wind."

Still, the results must have been beyond anyone's expectations. The Cleveland group was virtually deluged with calls and inquiries.

"The newspaper passed on hundreds and hundreds of names to me," Clarence said. "New York also gave me a lot of names in the area. I would hand them out on Monday morning like a sales manager—tell them to follow up and report to me on Wednesday. Nobody had a job at that time, so it was all right.

"For six or eight weeks, I didn't get more than three or four hours' sleep a night," he recalled. "After chasing drunks all day, I would write longhand letters to all the people who had written from Iowa, Indiana, Nebraska, and places like that. There were scores and hundreds of letters. The group grew and grew. People from Cleveland started groups in Indiana, Kentucky, New York State, California, Illinois," he said.

As Dorothy recalled, "When those articles hit Cleveland, people simply besieged the place. Our phone never quit ringing for about a month, and I did nothing but sit by the telephone and take inquiries. Ruth [Hock] was sending me lists of people who wanted help immediately. She even got telegrams in New York. I can remember one: 'This means life or death. Call me right now.'

"People had to be seen that day, and we only had about 13 people we could send out on Twelfth Step calls. I'd say almost 500 calls came in that first month. Every day, I'd call every one of these 13 men, and I'd give them a long list of people who had to be seen, and they would start out with five or six or eight calls every evening. How they ever did it, I don't know. But they made those calls.

"Within the space of about two weeks, our meetings grew from about 15 to 100," Dorothy said. "People couldn't get me on the phone, because the line was busy, so they'd come beating down the doors."

The *Plain Dealer* articles were responsible for helping A.A. get started in many cities and towns throughout Ohio. One example: the group in Ashtabula, some 45 miles from Cleveland.

After reading the articles, an alcoholic in Ashtabula told his wife, "I'm going to Cleveland to find out what this A.A. is about." As he recalled it, "I called the number, and they told me take a certain train. There were five of them to meet me. They took me to lunch, but I couldn't eat anything. They all ate great big meals and talked to me.

"The train got back to Ashtabula at 4:00 p.m. I walked from the depot past all the bars without having a drink. The next day, I went back and checked into Cleveland Hospital, where people came to see me day and night. All of them could shake the money in their pockets. They were clean-shaven and wore pressed suits, and I swallowed every bit of what they told me.

"After that, I would go to Cleveland for meetings. Everybody who knew me was talking about it, waiting for me to fall, but I didn't. The first one I got was my nephew. Then both of us would go to Cleveland. After a while, we got some others and started a group in Ashtabula. That was in 1940."

"We didn't have any literature except the book then," said Dorothy S. M., reminiscing with Bill Wilson. "You'd send us ten or 15 at a time. We thought that was really wholesale. Some people could afford to buy them, but most couldn't. I remember Ruth sent me ten books, and we gave them out hoping people would buy them. Some did—very few."

With the growth of A.A., there were growing pains—both in Cleveland and in Akron. Evidently, Dr. Bob and

Clarence S. each came in for his share of criticism at this time.

An October 3, 1940, entry in Lois Wilson's diary noted: "Met Williamses from Akron. Things muddled up there."

Later that month, Dorothy wrote to Ruth Hock and Hank P., "Things are happening fast and furious around here. I feel I have to sort of stand by to catch the pieces of Doc, Anne, and Clarence when they come hurtling in, torn limb from limb.

"The publicity that Doc got [not specified—perhaps the article in *Faith* Magazine] really roused the Oxfordites, and is there ever mud-slinging and reverberations! Doc and Anne took shelter at our house Saturday night, and they were both so stirred up and looked so old that it hurt me terribly. Hence my frantic efforts to get Bill down here. I really think Doc needs Bill for his own comfort. Doc looked pretty licked and tired. I'm so glad Bill is coming.

"The Akron group is pretty dead, and our successful meetings here [in Cleveland] had plenty of kickback down there," Dorothy continued. "Last week over 80 (and believe me, Hank, we are not counting scalps gleefully), and we expect about 100 this week.

"A few sourpusses pinned Clarence to the cross in no uncertain fashion last night, exploiting 'paid publicity, profit on the book, liar,' and whatnot, It hurt, I know, as they were all people he had helped. But how it is making him grow!"

Besides providing that early example of A.A.'s optimistic no-pain-no-gain philosophy, Dorothy also noted that demands for help were increasing, that more and more civic-minded people were interested in A.A., and that men in the program were working night and day with newer members.

As Clarence put it: "When the [first *Plain Dealer*] article appeared, it stirred up a hornet's nest. It wasn't great literature, but it had a tremendous effect. Someone said, 'This guy is a reporter. He's gonna put our names in the paper!'

" 'No,' I said, 'he's one of us—a rummy.'

" 'Yeah, he's a rummy all right, but he's a newspaperman.'

"It didn't make any difference. They were against it," Clarence said.

Remembering these events many years later, Warren C. said: "There was hell to pay when those stories broke. I mean, they really lacerated him. Of course, it was the greatest move that was ever made for A.A.

"A.A. started in a riot. It grows in riots. We got upset by the *Plain Dealer* business. We thought Clarence was going to get money, and voted him out of the group. He took others with him and started another group."

On November 10, Clarence wrote to New York that, effective that week, they would have three A.A. groups in Cleveland and "I expect two more at least by the beginning of the year. Right now, we have about 60 A.A.'s, most of them active, and an additional 15 to 20 being worked on in various ways. By splitting into smaller groups, the numbers should increase quite rapidly in the next 30 to 60 days."

Although he was silent about the problems he was having with the Cleveland membership, Clarence did note that the Oxford Group was "hopping up and down, as they have been trying vainly to get publicity.

"Can only think of eight who have slipped since our gang started six months ago," he said. "We find that putting the new fellows to work right away is the answer—putting them on their own and creating enthusiasm.

"The publicity has captured the interest of clergymen, doctors, medical people generally, welfare organizations, businessmen, and clubwomen. This seems the ideal time for Bill to visit here, and we are expecting him tomorrow."

Clarence moved on, "taking my friends," to establish the Borton Group, meeting at the home of T. E. Borton, a wealthy nonalcoholic, in Cleveland Heights. (It was not until many years later that the A.A. General Service Conference counseled against the practice of naming A.A. groups after individuals, in or out of the Fellowship, living or dead.)

A week later, Warren started a group on Cleveland's west side. It later became the Orchard Grove Group. "I was at both meetings," Warren said. "On the east side, we probably had 40 people—up from a mere handful. And on the west side here, we had 22 people as a result of the calls we made."

On November 16, Lois wrote in her diary: "Drove to Cleveland for meeting. Tremendous gathering. Clarence, Jack [perhaps Jack D. of New York, one of Bill's pigeons], and Bill spoke. Then, Bill and I dashed to second meeting. Met Mr. Lupton, Unitarian minister who is to give sermon on Nov. 26, and Elrick Davis, who wrote *Plain Dealer* articles."

Whatever his feelings regarding the Cleveland split, Bill was evidently playing no favorites. He went to *all* the meetings.

In December, Clarence wrote to Ruth: "Things are humming here, and it doesn't look like any letup. We have about 90 in our gang now in three groups, and lots of new ones being worked on at present. It looks like a busy winter for the girls and boys."

There was another significant development, which doesn't seem to have been recorded in earlier A.A. histories. Clarence wrote to Ruth Hock on December 12, 1939, that the "Matt Talbot Wagon Club" now had 88 members and "is doing a wonderful job." The "wagons" were used to collect old furniture, which members reconditioned and sold. As Clarence put it, they "had caught fire from the *Liberty* article and the *Plain Dealer*.

"We are working closely with them. They have no benefit of hospitalization or home setup. All are transients, stumble-bums, and social outcasts. There are nine of them working now. They are using our stuff and following much the same pattern in every way that it can be applied to their needs and setup."

The Wagon Club wasn't A.A., but there must have been some kind of cooperation, since they were using the A.A. program and materials. In any case, it seems to have marked the first A.A. effort to reach alcoholics outside the married, middle-class category, to which most early alcoholic members of the Oxford Group had belonged.

"We have long passed the 100 mark now," Clarence continued. "All three groups are growing steadily and rather rapidly. Almost time to start another gang. Having unusual success. Only four boys looped in last two months, counting the new ones. But all are well now."

Bill wrote later, "We oldtimers in New York and Akron had regarded this fantastic phenomenon with deep misgivings. Had it not taken us four whole years, littered with countless failures, to produce even 100 good recoveries? Yet there in Cleveland we saw about 20 members, not very experienced themselves, suddenly confronted by hundreds of newcomers. . . . How could they possibly manage? We did not know.

"But a year later, we *did* know," Bill recalled, "for by then, Cleveland had about 30 groups and several hundred members. Growing pains and group problems had been terrifying, but no amount of squabbling could dampen the mass demand for sobriety. Yes, Cleveland's results were of the best. Their results were in fact so good, and A.A.'s membership elsewhere was so small, that many a Clevelander really thought A.A. had started there in the first place."

Bill concluded, "The Cleveland pioneers had proved three essential things: the value of personal sponsorship, the worth of the A.A. book in indoctrinating newcomers, and finally, the tremendous fact that A.A., when the word really got around, could now soundly grow to great size."

XVI. Split between Akron A.A and the Oxford Group

About Akron A.A.'s break with the Oxford Group, very little was set down in writing. Nor did Dr. Bob ever say much about the matter—remembering to "guard that erring member, the tongue." No one interviewed could recall any direct comments he ever made, except to the effect that it became too crowded at T. Henry's.

As we have seen, the split had been a long time coming, and when it did occur, no one was quite sure about the exact circumstances. When Bill paid his visit to the area in mid-November, it was primarily to help Doc, although there is no record of what they talked about. Today, some members from Akron say Bill advised Doc to make the break. Others say he advised Bob to stay with the Oxford Group.

Some think that, when it came to movement matters, Dr. Bob was a bit of an autocrat. Bill, on the other hand, was likely to throw his ideas out to the whole membership for approval. "This was not his nature," Lois said. "He made himself do it."

Others have observed that Bill could be very persuasive when
he considered a question to be important to the Fellowship;
he would go to great lengths to get people to see things his
way.

At this time, according to John and Elgie R., "All of the
organizational stuff went on the Q.T. Bob and Anne would
take off and go to New York and talk to Bill, and then they'd
come back. The average member wasn't aware of it.

"They [Bill and Dr. Bob] didn't particularly want too
much interest in it. Maybe they came to think they'd better
keep as few people involved as possible in that part of it,
because it got to be a big brouhaha, and that just took time.

"Take the name A.A., for instance," said John. "The people here in Akron didn't like it, and they were saying no.
Wally G—— said, 'Hey, what's with this A.A. deal? We want to
call it Saint James' But Doc knew all the time that they were
going to call it A.A."

"He and Bill chewed that one out," said Elgie.

"Sure," said John. "They had it that way before we knew
it. Then it dawned on Wally that he was arguing against it and
they had already named it. Boy, that used to make him sore!
But he was a nice guy."

Elgie said, "Doc and Bill would sashay around and never
say a word. They'd ooze in and out of situations and let everybody just fight tooth and nail. All the while, it was going to be
a certain way, and that was it. When they announced it, everybody would accept it and that was the end of it. But in the
meantime, the other A.A.'s thought they had something to say
about it, and they would fight battles galore."

One oldtimer noted that in Akron they regarded Bill as

*The bond between Dr. Bob and Bill strengthened over the years,
from partnership to deep affection (next pages).*

"the man in the gray flannel suit," but Elgie said, "I'll never forget the first time I saw Bill Wilson. He was sitting behind me at this meeting. I turned around, and he had his foot up, and one shoe had a big hole.

"He was always pretty quiet. He never had too much to say in the larger group. He had so many things to do and so many people to see that it was all business. The time for sitting and chewing and arguing was over, as far as he was concerned. He didn't come here to do that. They had argued it all out in New York, and he figured that Doc had it settled here.

"I thought Bob, Bill, Anne, and Lois were very close. In fact, they had a good time together," Elgie recalled.

"Ideal all the way through," said John. "I remember, I first met Bill and Lois at Doc's house. The next day, here came Lois down the street, and she recognized me. I whispered, 'Let's go in and have a drink.' She looked at me. I said, 'A drink of coffee.' She turned around, and we went in and got a little shot of coffee, and I got a little more acquainted with her. I thought she was awfully nice."

At that time, Bill was in a good position—respected and listened to in the Akron-Cleveland area at least as much as Dr. Bob himself. We have only to read the letters through the early 1940's from Clarence and other oldtimers in the area asking for advice, visits, and moral support. Bill might have had his problems in New York; but in Akron and Cleveland, he was above it all—an elder statesman. Bob, though senior to all the others, was in many respects just one of the boys.

Whatever Bill's advice to Doc about the Oxford Group matter might have been, Bob E. felt that the women had a lot to do with the final split. This belief was not farfetched. The wives all considered themselves members of A.A. and had a great deal to say. Furthermore, Anne was extremely protective of Dr. Bob, who evidently was taking quite a beating at the time. Remember what Smitty said: His mother, though timid by nature, was capable of rising to great heights when someone threatened her family or the principles of A.A.

"Henrietta [Seiberling] didn't like the book," said Bob E. (who had joined the Akron group early in 1937). "She and Anne had a little falling-out over that. Then Clarace Williams and Anne had a falling-out over something. What it was, no one ever found out.

"There were some hot conversations on the telephone. It was a three-way thing between Clarace, Henrietta, and Anne. The women decided it, as was usually the case in things like that. And Doc went along with Annie."

About that time, Doc went to New York to see Bill, who, in a letter dated December 1939, said: "Thanks for your visit and also for your suits. I don't know what I'd have done without them." And not a word of *what* they had talked about! (They could hardly have foreseen the establishment of A.A. archives.)

It was probably following this visit that Dr. Bob went to talk with T. Henry Williams, who told Bill about the conversation in a letter two months later. Noting that "the boys were all over 21," T. Henry told Bill: "I have nothing to hold them here. Bob came over and insisted that the boys were not satisfied and felt we were unfriendly and insisted they meet elsewhere. He also insisted that I make a statement telling them they were free to leave. Do you think we would turn them out, after what it has meant to us? Our door is open, and we love every one of the boys, and they will always be welcome."

John and Elgie R. remembered when the decision was made. "There was a meeting that night," said John, who always managed to get in a good word for every person he mentioned. "Boy, I never heard two men talk like they did [Dr. Bob and T. Henry]. They passed confidence and praise to each other. And they both deserved it.

"It was a hard time for the group," John said. "There were a lot of us who liked T. Henry. And we didn't know whether to leave or not."

"At the last meeting, they voted," said Elgie. "The ones who were going to stay with T. Henry—okay. And the ones who were going with Doc—okay. That's the way they said goodbye. But they had argued over it all for a month or more."

Among those who stayed were Lloyd T., who had been Clarence's sponsor, and Bill J. Others, including Rollie H., the baseball player, stayed for a time and changed their minds later.

"Henrietta [Seiberling] told Dr. Bob that it was the worst mistake he had ever made," according to Elgie, who remembered her saying, "How could you do this? You'll be sorry."

"Bob and Annie just went," Elgie said. "There was nothing to say. I could never figure out why she was so incensed." (Although Henrietta later went with the A.A.'s, she was not active in Akron for long after that. A short time later, she moved to New York, where she remained until her death, in 1979.)

"Doc said, 'We don't have a place to meet—we'll meet at my house,' " Elgie recalled. "It was in November or December, because I remember the Christmas tree in their living room."

There is no record of what happened at the first meeting, except for a Grapevine account years later noting that it was led by Dr. Bob, who "put his foot on the rung of a dining-room chair, identified himself as an alcoholic, and began reading the Sermon on the Mount."

On the second day of the New Year, 1940, Dr. Bob wrote Bill: "Have definitely shaken off the shackles of the Oxford Group" (a choice of words that indicates his attitude then) "and are meeting at my house for the time being. Had 74 Wednesday in my little house, but shall get a hall soon."

Clarence S. wrote three days later: "Have attended two of Doc Smith's meetings since he has been holding them in his home, and they have been very well attended and very inspirational.

"Doc led our meeting, and never have I heard him in such fine fettle. Noticed a vast improvement since he pulled his gang out of the Williamses'. Now speaks with authority and no pussyfooting, and I believe he looks ten years younger."

"I'm not sure, but I think we had two meetings there," said John R. "You should have seen Doc's house! His little living room wasn't much bigger than this little house we live in. We were crowded up pretty good there."

The Smiths' house was indeed too small to handle that many people, it developed. After a few meetings, Wally G. checked King School, where his daughter went. From then on, it was every Wednesday night for the King School Group, which, however you figure it, traces its beginnings from the first meeting of Bill and Dr. Bob, four and a half years before.

On May 14, 1940, Dr. Bob was to write Bill about that memorable day: "Dear Willie: Know you are busy, so I cannot expect too much correspondence from you, but would love to hear from you. Perhaps you recall that it was five years ago last Sunday when I first met you at Hen's. I shall never forget it, though perhaps it may have slipped your mind. I shall never cease to be grateful to you and am very glad I have been able to pass the good word along."

XVII. 'As Dr. Bob said...'

As the Akron group began gathering at King School in 1940, a definite style evolved, which set the pattern for meetings in the area. Oldtimers remember early meetings as being pretty much the way they are now, with a few exceptions.

There was no chairperson or secretary to introduce the speaker. Through the mid-1940's, it was felt that grand titles and flowery introductions might go to an alcoholic's head. When the time came, the speaker would go up front, wait for quiet, and introduce himself. He opened with a prayer of his own choosing, then gave a five-minute "lead." Usually, it would be on a specific subject—a passage from *The Upper Room* or a verse from the Bible. Then he asked other members to make short comments.

Alex M. (who had joined the group in 1939) recalled that they started to take up regular collections to meet rent and custodial expenses at King School. Before that, it hadn't been necessary. "There were no dollars," he said. "Two bits would

have been pretty high for most of us." Passing the hat to meet
expenses eventually led to the custom known as the secretary's
break, at which the speaker was thanked and announcements
were made. In other Akron groups today, the secretary reads a
long list of announcements about meetings, anniversaries, and
speakers in the vicinity. King School is one of the few groups
where this is not done.

"There was no levity in the beginning," said Bob E. "We
all had our sense of humor, but for us, recovery was a life-or-
death matter. Nor was there any clapping. At that kind of
meeting, applause would have seemed out of place."

Norman Y. (the blind A.A. from Youngstown, Ohio)
agreed and quoted Dr. Bob as saying, "Don't applaud me.
Don't applaud any alcoholic." Characteristically, Dr. Bob
would motion for members to sit when he was given a standing ovation.

"Everyone had to have him on a pedestal, as I still do,"
said John S. of Coshocton, Ohio, in 1977. (John had been a
member since 1940.) "But he never had himself on any pedestal, I'll guarantee you that!"

Father J. F. Gallagher, who worked with Sister Ignatia,
said, "It is difficult to speak of Dr. Smith without going into
eulogistic superlatives. While he lived, he laughed them off,
and now, though dead, I feel he still laughs them off.

"I sat beside him many times at the speakers' table and
watched him squirm as some florid introduction was being
given him," said Father Gallagher.

Many a chairman strove to rise to the responsibility by
referring to Dr. Bob as "the founder of the greatest, most
wonderful, most magnificent, most momentous movement of
all time," etc. On one of these occasions, Dr. Bob whispered,
"The speaker certainly takes in a lot of territory and plenty of
time."

Dr. Bob's attitude toward high praise and standing ovations had something to do with his search for humility—a "thing with which most of us are not too blessed."

As he said, this was not "the fake humility of Dickens's Uriah Heep." Nor was it "the doormat variety. . . . I'm talking about the attitude of each and every one of us toward our Heavenly Father," said Dr. Bob.

"Christ said, 'Of Myself, I am nothing — My strength cometh from My Father in heaven.' If He had to say that," Dr. Bob asked, "how about you and me? Did you say it? Did I say it? No. That's exactly what we didn't say. We were inclined to say instead, 'Look me over, boys. Pretty good, huh?' We had no humility, no sense of having received anything through the grace of our Heavenly Father.

"I don't believe I have any right to get cocky about getting sober," he said. "It's only through God's grace that I did it. I can feel very thankful that I was privileged to do it. . . . If my strength does come from Him, who am I to get cocky about it?"

On his desk, Dr. Bob had a plaque defining humility: "Perpetual quietness of heart. It is to have no trouble. It is never to be fretted or vexed, irritable or sore; to wonder at nothing that is done to me, to feel nothing done against me. It is to be at rest when nobody praises me, and when I am blamed or despised, it is to have a blessed home in myself where I can go in and shut the door and kneel to my Father in secret and be at peace, as in a deep sea of calmness, when all around and about is seeming trouble."

Dr. Bob's character undoubtedly had a strong influence in shaping local meetings. As Akron's Bob E. saw it, one of the big differences between Akron and New York, and Akron and Cleveland as well, was that "we did not tell our drinking histories at the meetings back then, We did not need to. A man's sponsor and Dr. Bob knew the details. Frankly, we did not think it was anybody's business. Besides, we already knew how to drink. What we wanted to learn was how to get sober and stay sober.

"Bill was in favor of having an A.A. member qualify or tell how he became an alcoholic," Bob E. said. "And this idea did attract people and enabled the movement to grow.

"When the qualifying business began, it took some getting used to on our part," Bob E. said. "I remember one time when we were meeting at King School. Some people came in from Cleveland. They clapped and made a lot of noise. To us, it seemed strange and offensive. Gradually, we opened up under Bill's persuasive influence, but we still did not care for it when people would get carried away by their own voices and make their stories too sensational."

Almost everyone remembered that Dr. Bob and Anne had "regular" seats—pretty well back on the side, with Anne on the outside near the aisle. "I could go in the door, and I knew where Bill V——— H——— was sitting, where Wally G. and Ethel M—— and Dr. Bob would sit," said one oldtimer. (Ethel and Rollo M., both alcoholics, joined A.A. in 1941.) "They all had their own places. Nobody would think of sitting in their seats."

Speakers were not always chosen in advance, according to Norman Y. He recalled Dr. Bob's telling one fellow, "George, it's your turn this week."

"But I didn't prepare anything," the man replied.

"You didn't prepare to get drunk, either," Dr. Bob said. "Get up and talk."

Most oldtimers agreed that Dr. Bob usually made some comment at every meeting—and this was because the leader asked him to, not because he volunteered. "It was short, but to the point," said one. John R. said that he had heard Dr. Bob's last talk at Cleveland and there wasn't a thing in it John hadn't heard him stress over and over again at the regular meeting of the King School Group.

Except for the talk given in Detroit in 1948, Dr. Bob was noted for speaking very briefly. Both he and Anne were often quoted as having said, "If you speak more than 15 minutes, you're going to repeat yourself," or "No souls are saved after 15 minutes."

One story had it that when Dr. Bob was guest speaker at an out-of-town meeting, he got up and said that the world's finest talks had been short ones. For example, both the Sermon on the Mount and the Gettysburg Address had been given in less than five minutes. "With this point in mind," he said, "I also propose to give a short talk. In fact, I just did."

He sat down.

"He was a very calm speaker, and he sounded grateful," said Ed B., an Akron oldtimer. "Sometimes, he would point his finger or spread his arms, but he didn't gesture much. And he always wore a suit and a tie to meetings. When he came to an A.A. meeting, he was just another alcoholic. He wasn't a doctor or anything."

In Dr. Bob's comments, "he would always pick some good point the speaker had made," according to Ed. "It was more or less to encourage him. He never mentioned much about his own drinking."

Ed also noted that Dr. Bob spoke at many meetings in the area. "When we had an anniversary, we'd want Dr. Bob, and he never turned us down." Ed felt that Dr. Bob's reluctance to speak at big meetings could be ascribed as much to his distaste for being regarded as a big shot as to his shyness.

While Dr. Bob's remarks were usually kind, Dan K. (who had been one of Doc's many patients at St. Thomas Hospital) noted that if he thought a man was a phony, he would tell the man so. "And if he was sitting at a meeting and a man used bad language, Dr. Bob would say, 'You have a very good lead, young man, but it would be more effective if you cleaned it up a bit.'

"Another thing," Dan recalled. "When I was first asked to speak, I told him I thought you had to be an oldtimer. He said, 'Dan, your type of talk would be good for these two-suiters.' You see, we had a lot of rich people, and we called them two-suiters in those days."

Oscar W., a Cleveland member who was 29 when he first came to A.A., remembered speaking up at his first meeting and being told by one of the oldtimers, "When you are new, you should take the cotton from your ears and put it in your mouth. Sit down and listen!"

Then Dr. Bob got up and said to Oscar, "That's right, son, listen. But you watch and see what the man *does* as well as listen to what he says."

"After I had been in A.A. for a few months," Oscar continued, "I wrote my resignation and handed it to Dr. Bob. He read it and didn't laugh. Then he looked at me and said, 'Well, you're doing it properly.' Then he told me to go to the Mayflower Hotel, buy a bottle of whiskey, take a couple of good drinks, then cork the bottle. 'If you can stay there a couple more days without taking another drink, you don't need us,' he told me. I thought, 'There aren't enough bottles, and there aren't enough days.' But I didn't tell him.

" 'I'll tell you what we'll do,' Doc said. 'We'll keep some oats in the bin and some straw in the barn for you, because you're sure as hell gonna come back.'

"He was right. Six months later, I was back.

"When the Jack Alexander article [in the *Saturday Evening Post*] came out, in 1941, I worked with about 17 newcomers," Oscar said. "I helped them with the rent, brought them food and coal, and helped them get jobs. They all got drunk.

"I went down to Akron and complained to Dr. Bob, who told me that I was doing this for myself and *they* were doing *me* a favor.

" 'But I'm helping *them.'*

" 'No,' he said. 'Those men showed you what will happen if you pick up a drink. They did you a favor. And when they don't pick up a drink, they show you how the program works. Either way, they do you a favor.' "

Another quote in the same vein, attributed to Dr. Bob by Ernie G. the second, was: "There are two kinds of people to watch in A.A.—those who make it, and those who don't."

"Dr. Bob said you had to sponsor yourself as well," recalled Oscar, "that you should stand back now and then and look at yourself and sort of laugh, then help yourself.

"He was a great one for counseling. He'd say, 'Let's get together and talk it over and see if we can work things out,' whether it was personal or had to do with the group.

"Bill [Wilson] would never give a definite answer. He'd write a two-page letter, and you would have to read it twice to see what he meant. But it was all suggestion. He'd never give an order. Bob was the same way. A bunch of us would go down from Cleveland madder than hell about something. Then we'd counsel with Bob, and by the time we were heading back to Cleveland, everything would be okay, and we would have forgotten what we had gone down there for."

There is a problem when it comes to recording any remark supposedly made by Dr. Bob. Did he really say it? Or do people remember what they want to remember? Ruth G., wife of Ernie the second, admitted, "I suppose I remember him stressing the spiritual part because that was what I was listening for."

Joe P., who came into A.A. in 1942, noted that "the things Dr. Bob did say became so familiar. Everyone that leads a meeting uses them. And others are always repeating things Dr. Bob said that I *know* he didn't. Sometimes, people will say, 'Now Dr. Bob said . . .' in order to lend a little importance to what *they* are saying."

There are many things Dr. Bob definitely did say, and
many he might well have said—they sound characteristic of
him. Apart from "Let's keep it simple," however, it is difficult
to tell which are which. Different people had different per-
spectives on Dr. Bob. But regardless of their point of view,
they were looking at the same man—serious and humorous,
earthy and spiritual, outgoing and shy, friendly and aloof.

Dr. Bob did elaborate on his keep-it-simple theme as far
as the A.A. program is concerned, incidentally. In a September 1948 article for the Grapevine, he wrote:

"As finally expressed and offered, they [the Twelve Steps]
are simple in language, plain in meaning. They are also
workable by any person having a sincere desire to obtain and
keep sobriety. The results are the proof. Their simplicity and
workability are such that no special interpretations, and certainly no reservations, have ever been necessary. And it has
become increasingly clear that the degree of harmonious living which we achieve is in direct ratio to our earnest attempt
to follow them literally under divine guidance to the best of
our ability."

Dr. Bob, whose education at St. Johnsbury Academy and
Dartmouth had involved some 12 years of Greek and nine
years of Latin, sometimes wrote in a much more formal style
than he used in talking. His Grapevine article continued:

"Yet, withal, there are no shibboleths in A.A. We are not
bound by the thongs of theological doctrine. None of us may
be . . . cast into outer darkness. For we are many minds in our
organization, and an A.A. decalogue in the language of
'Thou shalt not' would gall us indeed."

That is, "There are no musts in A.A."

Another thing Dr. Bob put quite simply: "The first one
will get you." According to John R., he kept repeating that.

The widow of an oldtimer remembered Dr. Bob standing
up at the meeting with "the Good Book under his arm" and

recalled that he used to say the answers were there if you looked for them, because people back in the Old Testament were just like the people of this century and had the same problems.

And if he were here now, Dr. Bob might say the same thing about the early A.A.'s—that they were just like the members today and had the same problems.

Dr. Bob donated that Bible to the King School Group, where it still rests on the podium at each meeting. Inside is an inscription: "It is the hope of the King School Group—whose sobriety this is—that this Book may never cease to be a source of wisdom, gratitude, humility, and guidance, as when fulfilled in the life of the Master." It is signed "Dr. Bob Smith."

An early Chicago member wrote that they usually resorted to such quaint evasions as "the Fellow Upstairs" in order not to frighten or antagonize the agnostics who were coming into the program. "Dr. Bob was the first group leader I heard refer simply and without ostentation to God. He cited the Sermon on the Mount as containing the underlying spiritual philosophy of A.A."

Ed B. remembered that Dr. Bob used to tell stories at meetings to illustrate certain points—much as parables are used in the Bible.

"He would always stress that being at the meeting was itself part of a spiritual awakening, that it didn't necessarily have to come to you in a flash of light," recalled Ed. "And to make the point in a humorous way, he would tell about the cop shining the light on a couple making love in the park. 'It's all right,' the man said. 'We're married.' 'I'm sorry,' the cop replied. 'I didn't know it was your wife.' 'Neither did I until you shined the light on us,' the man said."

Ed had quite a collection of Dr. Bob stories.

"He told one about these 'shotgun' A.A.'s—the ones who had come in to get the wife off their backs. This farmer brought a man to the doctor's office. 'Here, Doctor, I shot my son-in-law full of buckshot.' The doctor said, 'You ought to be ashamed, shooting your son-in-law.' 'Well, Doc, he wasn't my son-in-law *until* I shot him.'

"Then you know how we talk about God never forgetting us. Dr. Bob had a story for that, too. One man was telling another about all the trouble his son got into, and the second fellow said, 'You know, Jim, if that was my son, I'd kick him out.' The first fellow said, 'If he was your son, I'd kick him out, too.' That was to stress that God didn't kick us out. We left of our own accord.

"Then about getting out of A.A. what you put into it. Doc told about the farmer asking this fellow if he wanted to work the harvest. 'What are you paying?' the man asked. 'I'll pay you what you're worth,' the farmer said. 'No thanks,' the fellow said, 'I'll be damned if I'll work for that little.'"

According to Ed, Dr. Bob would explain prayer by telling how the camels in a caravan would kneel down in the evening, and the men would unload their burdens. In the morning, they would kneel down again, and the men would put the burdens back on. "It's the same with prayer," Dr. Bob said. "We get on our knees to unload at night. And in the morning when we get on our knees again, God gives us just the load we are able to carry for that day."

"I remember one story he repeated over and over," said Ed. "It was about this boy who burned his hand. The doctor dressed it and bandaged it. When he took the bandage off, the boy's hand was healed. The little boy said, 'You're wonderful, Doctor. You cure everybody, don't you?' 'No, I don't,' the doctor replied. 'I just dress the wound. God heals it.'"

Finally: "There was the woman who called and asked, 'Are you the Dr. Bob who helps alcoholics?' When he replied that he was, she asked him to send her two bottles of that Alcoholics Anonymous for her sick husband. 'Don't you think one would be enough?' he asked. 'Oh no,' she replied. 'My husband is in the hospital. He needs two.' "

Jud O., who came into A.A. in 1939, recalled, "If there were any alcoholics who happened to get near the Akron area, they always tried to arrange to see Bob Smith. There was a group that drove all the way from Youngstown every Wednesday, come rain or shine," said Jud. "They stayed for the meeting, had coffee, then drove back. This kept up—with members from other cities and towns as well—until they got organized enough to start their own groups."

From all the stories, it is clear that Dr. Bob was always open to seeing and talking to an A.A. member—whether at his home, at his office, or at an A.A. meeting. "But he could be unpredictable," said Ed B. "I had a fellow come purposely to Akron to see Dr. Bob. I brought him up to where Doc was talking to a couple of people, and all Doc did was shake hands with him and go back to talking to the others. I could see the fellow was disappointed. But after the meeting, when we were having coffee, Doc sat down beside the visitor, put his arm around him, and talked to him. The fellow bragged about it all the way back to his hotel."

xviii. The wives' role in early A.A.

Following the meetings of the King School Group in Akron, members went downstairs to the school cafeteria for coffee and doughnuts. This was the province, not of a refreshment committee, but of the wives. As Oscar W. put it, "They were allowed to wash dishes, make coffee, organize picnics, and things like that."

After refreshments, a smaller group of A.A's usually went to Kessler's Donut Shop, as they had been doing after the meetings at T. Henry Williams's. There, they had more coffee and conversation, often lasting late into the night. In the years since then, this "after-the-meeting meeting" has probably become as much a part of A.A. throughout the world as the Serenity Prayer.

"You know, when this thing first started out, it was the wives that had to work," said Mrs. M. (Alex's wife), "because the men were supposed to stay in the meeting. Today, lots of the men work in the kitchen.

"And years ago, the women sat on one side and the men on the other. Now, it is so much better, because the women go in and they mix and they sit around with men.

"We used to make fancy desserts and everything just to please our men and make a success of our meeting. We made anniversary cakes for our husbands [at the Ravenna, Ohio, meeting]. Now, I won't let them buy a cake for Alex. I bake it. But once a month, they buy a nicely decorated cake for everyone who has an anniversary."

Virtually everyone agreed that the refreshment period was Anne's part of the meeting. "She would make it her business to go from table to table and introduce herself," said Dorothy O. (Jud's wife). "She told the new women they were in the same boat, that we were all friends and she would do all for us she could."

"Anne always looked to the newcomers," said Dan K. "She'd spot you, and after the meeting, she would go to your table and introduce herself. 'I want to welcome you and your lovely wife to Alcoholics Anonymous. We hope you'll keep coming back.' She'd give a little bit of background on A.A. and then maybe she'd go to another new member."

Anne's concern for the newcomer was both legendary and phenomenal—a greater concern, perhaps, than that of most A.A. members.

"Before our first New Year's party, someone had given Anne three new dresses, and I had never seen her without that one black dress she had," Dorothy S. M. recalled in a conversation with Bill Wilson.

"My brother had given me a new dress for Christmas, the first new dress I'd had for years. So I was discussing the party

Quickly outgrowing the Smiths' house, the first A.A. group moved its meetings to King School.

with Anne, and I said, 'Look at your three dresses. Which one are you going to wear?'

"She looked at me and said, 'You know, Dorothy, there are some new people that won't have anything, and I can't bear to wear any of them.' And she showed up at that party in the same old black dress.

"Anne did so much in her own gentle way. I was a little bit afraid of her, as much as I loved her. But she would give me a lesson in such a way that by the time I got back to Cleveland, I would know what she meant.

"I was so thrilled at my friends that after every meeting, I'd rush up to them and get into these mad conversations. One night, Anne called me over. 'Dorothy, people have been awfully good to you, haven't they? You've been pretty lucky, and you made so many friends.' Of course, I agreed 100 percent. 'Don't you think that you could pass that on, a little bit? There's a new woman sitting over there in the corner, and nobody's talking to her.'

"That's the one thing I've tried to remember all these years. If I didn't learn anything else from Anne, I learned it was the new people that counted. To really try and make them feel welcome and wanted—that's one way I can try to pay back.

"You remember how Anne always called everybody by their first name?" Dorothy said to Bill Wilson. "She could remember them. She knew all the children they had. It was that terrific personal interest she took in everybody. Even when she was almost blind, there at the last, she'd go up to them, and even if she couldn't distinguish who they were, she could tell by their voices, and she would recall every single thing about them.

"She used to gather clothes for anyone who didn't have anything to wear. I had a summer coat, and I had to wear it as a winter coat. Anne ripped the fur collar off somebody's old suit, and we sewed that on, and I had a winter coat. Then came summer, and we just ripped off the fur collar and put on a white collar. She did things like that for everybody.

"Lois, too!" Dorothy said to Bill. "I remember when you and Lois would come to Akron, and the word would go around that you were coming, and we would have absolutely everybody waiting there for you. Lois might be sitting there, mending one of your coats. She always seemed to have some darning or mending to do to fix you up so you could go out into the world again."

The wives' role was extremely important in the earliest days of A.A. It is no exaggeration to say that there would have been no A.A. without those wives.

First, it was often the wives who sought help for their husbands, as Anne did in going to the Oxford Group. Then, they helped with the meetings, opened their homes to recovering drunks, did twelfth step work, and considered themselves as much a part of A.A. as their husbands. They may have remained in the background, as Anne advised Henrietta D. (wife of Bill, A.A. number three) to do, but their influence was strong.

"The meetings were definitely open. They insisted on it," said Ernie G. the second. "Doc didn't believe in closed meetings. He told me, 'You bring Ruth. If you don't, I'm going to come and get her.' He was emphatic about it. That was good, because Ruth thought I was the world's worst drunk. When she came to a few meetings, she found out there was hope."

"I told him I felt the presence of God at that meeting, more than any other place I've ever been," said Ruth. " 'This is for us,' I said. 'Let's grow up here together.' We decided, and we both made it our life's work — to build our lives around the spiritual aspects of Alcoholics Anonymous."

"There was more appreciation in it as far as the women were concerned," said Alex M.'s wife. "They'd get down and kiss the ground their husbands were walking on, just because they were behaving themselves. Now, they've got it more in perspective, because that's the way they [the husbands] should have behaved in the first place. Well, it was the Depression, and we had to stick with them whether we wanted to or not. We had to eat, and the kids had to eat.

"The women would work and slave to do everything they could to make the A.A. group successful. Three of us went into the kitchen, and we did it for four or five years—maybe longer—before we could get anyone else to help. But we never once thought of asking our husbands to do anything."

Dorothy O. (Jud's wife) recalled how "another girl and I did all the calling to see that members would visit patients in the hospitals. It wasn't just left to chance. Then we went to meetings and assisted there."

Elgie R., who was only 26 years old then and might have been a bit more independent and outspoken than the other wives, recalled that when her husband came out of the hospital, she asked Dr. Bob "as hard as I could if there was anything I could do to help.

"I used to stay with Anne when Bob went out to speak, because she wasn't feeling up to going all the time and she got a little worn-out. I also made address books. We didn't have an office, and they were using my telephone. It was going day and night. It was a riot!

"The thing about A.A. in those days was, you ran into so many fantastic situations," said Elgie. "You never knew what was going to happen. You just did the best you could."

For example, a man who was on pills was staying with John and Elgie. He kept getting up and going to the door. He'd say (to nobody at all), "Hello. What do you want?" Then he'd go back to bed. "I was scared to death," said Elgie. "I asked Doc what we were going to do if he went out of his mind. 'I don't know,' Doc said. 'Let's wait and see.'

"One day, I had to go to my doctor. I took the fellow with me, because I couldn't leave him. My doctor was quite interested in A.A., but when I told him about this character, he said, 'My goodness, a woman like you shouldn't have to do things like that.' The fellow stayed with us for ten days, and he was all right. As far as I know, he stayed sober.

"I was very active until one day I made a statement at a meeting," said Elgie. "I don't remember what it was, but one A.A. got up and said, 'What are you talking up for? You're not an alcoholic. Why don't you mind your own business?'

"So I said to myself, 'You know, that's a good idea. I think I will.' That was it. I just quit. I figured there were enough alcoholics to take care of things. They didn't need my two cents' worth. I did ask John if I was helping him by doing all that. And when he said no, I thought it was kind of silly for me to keep it up, because that was what I was doing it for."

Elgie's decision was individual and personal, but it reflected a gradual, general change in attitude toward recovering alcoholics, and in these alcoholics' attitude toward themselves.

In Akron in the very early days, alcoholics had almost no say. Their wives got them to the meetings, which were, in turn, run by Oxford Groupers. The men chafed a bit, but allowed it to go on. When the A.A.'s did break away from the O.G., their wives very likely had a lot to do with the move, as we have seen.

Then, especially as single men and women alcoholics began coming into the program, there was friction with the wives. This resulted in "closed meetings" for alcoholics only, as well as "open meetings" at which the nonalcoholic wives were not allowed to speak. Later, the situation was to balance out, with the establishment of such compromises as "open discussion meetings," in which wives and other nonmembers were invited to participate.

"When they had this Al-Anon and Alateen, I thought it was a wonderful idea," said Elgie.

Al-Anon Family Groups took its present form in 1951, though "family groups" composed of A.A. members' relatives had been developing over the preceding years. It soon became a source of help for wives and others close to drinking alcoholics, as well as to those sober in A.A. The special needs of alcoholics' teenage children were answered in 1957 by the formation of Alateen, a part of Al-Anon. Both use the A.A. program with only slight adaptation, but are entirely separate from A.A.

"I think now what a relief it would have been if I could have gone in a program that would have kept me occupied," Elgie said. "That's why I got involved. I wanted to help. It wasn't that common. There were two or three of us who did it.

"Dr. Bob said that when you come into A.A. and your husband has been drinking, you are at the point where you are as crazy as he is," said Elgie, "and it is going to take you a long time to look at things normally.

"He also said that the man won't stay sober if the wife isn't with him. And the families won't get back together unless everybody works at it. That was the way he put it. Nothing fancy. Just practical psychology."

xix. Minorities within A.A. gain acceptance

As we have seen, early A.A. members were predominantly white, middle-class, and male. There were membership requirements—belief in God, making a surrender, and conforming to the precepts of the Oxford Group—in addition to having a desire (honest, sincere, or otherwise) to stop drinking.

The requirements might be summed up by saying you had to believe before you began. The fact that some members saw it the other way around—as indicated in the later A.A. saying "I came; I came to; I came to believe"—was at the heart of the conflict between the A.A.'s and the Oxford Groupers. It then continued in A.A. between the rule-makers and the rule-breakers.

There had to be a first time when a man wandered into a meeting with a couple of drinks in him, the "snifters" started to throw him out, and somebody said, "Let him stay. Maybe something will seep in." ("Snifters," an early member explained, were "men who stood by the door, sniffing each man who came in.")

And when that drunk, for some mysterious reason, stayed just as sober as the fellow who had been hospitalized or visited by ten members, there went another rule. In the end, pioneer A.A.'s broke so many of their own rules that there were no rules left!

At the same time, the earliest members began reaching out to those who might either have seemed or have felt themselves to be different. By 1939, the prevailing A.A. attitude was summed up in the foreword to the Big Book, stating, "The only requirement for membership is an honest desire to stop drinking."

Most A.A.'s simply wanted to get people into the program, rather than keep them out. This might mean overcoming inbred prejudices and crossing social, religious, racial, and national boundaries in order to carry the message of recovery to anyone, anywhere, who needed help. It also meant doing the very same things in order to accept help. And if A.A. as a fellowship never had any greater achievement, it could say that most members have done more than pay lip service to this idea.

As the discussion of the Third Tradition in the book "Twelve Steps and Twelve Traditions" shows, there was a great deal of fear about alcoholics who might be odd or different. In A.A.'s second year, a man came to an A.A. group and said he was the "victim of another addiction even worse stigmatized than alcoholism."

The group's "oldest member" spoke in confidence with two others. They discussed "the trouble this strange alcoholic might bring" and the notion that it might be better to "sacrifice this one for the sake of the many." Finally, one of the three said, "What we are really afraid of is our reputation." And he asked a question that had been haunting him: "What would the Master do?" No answer was necessary.

Letters written by Bill in 1938 and 1939 placed this situation in Akron, thereby implying that "the oldest member" was Dr. Bob. Retelling the anecdote in 1969, Bill finally confirmed this identification by using his partner's name.

However, Dr. Bob showed somewhat less assurance upon first confronting the most troublesome and, in some ways, the most unwelcome minority in A.A.'s olden days—women!

We have already seen some examples of his dismay at the thought of a woman's coming into the Akron group. "He didn't know how to handle them," said Smitty. Others said Dr. Bob felt that the program would not work for women. Just the same, he tried to help several.

Bill recalled "explosions" that took place around the "out-of-bounds romance" and the arrival of alcoholic women at meetings. "Whole groups got into uproars, and a number of people got drunk," he said. "We trembled for A.A.'s reputation and for its survival."

Women alcoholics had to overcome a double standard that was even more rigid in the 1930's than it is today—the notion that nice women didn't drink to excess. This made it difficult for a woman to admit to the problem in the first place, to say nothing of being accepted in A.A.

Women who joined the Akron group in the earliest days had adequate, if not impressive, social credentials. Jane was married to the vice-president of a large steel company, and Sylvia was an attractive heiress. As far as we know, "Lil" never got far enough along to attend a meeting.

No women ever responded to the *Plain Dealer* articles, and the first one Warren C. remembered was thrown out of A.A. by the wives. "She was so bad, they wouldn't allow her in their homes," he said.

But this woman eventually did get sober, according to Clarence S.'s recollections. She started working with children and moved to Florida, where she made a good deal of money in real estate. She stayed away from A.A., however, because of that initial rejection.

Dr. Bob always agreed to talk to the few women who came his way; then, he usually turned them over to Anne and other wives who were willing to work with them.

Elgie felt that Anne had a lot to do with his eventual change of attitude. "Doc used to shake his head and say, 'Well, I think I'd better work with the men, because the women . . . I'm not sure. I don't know.'

"And Annie would say, 'Let's try and see.' She always felt if you don't try, you never know. The thing that bothered him was that most of the women came in with the label 'nymphomaniac.' Most of the wives would back away, and the men got leery because they were afraid they would get into some situations. So, in the beginning, the woman was looked on as trouble. Nobody wanted to handle it.

"But I felt, 'Why not? What difference does it make? They're just as drunk as the men are.' "

Ruth T. from Toledo was another well-to-do woman who came to A.A.—because her father and a lawyer contacted the Akron group—in the spring of 1939.

Doc asked Elgie to take her in, "which was funny," Elgie commented, "because we'd just been married a year, and we lived in a little house in a less-than-ordinary part of town. I didn't know her background or anything then. I welcomed her and took care of her and talked with her. I just felt sorry for her. We went to the meetings. We worked with her, and she seemed to be taking everything in.

"Then it came time for her to go home, and the court would not agree to her being in the house with her children unless there was someone there who was responsible and would see that everything was all right.

"So Doc said, 'Well, Elgie, you don't have any children. I

think John is going to be okay. Why don't you go home with her? That way, the kids can come home from school, and you can get them ready for camp.'

Elgie did go to Ruth's house for a week. "On the weekend, Bob and Anne and Roland and Dorothy J—— came up and stayed. We talked about starting a Toledo group, and Doc said he thought Ruth could do it. When she saw that they were going to depend on her to do something, she sort of snapped out of it, and she became interested in going ahead. I don't know how long she stayed sober. I know the group did form, and they had meetings there."

According to Elgie, the idea that men should help men and women help women evolved as a means of A.A. self-preservation, before experience proved it wise for the newcomers' sake. The only trouble was that there were so few women A.A.'s to help new women. So the wives continued to do the job. In November 1940, for instance, Dorothy S. wrote that they were working on two women and were trying to start a really anonymous group for them.

Finally, Ethel and Rollo M. came into the program together in May 1941. John and Elgie took the call and went to talk with the couple.

As Ethel related at a meeting some years ago, she had earlier told some fellow in a bar that she was thinking of calling A.A. "He said, 'Sister, you think you're nuts now—wait till you join *them*. They holler and roll on the floor. But I know some of them and I can get you in.' "

Needless to say, Ethel thought it all over a while longer. "Then, a woman in a bar told me that her husband was a member and that he could help me. He and some other people came to see me and Rollo."

"She weighed 300 pounds," Elgie said, "and her husband, Rollo, was a skinny little fellow about half her size— maybe five feet two. They were hilarious, like Mutt and Jeff, talking back and forth all the time. John asked them a few questions, and then we let them say a few words and argue," Elgie said. "Then we left and said we'd be back. We knew then, and it's still true, if they're not ready to accept A.A., there's no point in wasting your time.

"Doc used to say, 'If they're ready, work with them; if they're not, you might as well walk away, because they're not going to stop drinking.' "

"I knew several people at my first meeting," said Ethel. "I felt accepted and loved right away. I remember Annabelle G—— saying, 'I understand you drink, too.' 'Yes,' I replied. 'That's why I'm here.' I did think that maybe the wives would look down on me, but it didn't last long. I became very close to Henrietta D——."

"Ethel and Rollo worked as a team, and that was safer," said Elgie. "Everyone felt at ease. But every woman who came in alone was like a warning signal to all the wives. They were scared to death of them."

"Yes, we were mistrustful of the women who were just starting to get sober," said Emma K. (who was to care for Dr. Bob in his last illness). "I think we looked down on them, were not quite sure of them, because 'no lady would do a thing like that.' The women had more to overcome than the men. Now, I guess there are as many women in A.A. as there are men." (By 1978, when Emma was interviewed, that was likely to be true only in some big-city groups. Women made up about one-third of the membership as a whole; but that proportion was rising rapidly.)

"Ethel was very active from the beginning," Emma recalled, "and after Rollo died, A.A. was her whole life. She became sponsor to many women who came into the Fellowship in later years."

According to Oscar W., there was another woman around who was built like a football player and wore a big hat flat on her head. "If she sponsored you, and you got drunk, she'd pick you up and slap you around. Then she'd tell you, if you didn't get sober, you were gonna get some more."

Even Sister Ignatia found it difficult to understand how a "nice" girl could have a drinking problem, according to Anne C. "She knew my mother and my dad and the whole family before A.A. was born. When she found out I was in the program, she said, 'How could this have happened to you with that wonderful family of yours? It can't be!'

" 'Aren't you glad that I'm here? Or do you want me to go back to where I was?' I'd reply.

"'Oh no, no.' But for years, she would tell people she didn't know *how* I became an alcoholic."

Vi S., who came into A.A. with her husband, Freddie, in Cleveland in May 1941, remembered that every time she saw a couple of wives talking, she thought they were talking about her—"what a drunk I was. I couldn't open my mouth. I'd say hello, but that was as far as I would go. And there was no other woman I knew of in A.A. I was scared to death of the wives. I think they really tried to accept me, but I was too standoffish.

"I stood up publicly once," Vi said, "and thanked Clarence for letting women come into A.A. That was because I knew they didn't want me there. They the same as told me that I wasn't old enough, I didn't drink enough, and I didn't need the program. Their idea was that if it helped Freddie, they would let me in.

"We started a woman's group. I never talked anyplace but there, until I'd been in five years and we went to Akron one night. Freddie, in his usual way, got up and told what a drunk I was. Dr. Bob was on one side of the room and Paul S—— on the other. Both got up about the same time, and they said, 'Fred, let Vi tell her own story.'

"I couldn't get my head up. I don't even know what I

said. I told Dr. Bob afterward, I was thinking of the things I should have said. 'Don't let it worry you,' he said. 'I do the same thing.'

"Bill D—— [A.A. number three] used to go to all the meetings. Fred asked him how come. Bill said, 'Well, Fred, that's how I stay sober.' So we figured, if that's what *he* needed, that's what *we* needed."

To give some idea of the dangers involved with women, Oscar W. recalled the first man killed on a Twelfth Step call.

"He called on her after the husband had left for work," said Oscar. "The neighbors saw this and told her husband. One night, the husband lay in the weeds outside the house, waiting for the guy, and when the A.A. came along to take the woman to a meeting, the husband blew him in half with a shotgun. This was in upstate New York, and it was said that they named a club after the fellow.

"They started a nursing home for women in Cleveland, because they couldn't get them in hospitals," Oscar said. "They had been taking them in homes, but now they needed more room. They rented a duplex, and a nurse in A.A. and her husband lived there.

"The neighbors noticed a lot of women going in and out. Some of them were obviously drunk. So they called the cops, who came and found them all in nightgowns and so on. Imagine telling the desk sergeant you're helping them get sober. He just looks at you and grins."

Gradually, the situation changed. "They wanted to do more for you if you were a woman," said Polly F. L., who came into A.A. in Chicago in 1943 and later went to work in the A.A. General Service Office in New York. "The men would say, 'If a woman can stay sober, then I can stay sober.' I could see some of the suspicions that wives had, but they were friendly with me. In fact, a lot of them would ask me to see if I could get their husbands to do things."

Peg S., who came into A.A. in the mid-1940's, reported that "A.A. wives just bent over backwards to be kind and help me. I was at a meeting one night, and a couple of other women members were standing in back of me. One said to the other, 'Be darn careful how you handle yourself around these wives. They think you're the babe their husband went out with.' I thought about it awhile, then turned around. 'No, you're mistaken,' I said. 'Maybe there are some like that, but I have never run into them.' "

Formation of the first black group in Cleveland was centered around a woman; so two minorities were involved. "We got a call at three in the morning from this colored woman who worked in a nightclub and was disgusted with her life," said Oscar W. "I went to see her and read the book [the Big Book] to her and talked to her. Then a guy broke in and chased me downstairs, throwing milk bottles after me.

"A day later, the woman called me and said she was still sober and wanted to know what to do. I took her to the Lake Shore Group. They said she could be in A.A. but she had to attend a different group. With all our liberal attitudes, we couldn't accept a colored woman," Oscar admitted. "We sat in the lobby talking with a couple of fellows, but the manager came up and said we had to leave. She was the only one, so we had to form a group for her.

"A lot of fellows helped me. We formed a group around her in a black neighborhood, on Cedar Avenue, and the news spread about 'some crazy people who could help you stop drinking.' We also got her a job running an elevator, which she didn't like, because she didn't make as much money.

"A chauffeur from one of the big families was one of the first, and he got two or three more, and pretty soon there were about 15. By this time, I was getting ready to quit the group, and one day the chauffeur comes down to the meeting in a big Rolls-Royce. He opens the door for this white man to get out. They both walk in, and the chauffeur introduces his boss as a new member."

Noting that "we were biased then," Oscar recalled the April 1945 Cleveland *Bulletin* (an A.A. newsletter), which said, "We whites, if we preach brotherly love, must practice it. And should a Negro appeal to us for help and guidance, it is our Christian duty to give the best that is in us, recognizing that a human soul is given into our hands to help or destroy."

Clarence S. remembered how they continued to work with another minority—the down-and-outers on skid row. In 1942, the A.A.'s went to a Salvation Army shelter and began talking to the men, who would never say anything in reply. Finally, a fellow who seemed to be their leader asked a question. The answer seemed to satisfy him, and he asked another. "That was the start, and it grew rapidly," said Clarence.

"We made a deal with the Salvation Army to use their lower rooms," said Oscar W. "First, we tried to get the men in with coffee and doughnuts, but they didn't want any part of it. So we got smart. We'd stand outside with a pocketful of change. They'd come up to us and ask for a nickel for a cup of coffee or ten cents for a flop. 'Be honest,' we'd say. 'What *do* you want it for?' They'd say, 'We need it to get some smoke at Smoky Joe's,' and we'd give it to them.

"The word got out that there were a bunch of fools who wouldn't give you anything for food or a bed, but they would give you some change if you wanted a drink. They began to trust us, and we got three fellows in the Citadel. It so happened that the first one we got sober was the son of a Salvation Army couple, and they thought we were wonderful.

"They backed us up completely, gave us 40 beds. And the only way a bum could get in was if he had an A.A. sponsor. They would see a doctor and a dentist and have food and a bed for 90 days. And sometimes, they would work at the same time.

"The A.A.'s ruined it by going in and telling the 'Sallys' how to run their business. And not too many got sober," Oscar said.

Another minority in A.A. consisted of members who spoke languages other than English. In early 1940, Dorothy S. noted in a letter to the New York office that a couple of Mexicans from Cleveland's west side were reported to have "fixed" someone in Mexico City.

One of the Cleveland Mexicans was Dick P., perhaps A.A.'s first Spanish-speaking member, as well as the first to try to carry the A.A. message south of the border. Then in the United States illegally, Dick came into the program in 1940 as a result of the story about Rollie H. in the Cleveland *Plain Dealer*. In 1963, long after Dick's immigrant status had been straightened out and he had achieved citizenship, he became manager of the Cleveland Central Office.

Dick recalled his own arrival in A.A.: "Harry R—— came to see me and told me I could go to the Orchard Grove Group if I stopped lying and mooching and I didn't drink. I stayed sober, and I started to visit other Mexicans I thought needed A.A. I didn't have anything but my own words, and my wife decided to translate different sentences of the Big Book. It got longer and longer, and after a while, she suggested doing the whole thing. It was finished in 1946. When I got my first vacation, I took it to New York and gave it to Bill."

Earlier, Dick had gone to Mexico with some literature, which he gave to priests and social workers. "There was a meeting, and the newspapers gave us some help, but nothing much happened," he said. "A group was finally started in Mexico City by an American woman whose husband had been transferred there from the United States."

Yet another minority was the handicapped. Norman Y., the blind A.A., had the Big Book done in Braille in 1940 and sent out from the Cleveland Library to other blind members.

"There were 19 of us corresponding back then," he said.

The odd thing is, Norman never read the book himself.
"I never read a word in A.A.," he said. "You don't have to
read. You don't have to have all these pamphlets they put out.
You can learn to live this program by learning to think.

"A.A. is a wonderful thing to know and apply," he said,
"—but in your life. You've got to live it out in the street. You
see somebody having a little problem, help them, no matter
who they are. That's A.A."

xx. Toledo A.A.'s find division is not disaster

In May 1940, there was more publicity out of Cleveland. This time, it involved the baseball catcher for the hometown Indians, Rollie H., who had just caught a no-hit game pitched by Bob Feller.

Rollie had been sober in A.A. for a year, and the story, when it broke, was big news—not only in Cleveland and Ohio, but in the sports sections of newspapers throughout the country.

Rollicking Rollie, as he had once been called, set fire to cars, raised hell on trains, caught a ball dropped from Cleveland's Terminal Tower when drunk (he did it again after he was sober), and was on the way out of the big leagues when Dr. Bob called John R. in April 1939.

As John recalled: "Doc said, 'You're the only one around here who knows anything about baseball. Do you know a player named Rollie H——?' I said, 'Yes, sure I do. He's a catcher for the Cleveland team.' 'He is?' Doc said. 'Well, someone brought him down here, and we've got him over at the hospital. You come up and talk to him.'

"I forget what name they put him under," said John, "but it made a sportswriter at the *Beacon-Journal* damn mad that Doc wouldn't reveal it. Then Rollie came out and went to T. Henry's. He went all the way, too.

"We were over there one night, and Rollie said, 'You know, I don't have any quarrel with any of this. But when I travel, I just have a little bag, and I can't get a Bible in there.'

"That summer, Rollie would send tickets down for baseball games, and Annie, Doc, Elgie, and I would go out to see Rollie afterward and shoot the breeze. When Rollie got sober, his wife trimmed down and put lipstick on and boy, she was smart-looking! I think she used to eat to keep her nerves calm."

Clarence S. recalled that Rollie, who owned a brand-new Packard roadster, wanted to go to one of the A.A. picnics and asked directions. "Just go to the park and look for a bunch of cars that look like they belong in a junkyard, and you'll find us," he was told. "You know, we invented cars without running boards," Clarence said.

On another occasion, a teammate offered Rollie a drink. "No thanks," he said.

"What's the matter?" his buddy asked. "You afraid you'll make a damn fool of yourself?"

"Yes," Rollie replied. "So you have it for me and make a damn fool out of *your*self."

When the Akron A.A.'s left the Oxford Group, Rollie stayed with T. Henry for a time. So, when the story of his alcoholism broke in 1940, credit for his recovery was given to the Oxford Group. At that time, however, Rollie broke his silence and said no, the credit for his sobriety belonged to Alcoholics Anonymous.

In addition to bringing hundreds of new members to

A.A., the story was the Fellowship's first anonymity break at the national level. It caused some concern among A.A.'s; but in all fairness, Rollie couldn't have been blamed for it.

Commenting later on what he thought to be the difference between the Oxford Group and A.A., Rollie said, "You know, if someone gave me tips about baseball and I found out he never played, I wouldn't pay much attention to him. It's the same thing with alcohol."

One of those who got sober as a result of the story was a Toledo-based salesman, Duke P. His boss read the account and called Duke and his wife, Katie, in for a conference. He said, "Duke, I think this A.A. will appeal to you, because it's psychologically sound and religiously sane. There will be a couple of men come to see you. Do anything they say. If they want you to go to Akron and spend the weekend with them, go ahead. We'll pay the bill."

The men who came were Charles ("C. J.") K. and Eddie B., both of whom had been in the state insane asylum at Toledo on voluntary commitments in the summer of 1939 when they were shown the manuscript of the Big Book. They were so impressed that they got themselves out of the asylum and went to Akron to live. C. J.'s father then told him that he would pay his living expenses as long as he stayed out of Toledo.

According to Ernie G. the second, A.A. in Toledo went back further than that: "When I came into A.A. in May 1939, there was a fellow who came down from the hospital," Ernie said. "He never made it, but he got hold of the manuscript and carried it into the state hospital in Toledo. That's how Walter C—— got it."

In any case, C. J. had to ask his father for permission to come to Toledo and talk to Duke. Katie, who kept wiping tears from her eyes in an interview some 38 years after the event, went along with the deal but recalled thinking, "What kind of sucker are you to send your husband down to spend a week-end in Akron with the alumni of an insane asylum?"

"I was admitted to City Hospital with 'acute gastritis,'" said Duke, noting that, in those days, hospital rooms were cheaper than hotels. "But I went that night to Wally G——'s home. I was amazed—a dozen people sitting around calling each other rummies and alkies and not getting upset. Wally had iron-gray hair and looked like Warren Harding. He didn't seem to have a worry in the world. Yet he had been fired from the W.P.A." (The Works Progress Administration was a Federal job program instituted during the Depression of the 1930's.)

"The next morning, who should come to see me but Dr. Bob! He just radiated charm, love, and confidence—all the things I didn't have. He said, 'Duke, everything's going to be all right.' And I knew it would be all right.

"After he left, I had a sense of peace. The fear was gone. I knew that when I saw Katie, I was going to tell her every-thing. And when I did, she knew that I was telling the truth for the first time.

"That Monday, Katie went with me to Youngstown, Ohio," said Duke. "When I got there, I met Neil K——, who had been forewarned that I was coming. He invited us to dinner that night. I phoned Katie and told her. When I got back to the hotel, she was in tears. 'What can I talk to that woman about?' she said. 'We don't know these people.' 'We've got to,' I said. 'We don't *do* things like that,' Katie said. 'We've never been introduced.' 'This is a new way of life,' I said.

"And of course, you know we hadn't been there five min-utes, and we were on a first-name basis. I even did a Twelfth Step that night. They brought a new man over, and we sat on the front porch. He was nervous and excited, and I began to talk—me, a veteran of 36 hours! He said, 'It's all right for you people because you've known each other so long.' He couldn't believe that I was an absolute stranger, the same as he was."

Like the small number of A.A.'s from Youngstown and other Ohio cities, Duke and Katie traveled from Toledo to Akron on Wednesday nights to attend the King School meeting. "In five minutes, from his seat, Dr. Bob would give Katie and me enough inspiration to keep us going until next time.

"Later, at Kessler's Donut Shop, we used to sit next to Dr. Bob if we'd get the chance. He'd regale us with stories. If there was some slang expression he could use to replace a word, he'd do it. A dollar bill was a frogskin. And when you'd ask him a question, he'd say, 'Why ask me? I'm not an oracle.' We'd stay there for hours and hours.

"He made life so pleasant and entertaining," said Duke. "He was just like your father or uncle, and he loved everybody. But he particularly loved Bill Wilson.

"He had a lot of concern about Bill. 'I'm doing all right,' he'd say. 'I do an operation once in a while. We ought to do something for Bill.' Then Bill would say, 'I'm doing all right, but we ought to do something for Smithy.' There was a love between those two that was like David and Jonathan. It's great to sit back and think about it.

"Anne gave us a feeling of stability," said Duke. "She always had the right thing to say, no matter what. You couldn't have a feeling of anger or animosity toward anyone when she was around. She always said, in order to know someone's feelings you had to walk a mile in his shoes."

"I remember that she told me not to be surprised when Duke started to drink again," Katie said. 'Why should he?' I asked. 'He hasn't had the problems most of the men have had,' Annie told me. 'He's never really been in trouble.' 'It seems to me he's been in constant trouble,' I said."

Duke never did pick up another drink. A few months later, in September 1940, he and the other Toledo members started their own group. Duke remembered 13 people being there at Ruth T.'s big home on the river. Eight were alcoholics. Among those present were Ruth and Ernie G., who had just moved from Akron. In fact, the meeting had been postponed for one week so they could attend.

Ernie remembered Dr. Bob's saying at the time, "I'm awfully glad you're going to Toledo, because they need some help there." Ernie added, "And Anne told us to keep the meeting on a spiritual plane and we would succeed.

"On Saturday, we'd go down to Akron and see Dr. Bob. We'd talk over what was happening, and if we were having problems, he'd pray about it. 'Keep it on a spiritual basis,' he'd say. 'If you keep principles ahead of personalities and you're active and sharing your program with other people, it will work out.' He said, 'Alcohol is a great leveler of people, and A.A. is, too.' "

As Duke recalled, there was another fellow, Chet M., who had also been in the state hospital. Chet would get patients from Dr. Kaiser at the hospital, leave a receipt, and take them to the Toledo meeting. "That's the way we got our first new members up until December 1940," said Duke. "Right out of the booby hatch."

The Toledo group met at Ruth T.'s home until January, then hired a hall for $10 a month. "The owner was delighted to rent it to A.A., because he was very much in favor of athletic associations," said Duke. " 'I have a rule,' he told us. 'I will not permit hard liquor in this hall. I don't mind half a keg of beer once in a while, but I have an absolute rule against hard liquor.' And you know, he never did find out that A.A. wasn't an athletic association.

"Katie was our first treasurer, since there was a resistance to having a member do it," Duke said. He also gave his wife credit for evolving "the greater 24-hour plan."

This involved a couple who were in such conflict that there was electricity in the air. "Katie said to the husband, 'You have pledged to stay sober 24 hours. Now, how about loving Grace for 24 hours?' Then she suggested the same thing to Grace. The following Friday, the couple came to the meeting hand in hand."

Then there was a man named Bob, who was brought to the program just as he was about to do himself in. A few days later, Bob went on a Twelfth Step call with Walter C. The prospect listened to them and said, "What you have to say is very interesting, but I don't think it's for me. However, I have a friend whose brother could really use your help."

"Who is he?" asked Bob.

"I don't know his name, but his sister is Edith M——."

"Why, that's *my* sister," said Bob—who had just been advised to make a Twelfth Step call on himself!

Toledo's first hospitalization arranged by A.A.'s wound up in the obstetric ward of the Women's and Children's Hospital, according to Duke, who said that was the only place they could get the new man in. He was tapered off on an ounce of whiskey every five hours. After a time, when he asked for his allotment, the nurse said, "Mr. B——, aren't you paying *any* attention to what these men are telling you? Let's see if you can't miss this next one." And he never had another drink after that.

"There was a trauma when we grew so big that we had to create more groups," Duke said. "One guy got drunk over it. 'You're going to divide,' he said. But it wasn't dividing; it was expanding. We had a plan, divided the money, and set up the meetings on a geographic basis. It wasn't a split because of resentment, but there were resentments just the same. When we [Duke and Katie] left Toledo on Easter, 1942, there were several groups.

"We also went to the first A.A. meeting in Youngstown. I say 'we' because all communities helped the others. It was in the front room of Neil K——'s house. Dr. Bob led the meeting, leaning against the mantelpiece and just talking to us."

At this time, traveling salesmen were also playing an important part in spreading the word about A.A. out of Cleveland and Akron, where they had joined the Fellowship. They stopped off in towns along their way to see prospects or "lone wolves" whose names had been referred to them in one way or another—often, by A.A.'s in New York.

Now living in Toledo, Ernie G. the second (who, when interviewed in 1977, was working with a youngster six months sober and in his early twenties) was responsible for helping a number of groups in western Ohio and southern Michigan get started, as was J. D. H., who also did a good deal of traveling in his job.

"Alcoholics Anonymous" was published three years after J. D. joined the Akron group. Then, he said, "I used to carry three or four Big Books in my car. If they didn't have any books at a particular group, I'd give them one and some pamphlets—or I'd know who the secretary of a neighboring group was, and arrange for them to get in touch with each other. Sometimes, you'd have a lone wolf. You'd drive 30 or 40 miles out of your way to hit a town of 400 to see a guy whose name you got from the office."

J. D. spoke of a friend, Doherty S., "who is responsible for more groups in Indiana than anybody. He'd get a lone wolf from one town together with another one for Sunday breakfast. I had to go up there Saturday nights and spend half the night getting there. It was a lousy trip, changing trains and all. Then I'd get out of there about noon to get home. It took about ten or 12 hours to get 160 miles. But it was a very interesting experience."

Sometimes, it was more than interesting. "I came back to visit one group I helped start in my travels," said Oscar W., "and there were four ministers sitting in the front row. I said, 'Isn't this wonderful? We have four ministers in A.A.'

"One of them stood up and said, 'We're not drunken ministers. We are the screening committee for Alcoholics Anonymous, to determine who is fit for membership.' "

One of the most famous early itinerants out of Cleveland was Irwin M., who sold venetian blinds to department stores in the Deep South. "Irwin weighed 250 pounds and had energy and gusto," Bill Wilson wrote, noting that "the prospect of Irwin as a missionary scared us rather badly."

Still, in his territory there was a long list of prospects, which was reluctantly given to him even though he had "broken all the rules of caution and discreet approach to newcomers." He ran each and every one of them down, working day and night. In addition, he wrote them letters and got them writing to each other. "He had cracked the territory wide open," wrote Bill, "and had started or stimulated many an original group."

Larry J. was a newspaperman who went to Houston, Texas, from Cleveland. There, he wrote a series of six articles about A.A. for the Houston *Press*. They were a condensation of the Big Book. Among those who contacted Larry after reading these articles, Roy Y. was the first Texan to get sober and stay sober. This was the start of A.A. in Texas.

Roy later went into the Army and, while stationed in Tampa, started the first groups on the west coast of Florida. Another Houston member moved to Miami to become one of the A.A. pioneers there.

As the years passed and groups became established, the A.A. travelers continued to stop in at their meetings, bringing messages and literature, getting group secretaries in touch with one another, sharing experience, and giving guidance when it seemed appropriate. The travelers witnessed the same growing pains in these new groups that groups in the Akron-Cleveland area had gone through, and were quite often able to help them speed their progress past the early stages. It was found that A.A. groups, like A.A. members, didn't always have to learn through their own experience. They could learn and grow through the experience of others.

XXI. Group concerns and angry rumors

Meetings in Cleveland evolved somewhat differently from those in Akron. "We opened with an audible prayer," said Clarence S. "The speaker, who was chosen four weeks in advance, spoke for 45 minutes, and we closed with the Lord's Prayer.

"Then, we would reopen for informal comments, questions, and so forth. The total meeting might go on anywhere from one and a half to two hours. No smoking was allowed in the first part of the meeting, only in the informal part.

"That's the trouble," Clarence said. "They take it so casually today. I think a little discipline is necessary. I think A.A. was more effective in those days. Records in Cleveland show that 93 percent of those who came to us never had a drink again. When I discovered that people had slips in A.A., it really shook me up. Today, it's all watered down so much. Anyone can wander in now."

Warren C., also an early Cleveland member, had a somewhat more optimistic view of A.A. when interviewed in 1977. "I think the program is just the same," he said. "The principles are there; the Steps are there; the practices are there; and the opportunities are there. If you do as the Big Book says, then it is the same program that existed when I came in, in 1939.

"We have more people in and out of the program now," he said. "But that's understandable, because we have more people. The people who wanted to stay sober then were the ones who did what the program suggested. Today, the people who want to stay sober are the ones who do what the program tells them to do. The only difference is that I don't know everybody in the program anymore.

"One big thing is that today people come in who have lost every dime, their wives, and their kids. That wasn't true in the early days. There wasn't much money, but most of the men still had their wives and families.

"The other thing is that there are so many young people. For example, my son came in when he was 31. I came in when I was 38. Those seven years made a tremendous difference.

"I was washed up at 36," Warren said. "Now, here I am 76. When you are sober in the program as long as I am, they look at you and want to hear all that you have to say whether it means anything or not. They [the newer members] might have something far more important to offer."

By September 1940, Cleveland was reporting to Bill in New York that, in addition to its own six meetings and 400 to 500 members, Ohio had meetings in Akron, Toledo, Youngstown, Dayton, Ravenna, Wooster, and Canton.

Dorothy S., Clarence's wife, inquired about the possibility of a mimeographed directory, "showing where people are," and also suggested a newsletter that could be sent to all groups and "bring everybody closer together." Up to then, Ohio A.A.'s had simply been reading letters from Bill at the meetings, just as Bill would read letters from Akron and Cleveland at the New York meetings.

The active or even recently active alcoholic was definitely not welcome at early meetings in Cleveland. In September 1940, Clarence wrote Bill that "several groups do not permit a rummy to attend unless he has been hospitalized or talked to by ten men." Clarence noted that they then had a "definite setup" with three hospitals and two sanitariums, and that there were ten to 15 hospitalized at all times.

By January 1941, requirements had eased up—slightly. Clarence wrote that "most groups" required either hospitalization, being talked to by at least five members, or being passed by a committee before a new person could attend meetings.

In Youngstown, it was usual for two couples to visit the prospective member before he attended his first meeting. The husband would tell the man about A.A., and the woman would talk to the wife. "That way, they would know what it was all about when they finally got to A.A.," said Norman Y.

"Various groups have various distinctions," Clarence wrote. "But the general idea is to try and prepare a fellow and give him a pretty good understanding of the aims and principles of A.A. before he comes to meetings. This eliminates much of the nuisance of entertaining boys under the influence at our meetings."

"If a drunk showed up at a meeting, three or four guys would take him outside and counsel with him," another early member recalled.

"Cleveland did not allow outsiders at meetings, but did allow families," according to Warren C. "Some groups allowed families to stay for the first part of the meeting, but then said, 'Will the women please leave for the second part?' One of the first women members got up, thinking this meant her."

As noted in a foregoing chapter, the status of women in

present-day A.A. is markedly different. But some of the early Cleveland groups' concerns—such as clubs for A.A.'s and members' anonymity—still have a familiar ring.

"There were some clubs," said Warren, "but they developed into poker games and didn't last. We felt that this wasn't right, and discouraged their formation. All the groups were independent. They had their own secretaries and officers.

"As far as anonymity was concerned, *we* knew who we were. It wasn't only A.A., but our social life. All of our lives seemed to be spent together. We took people home with us to dry out. The Cleveland group had the names, addresses, and phone numbers of all the members," said Warren. "In fact, I remember Dr. Bob saying, 'If I got up and gave my name as Dr. Bob S., people who needed help would have a hard time getting in touch with me.' "

Warren recalled, "He [Dr. Bob] said there were two ways to break the anonymity Tradition: (1) by giving your name at the public level of press or radio; (2) by being so anonymous that you can't be reached by other drunks."

In an article in the February 1969 Grapevine, D. S. of San Mateo, California, wrote that Dr. Bob commented on the Eleventh Tradition as follows:

"Since our Tradition on anonymity designates the exact level where the line should be held, it must be obvious to everyone who can read and understand the English language that to maintain anonymity at any other level is definitely a violation of this Tradition.

"The A.A. who hides his identity from his fellow A.A. by using only a given name violates the Tradition just as much as the A.A. who permits his name to appear in the press in connection with matters pertaining to A.A.

"The former is maintaining his anonymity *above* the level of press, radio, and films, and the latter is maintaining his anonymity *below* the level of press, radio, and films—whereas the Tradition states that we should maintain our anonymity *at* the level of press, radio, and films."

Ernie G. of Toledo, commenting on what he saw to be an increase of anonymity within A.A. today as compared with the old days, said, "I made a lead over to Jackson [Michigan] one night, and everybody's coming up to me and saying, 'I'm Joe,' 'I'm Pete.' Then one of the guys said, 'Safe journey home. If you get into any trouble, give me a buzz.' Later, I said to the fellow who was with me, 'You know, suppose we did get into trouble on the way home. How would we tell anyone in A.A.? We don't know anyone's last name.' They get so doggone carried away with this anonymity that it gets to be a joke. I had a book [evidently, one of the small address books compiled by early members or their wives] with the first hundred names—first *and* last—telephone numbers, and where they lived."

Dr. Bob's views on anonymity remained clear in the recollections of Akron's Joe P. (the Dartmouth grad). Though it was not the custom in the mid-1940's to give A.A. talks to anyone except drunks, Joe noted, a few members formed an unofficial public information committee that started to speak to Rotary and Kiwanis Clubs throughout the state.

"Of course, we first had to get permission from Bob. He said you were not supposed to break your anonymity in the newspapers or on the radio, but he didn't think we would get anyplace if people didn't know we belonged to A.A. He had the firm conviction that you should let yourself be known as an A.A. member in the community, and he was always sure to tell you about it every time you met him."

The great regard that most local A.A.'s had for Dr. Bob's thinking and for the man himself was formally expressed in the fall of 1941. Clarence S. and other Cleveland members planned a Doc Smith Day, which would consist of an afternoon program of talks and fellowship, then a dinner. He

invited Bill, noting that "Doc would be tickled to see you." At the same time, Clarence wrote, "I was down to Akron and am frankly quite apprehensive about Doc's condition. He is not at all well and should be taking things easy. In his position, it is quite difficult. While Doc is so conscientious that he will put up a front, he should be spared any details possible. So many people don't stop to think that Doc is not a chicken anymore, and they continue to put pressure on him."

Tickets for the dinner and other events were $1.35—and it doesn't take much imagination for anyone who has ever worked on a dinner committee to hear a few members complaining about how expensive it all was.

In any case, 900 A.A.'s and family members turned out. Speakers included Dr. Bob, Bill Wilson, Bill D., and Henrietta Seiberling, among others. And as Duke P. recalled, they chipped in to buy a $75 War Bond (which cost only $67.50) for Doc. The members of the Toledo group raised additional money for Bill's fare round-trip from Cleveland, so he could visit them, too. "We couldn't afford to put Bill up at a hotel, so he stayed at our house," said Duke. "Other members came over, and we spent the whole night talking."

A.A.'s co-founders were not always greeted with tributes. In 1942, a story got around Cleveland that the New York office and the Big Book were nothing but a racket. The rumors chiefly involved royalties on sales of the book.

Clarence S. said he had not known that either Bill Wilson or Dr. Bob was receiving royalties until "I met Bill at the depot when he came in for the shindig" (Doc Smith Day).

"He told me then," said Clarence. "I was stunned. I thought it was a labor of love—no one was supposed to get

Revered as a co-founder, loved as a tough sponsor, Dr. Bob still was not spared when critics spread rumors.

any royalties. But Bill didn't make any bones about it. People in New York knew, and he assumed that Dr. Bob would tell them in Akron.

"Bill was willing to tell them in Cleveland—about himself, but not about Dr. Bob," said Clarence. "He would admit anything. I told him, 'Not right now,' that I would work it out."

Sometime after that, Clarence had a confrontation with Dr. Bob that "kind of injured our relationship. I looked up to him and was disillusioned," Clarence said. "Annie got very disturbed about it. It's one of those things that you wish never happened, but it did."

It probably would have been better if Bill had followed his instinct to speak out to the Clevelanders right away on the matter of royalties. In spite of Clarence's assurance that he would take care of it, somone started to circulate the stories. Needless to say, it all became highly distorted.

Deciding to meet the situation head-on, some Cleveland A.A.'s organized a dinner for both Dr. Bob and Bill, at which the co-founders were invited to speak. After the dinner, which wasn't too well attended, the two "guests of honor" were asked to join the chairmen or secretaries of all the local groups, along with a lawyer and a certified public accountant, in a private session. The A.A.'s said they had heard that Bill and Bob were making fantastic profits from the book and had shared a total of $64,000 in 1941.

At the time, in fact, Bill was receiving $25 a week from the publishing sales. In addition, both he and Dr. Bob were receiving $30 a week, supplied by contributions from well-to-do non-A.A.'s friendly to the Fellowship. (A.A.'s Seventh Tradition — of self-support by both groups and A.A. as a whole — did not evolve until four years later.) Records show that Dr. Bob received a total of $1,000 during 1941; evidently, even their weekly $30 was not always forthcoming.

Bill just "happened" to have brought with him to the

dinner a certified audit of all A.A. financial affairs from the beginning. The C.P.A. for the investigating committee read the statement aloud and testified to its correctness. Both Bill and Dr. Bob received apologies.

The group officers present promised they would do all they could to stop the spreading of these tales, but never quite succeeded, according to Bill. The "racket" talk went on for years.

One of the ironies in this matter is that Dr. Bob had written the Alcoholic Foundation (A.A.'s board of trustees) early in 1941 that he considered the idea of royalties "unwise," that the book should be "the property of the foundation 100 percent." This was Bill's belief as well, though he was not opposed to royalties; he had turned over to the foundation his shares of stock in the company formed to publish the Big Book—but with the proviso that Dr. Bob and Anne receive royalties for the rest of their lives.

Each co-founder was given to worrying (with reason) about the other's financial situation. Dr. Bob's first reaction was that Bill needed the royalty money more. But his own income fluctuated, however optimistic he might have been at times, and he had a family to care for. So Dr. Bob's reluctance to accept the money faded under the impact of reality.

Actually, talk of "royalties" had been largely academic up to this point. Sums entered under that category had been going chiefly to support the headquarters office. But by the end of 1942, sales of the Big Book were steadily on the increase, and each of the co-founders received a total of $875 in royalties for that year—still a long way from the mythical $32,000 apiece.

xxii. Oldtimers' impressions of Dr. Bob

As the question of the royalties indicated, A.A.'s attitude toward its co-founders has fallen somewhat short of veneration, ranging from love and gratitude among most members to occasional antagonism and suspicion among a few. This freedom of opinion is entirely appropriate for a fellowship founded upon equality—one drunk talking to, never *down* to, another.

Neither Dr. Bob nor Bill ever wanted to be regarded as anything other than what they actually were—fellow alcoholics, fellow human beings.

By 1942, Bill was not in such favor with Clarence and his faction in Cleveland as in earlier days. In the years to come, there were further clashes, over finances, policy, the start of the A.A. General Service Conference, and other matters. The criticism was directed more at Bill than at Bob.

"People in New York decided they were *it*, and we were jealous," said Oscar W. "Bob wasn't that way. He had a marvelous nature. I don't know why we had that built-in animosity. Clarence didn't like Bill and would cuss him out, so you can see my animosity came secondhand," Oscar said. "If anything bad came out of New York, I blamed Bill. I had to blame someone.

"Most of us in Akron didn't like all this praying," said Oscar. "We had enough of it in the Oxford Group. I still don't like praying in A.A. I don't like the Serenity Prayer. New York brought it in, and we resented it. We thought they were bringing back the Oxford Group.

"They wanted to expel me from A.A. because I didn't like it. Bill wrote back that in that case, they would have to expel everybody in A.A., because we were all alike" (all, presumably, prone to complain at times).

This is not to say that Dr. Bob did not have his detractors, too. "He was liked and disliked," said one member. "Some felt he didn't give enough credit to Henrietta [Seiberling] or the Oxford Group; others, that he was too conservative or too strict—that you went to him once, and he would read the law and edicts to you, and that was it. And if you wanted to see him, *you* had to go to *him*."

"He did not play politics," said Ed B. "That would upset one faction or the other. There was a fellow, Sam C——, we were having trouble with. He started a meeting of his own and asked Dr. Bob to speak at the opening. We sent Ed M—— down to tell Dr. Bob not to go. I don't know exactly what Bob told him, but it was something like this: 'These people are organizing a group to help other alcoholics. I was asked to go there, and I am going. I'm not going there for Sam. I'm going there for the people who are there.'

"And he wouldn't listen to gossip," said Ed. "They would come to Dr. Bob with it, and I remember him telling them, 'Before you mention anything about that man, you bring him over here *with* you.' He stopped that very quickly."

"Dr. Bob was the most tolerant man I ever knew, and I do not believe he held any enmity toward anyone," said Lavelle K. "He was always quick to praise and very slow to condemn. He could always find some possible excuse for anyone's unseemly conduct."

Henrietta D. (wife of A.A. number three) recalled Dr. Bob's saying, "If the speaker doesn't say exactly what you think he ought to say, don't criticize. He may be saying exactly what the man in the back row wants to hear."

But "we are not saints." At times, Dr. Bob could be stubborn or dogmatic, and he relished an argument now and then. "I tell you he was a forceful fella," said John R. "If you both had a thought, and he had his thinking one way, you were absolutely wrong, and he was right."

The fact that Dr. Bob was "forceful"— stated his thoughts bluntly and straightforwardly, sometimes presented the A.A. program on a take-it-or-leave-it basis — probably did much to convey an impression of intolerance and rigidity. In truth, not only was his mind open to new ideas, but he was amenable to change and had an insatiable curiosity.

Tolerance did not come easily to Dr. Bob. "I have heard him say it was difficult for him to be tolerant," said Smitty, "that it was not his nature and a real hurdle. He got it [tolerance] from Mom, and he had to work on it real hard."

As Dr. Bob himself put it: "Another thing that was difficult for me (and I probably don't do it too well yet) was the matter of tolerance. We are all inclined to have closed minds, pretty tightly closed. That's one reason why some people find our spiritual teaching difficult. They don't *want* to find out too much about it for various personal reasons, like the fear of being considered effeminate. But it's quite important that we do acquire tolerance toward the other fellow's ideas. I think I have more of it than I did have, although not enough yet. If somebody crosses me, I'm apt to make a rather caustic remark. I've done that many times, much to my regret. And then, later on, I find that the man knew much more about it than I did. I'd have been infinitely better off if I'd just kept my big mouth shut."

Dr. Bob wrote on tolerance in the July 1944 Grapevine:

"Tolerance expresses itself in a variety of ways: in kindness and consideration toward the man or woman who is just beginning the march along the spiritual path; in the understanding of those who perhaps have been less fortunate in educational advantages; and in sympathy toward those whose religious ideas may seem to be at great variance with our own.

"I am reminded in this connection," he continued, "of the picture of a hub with its radiating spokes. We all start at the outer circumference and approach our destination by one of many routes. To say that one spoke is much better than all the other spokes is true only in the sense of its being best suited to you as an individual. Human nature is such that without some degree of tolerance, each one of us might be inclined to believe that we have found the best or perhaps the shortest spoke. Without some tolerance, we might tend to become a bit smug or superior—which, of course, is not helpful to the person we are trying to help and might be quite painful or obnoxious to others. No one of us wishes to do anything which might act as a deterrent to the advancement of another—and a patronizing attitude can readily slow up this process.

"Tolerance furnishes, as a by-product, a greater freedom from the tendency to cling to preconceived ideas and stubbornly adhered-to opinions. In other words, it often promotes an open-mindedness which is vastly important—is, in fact, a prerequisite to the successful termination of any line of search, whether it be scientific or spiritual.

"These, then, are a few of the reasons why an attempt to acquire tolerance should be made by each one of us."

There were also those, of course, who had an extremely negative reaction to Dr. Bob on first acquaintance or at one certain moment—and then had occasion to change their minds.

Ed. B. was one of these. He had been in A.A., then had gone out to experiment. He woke up to find himself in the basement ward of a little community hospital.

Dr. Bob, he recalled, "came down to see me and asked, 'What happened, Ed?'

"'I don't know, Doc. Somehow, I found myself in a bar, and I don't know how I got there.'

"I remember him getting up from the chair and pointing a finger at me. 'Now wait a minute,' he said. 'Before we go any further, one of the requirements—and an important requirement—is honesty. And you haven't got any honesty about you at all.

"'Nobody pushed you in that bar. You walked in there, and you ordered that drink, and naturally, you drank it. So don't tell me you don't know how you got there. Now, you're lying here using a bed that could be used by somebody who needs it more than you. And you're taking up my time, and I have better ways to spend it than to talk to you. If I were you, I'd go out and get drunk and stay drunk until I made up my mind what I wanted to do. As far as I'm concerned, you stink!'

"I was really mad. I thought, 'If they have people like that in A.A., it will never be a success.' That same night, I called Annie [Ed's wife] and asked her to take me out of there. That was August 1944, the night I had my last drink.

"Of course, the first meeting I went to after I came out of the hospital, I made it my business to thank Doc for coming to see me," said Ed. "He was very nice about it. 'I'm helping myself by helping you,' he said. 'I want you to do the same thing.'

"You know, we became good friends after my second trip, because I realized after I sobered up that he had actually done me more good by giving me hell than if he had been sympathizing with me. He *knew*. If you needed sympathy, he'd give it to you, and if you needed hell, he'd give it to you."

Alex M. agreed. "Dr. Bob was not patient with people who slipped, but he didn't let them down. He could give it to you in a rough way if he had to. If a guy got smart with him, he would set him down real quick. But he had compassion."

Dan K. didn't get off on the right track with Dr. Bob, either. "Our first meeting wasn't very friendly," he recalled, "due to the fact I brought a couple of magazines to the hospital in my little suitcase. He wanted to know where I got them.

"I didn't know who he was, and I told him I brought them with me and I paid for them. 'In here,' he said, 'we have literature pertaining to Alcoholics Anonymous. If you don't want what we have for you, this bed space is very valuable, and we have someone else waiting for it.' "

John S. (an Akron member beginning in 1940) remembered: "He pointed his finger at me—he had a finger on him like a yardstick, skin and bone was all it was—and said, 'You want to do something about your drinking, do you?'

"He was kind of rough and tough, you know. He said, 'You got any dough?' That was for the book. I didn't know what he had going. I thought maybe he was a book agent or something.

"Then, he'd come in the room after I'd read the book. He'd ask me a lot of questions. It was like a second grade teacher coming in and asking about the lesson. And you better have some of the answers.

"He asked me when I was going to take the Steps. 'Right now is as good a time as any,' I said. This was admitting to God, to yourself and to another person. So that's what I did." (Evidently, John had reached the Fifth Step.)

"At this time—January 1940—he wasn't making you get out of bed to surrender on your knees, to pray with you. I'm not sure that would have worked too well with me."

Even John R. wasn't particularly drawn to Doc on first acquaintance. "When he came over to my house and he was telling me that he hadn't had a drink in three and a half years, I looked at him and boy, I was doubting that! I said, 'There was a gray-haired fellow here to see me today. Do you know who he was?' Doc laughed and told me it was Bill D——. I said, 'Can you see if he'll come and see me again?' He telephoned, and Bill came over to see me right then."

Of course, Dr. Bob didn't succeed with all his pigeons. "I met Dr. Bob in 1942 or '43," recalled Bruce M. "One of my doctor friends brought me. We had quite a chat. I'm sorry to say it was to no avail. Dr. Bob was most gracious in a typical Vermonter's way—short and to the point, with no hemming or hawing.

"He told me that he and some friends had worked out a program whereby people who had a drinking problem could receive help if they wanted. Then he told me some of his own experiences, one of which I remember vividly—that while he was practicing and while it still worked, he would put a tumbler full of whiskey on the nightstand. In the morning as he woke up, before he'd get out of bed, he'd reach over and drink that glass of whiskey. My reaction was, he drank too much whiskey. *I* used to take a little orange-juice glass of whiskey and put it on my dresser.

"He told me about the hospital, but he was rather vague about what they would do, except that I could lie in bed and meditate and read the Bible, at which point I concluded he not only drank too much, he was nuts and apparently a religious fanatic.

"When I left, he was just as nice as he could be," Bruce recalled. "He said, 'Young man, I don't believe you're ready for what we have to offer.' And I well recall saying to myself, 'I'll say I'm not!' He was a one-shot salesman, and he didn't run after you. I didn't see him until after 1945, when I came into A.A. in Canton" (Ohio).

Henry W., a Cleveland A.A., went to a big meeting in Akron in 1949 where he heard, not only Dr. Bob, but Bill Wilson, Bill D., and Sister Ignatia. Then he went out and got drunk.

"In 1950, when I finally sobered up," Henry said, "Dr. Bob told me, 'Young man, keep that enthusiasm. That will carry you through.' Then I told him, 'After hearing you, Bill Wilson, Bill D——, and Sister Ignatia, I went out and got drunk.'

"Dr. Bob just laughed and said, 'Well, Bill is my sponsor, and I went out and got drunk after he talked to me.' "

"We didn't really get to be friends in the usual sense of the term," said Bruce M. "He seemed to me to be a little standoffish. I've since known others from Vermont who were the same way. They stand aside and don't make conversation easily, and when they do, they don't engage in it for long.

"His appearing kind of unapproachable could have been my own reaction," Bruce said, "because I'm shy, too. And I've found out since, he did talk to people. Later, I got to know Bill [Wilson] very well, but I never felt it was my privilege to speak to them as if they were my friends."

"Sure, he was easy to talk to," said John R. of Dr. Bob. "I used to peddle jewelry, and I spent a lot of time around Dartmouth and the New England states. All you had to do was mention something about Dartmouth, and Doc was off. I had a barbershop in those days, on West Exchange Street. Doc would stop by maybe just two minutes in the morning. Then he'd go over next door, to Ed M——'s meat market, stop there, then get in his car, and go on into town. Then maybe in the evening, he'd stop by again."

Said Elgie R., "In the beginning, he talked to everybody. He worked so hard. But when people started coming to him, the pull got so strong that he backed away. He would use other people to screen them. For example, he would turn someone over to me, or he would call Annabelle G——, or if Dorothy S—— was in town, he'd use her. Anything to keep the pressure off, because it got to the point where he couldn't take it anymore. You know how people are—when they start pushing, they just won't let up. I think it was his way of protecting himself, because he could only do so much."

Speaking of Dr. Bob and Anne, Dorothy S. M. said, "They loved everybody, and their home was just full of people. It was like Grand Central Station. They'd come up to our house to get away from the tremendous pressure—people dropping in on them all the time. I always felt privileged."

xxiii. His prescriptions for sobriety

Dr. Bob's financial condition improved during the 1940's. "As the movement grew and A.A. membership expanded, Dad's practice was also growing," Smitty said. "He regained the respect that he had had in the community, and he was recognized for his talents as a surgeon, as well as for the efforts he and Bill were making with A.A.

"He was in dead earnest with regard to his lifework and tried his utmost to live up to the oath of the doctor," Smitty said. "He was very competent and strived constantly to keep abreast of the newest developments in the field of medicine. I do not believe he ever lost sight of the ideals that were instilled in him during his medical training, or ever wavered from his principles. They were very real to him, and I know that he was hurt when he heard of doctors' operating needlessly for the sake of additional money, although he never mentioned any names, even to his own family."

Dorothy O. (Jud's wife), who returned to nursing at the

beginning of World War II, said, "I imagine there were some times before when he didn't have all the patients he would like; but when I knew him, he had a good practice. He was busy during the war, because he was an older man and so many of our younger men went into the service. He knew the days I worked and always came up to see me. When he talked about his patients, he was quite professional. Otherwise, we just spoke in a friendly way."

"He was just as serious in his efforts to help the A.A. movement grow," said Smitty. "He tried his best to do the work, although there were some phases of it which he disliked—making talks to large groups, for instance. It not only made him nervous, but I don't think he wanted to play the big shot. Again, he was a man of principle with regard to the goals of the A.A. program. He tried to make every decision in the best interests of the group, to the exclusion of personal advantage. The results always amazed him. He never ceased to be surprised that so many people sought him out, but felt that he had only been God's agent and so was not due any credit for personal accomplishments."

If there is any question about Dr. Bob's priorities, A.A.'s in the Akron area have no doubt what came first. "A.A. was the most important thing in his life," said John S. "A couple of us went into his office one afternoon. There were four or five other people in there for professional reasons. He looked up and saw us and said, 'Come on in, boys. Hell, I can talk to people with a sore ass anytime. But I don't often get a chance to talk to A.A.'s in the office.' "

His office was open to A.A. members' wives as well. One woman remembered going up to see him at a time when she was very discouraged about her husband. "'Don't push,' he told me. 'You can't push him and you can't nag him and you can't *make* him do things. Have faith in him.' "

At the same time, Dr. Bob's home remained open to any

who needed his or Anne's counsel. "I used to stop in every time I went over to Akron on the weekends," said Alex M. "I'd get kind of leery, walking that Main Street, shopping. There was a lot of action then. You'd hear those jukeboxes. I'd think, 'Oh, what a drink would do for me now!' You'd hear them laughing clear inside—half a block away. I'd go in Stone's grill for a meal. Then I'd get leery of the back bar and get the hell out, take a taxicab over to Doc's.

"He'd say, 'Stay away from that place. They got nothing in there that you can't get somewhere else, whether it's food, cigarettes, or a Coke.'"

Remembering his own disastrous trip to Atlantic City and Bill's experiment with keeping liquor on the sideboard to prove it was no longer a temptation, Dr. Bob advocated that members stay in dry places whenever possible. "You don't ask the Lord not to lead you into temptation, then turn around and walk right into it," he said.

"You could always go to him, and you'd always get an answer out of him," said Alex. "He could just look at you and tell that you were in trouble. I used to shake hands with him, and he'd say, 'There's something bothering you.' I'd say, 'Yeah. *You* are, for one thing.'

"That was because I had trouble getting the program spiritually. 'I want to make something easy for you,' he said. 'Try to find your own God—as *you* understand Him.'

"We had a lot of talks, but I didn't want to take up too much of his time, because everybody was after him. He was setting the example, and he was supposed to know all the answers. And he did! Whatever you asked him, he had the answer for it. But he wasn't God. He was a human being. A real man all around. He was a man's man."

Dan K. remembered doing more or less the same thing five or six years later. "I'd walk to 855 Ardmore, and I'd sit on the steps. Doc and Anne would come out to meet me. I'd say,

'I'll just sit here.' And Dr. Bob would look at me and say,
'What is it, Dan? What's your problem today?' He could see it
on my face. I was young, and I was struggling.

"   'You know, Dan,' he told me, 'many people coming into
A.A. get the wrong conception of "Easy Does It," and I hope
you don't. It doesn't mean that you sit on your fanny, stay
home from meetings, and let other people work the program
for you. It doesn't mean you have an easy life without drinking. "Easy Does It" means you take it a day at a time.'

"He told me that before I could be honest with him or my
sponsor or anyone else, I had to 'get honest with that joker in
the glass.'

"I didn't know what he meant by 'that joker in the glass.'
He told me that was the man in the looking glass. 'When you
shave tomorrow, get honest with the man who looks back at
you from the looking glass.'

"Dr. Bob said that even then, it wasn't 'Easy Does It' for
him. 'In the morning, when I get up and put my feet on the
cold floor' [evidently, they didn't have wall-to-wall carpets], 'I
have a battle all day to stay away from that drink. You know,
Dan, there were times in the early days of Alcoholics Anonymous when I passed those saloons that I had to pull my car
over to the side of the curb and say a prayer.'

"And when I had a problem with other members because
I was young," Dan continued, "he told me they resented the
fact they didn't do something about it early, like I was doing.

"Dr. Bob and Anne drove me to the meeting for about a
year and a half because I didn't have a driver's license. And
another thing—I'd call Dr. Bob and say, 'I've got this speaker
for the consolidated meeting [a once-a-month, citywide meet-
ing]. Would you mind if he comes over to visit you?' 'Why, no,
Dan.' He never turned me down once."

So we see that Dr. Bob was easily available and consulted
constantly by various A.A. members virtually from the time

A.A. began until illness made it impossible for him to see anyone.

"He was one fine person," said Madeline V., in one of the sweetest and simplest of remembrances. "He wasn't the type to get up and mix. They would say, 'Hello, Dr. Bob,' and all they would get back was 'Hi.'

"I was real close with him, though. And I knew Bill. I was nervous inside of me because every time Bob or Bill would come, they'd say, 'Where's Madeline? Where's Madeline?' And I'd be right there.

"Bob said to me, 'Stay up and aboveboard. You're all set now. Stay all set. And if you need help, you can come here to A.A. We're willing to step out and share the program with you.'

"Anne was a lovely person, I liked her. She'd always come over and sit with me. She'd say, 'I want to go over with Madeline.' She'd tell the people next to me, 'I'm sorry I want to sit with Madeline.'

"They never said much, only, 'If you want help, you have to ask for it.' And they'd say, 'We can't tell you what to do, but we can help.' If you got to the meeting, you didn't have to worry about getting home. They'd say to me, 'You just get to the meeting, and we'll see you get home.'

"Some of the oldtimers would say, 'Go to the meeting, and you'll meet Madeline. She'll shake your hand.' And that's what I did. I would shake their hands and say, 'I'm glad you got here. Thank God for that. I hope you'll enjoy it.'

"And Sister Ignatia. She was my dear friend. When she was invited somewhere, she often asked me to go with her. If I hesitated, people would say, 'Don't you see Sister wants you to go with her? And if you don't go, maybe she won't go, either. We're glad she said she would go, and we told her that we'd get you to go, too.'

"I started A.A. in my forties. I stopped [drinking] and

never broke over. Thank God for that. And I never pushed
A.A. on anyone. Dr. Bob used to always say to me, 'Madeline,
whatever you do, whoever you talk to, don't push.' 'Well, who
said I push?' I would say. 'Because I'm not pushing.'

"Then he'd get to laughing, and then he'd say, 'Don't
push. Just tell them that you found yourself in A.A. and how
grateful you are and how things have changed. Talk about
yourself. Then tell them, "If you need help, want help, join
A.A." '

"I didn't have to go to *him* when I needed help. In fact,
every time he'd come over to St. Thomas, he'd yell out,
'Where's Madeline? Where the devil is Madeline? Isn't she
around here tonight?' I'd be in the kitchen helping the new
girls get things ready, and I'd have a fit. 'What do you want
me for?' I'd say. 'What can *I* do? You're on your own.' Then
he'd give me a sassy answer, and we'd laugh. And they'd say,
'Well, Bob and Madeline have made up.'

"You see, it was just a joke," said Madeline, who in 1977
was staying at a beautiful old-folks home—"where there's no
drinking, just good people"—on the outskirts of Akron. "I
never fought with him. I was grateful, and I am today—so
grateful for the help I got from the group and Dr. Bob and
Bill Wilson and Ethel M——[Rollo's wife]. She was a big girl and
a marvelous example. I helped her start the women's group.

"I had a wonderful husband. We were so happy. He
would take me to the meeting, and he would always say,
'Madeline, you stay on the beam and don't worry.' When I was
drinking, I was not the real woman I became when I joined
A.A.

"Yes, I'd go to King School, and they'd all scream out,
'There's old Madeline.' I'd say, 'Where do you get that *old*?'
And they'd say, 'We're only kidding.'

"I haven't seen any of the people since I came out here.
They used to call me and ask me what meeting I was going to

be at. If you know anyone, tell them to talk about A.A. Say you spoke to a woman who talked more about being sober than about her drinking.

"I knew all the oldtimers. I call them the good oldtimers. Here we are, the good oldtimers, together again. And I think, 'Madeline, you're so lucky to be in A.A.' I got all the help I could in A.A., and I'm grateful for that.

"I'm so glad you came and that you're going to write a book about Dr. Bob—about the old days. Call it 'The Old-timers'—'The Good Oldtimers.' "

XXIV. Dr. Bob's influence on Ohio A.A.

It was probably in the early 1940's that Dr. Bob began to delegate more authority to others. Through the late 1930's, he had usually been the one to have initial interviews with prospects and determine whether they were ready for the A.A. program. Now, there were too many, and demands on his time were increasing. John R. recalled that Dr. Bob had him going out to see new people, and that he "sent me on some pretty wild goose chases.

"It was when things started to get organized that he moved back," John said. "Not that he wanted to. He was almost forced to. Everyone wanted to see Doc! So he put that job on some of the rest of the members. I think he did it the right way, too. Doc didn't have much money when he came in, and he had to get on the ball and make a livelihood. During the war, he *was* busy."

"Dr. Bob was a good listener, and he knew how to manipulate people," said Elgie R. "He'd pick this one and that one to get done whatever kind of a job in A.A. he wanted done."

As Joe P. saw it, it was just good old-fashioned A.A. for Dr. Bob in the 1940's. "Originally, he would explain to five or six of us what he would like us to do, and we would. Then, he'd judge whether we'd done it the right way or not. He was a rather stern executive. Gradually, with his own 'medicine,' he cooled down to being a very gracious and friendly person. But he still wanted to get things done.

"He was busy in all possible forms of A.A.," said Joe. "He was always consulting in towns nearby—how to start this, what to do when problems came up. He normally took off at least a day or so to go to a new group's first meeting.

"When I came into A.A., there were 12 or 14 groups around. Now [1977], there are 92 in the area. He was probably present at the beginning of 75 of those. I don't know whether I read his mind or not, but he used to agree with us, at least, that a group should not get too large—that it begins to lose a little of its effectiveness when it does.

"I don't have the feeling he was inhibited by being a founder," said Joe. "It worked the other way. A.A. became a lifework, and he felt that he should do everything he could to help make it succeed, and that it was his responsibility to do what he could to help it continue to succeed after he was gone.

"At St. Thomas, he was the spark of the whole hospital setup. I would say that he increased his interest in A.A. as he went along. And if a saint can see the future, Dr. Bob was looking at it."

Dr. Bob did present his ideas on the future of A.A. in his last major talk, in Detroit in 1948:

"We know what A.A. has done in the past 13 years," he said, "but where do we go from here? Our membership at present is, I believe, conservatively estimated at 70,000. Will it increase from here on?

"Well, that will depend on every member of A.A.," he continued. "It is possible for us to grow or not to grow, as we elect. If we fight shy of entangling alliances, if we avoid getting messed up with controversial issues (religious or political or wet-dry), if we maintain unity through our central offices, if we preserve the simplicity of our program, if we remember that our job is to get sober and to stay sober and to help our less fortunate brother do the same thing, then we shall continue to grow and thrive and prosper."

"He had a lot of good friends who were not alcoholics, and he kept them separate from his A.A. activities," said Joe. "He was active in medicine. He was active socially. However, he didn't boast about what he had done. You'd just learn, because it came out some way or another.

"He got into this with Goodrich and then with Goodyear. Finally, we had a deal with three rubber companies that if they had anyone they wanted us to try and sober up, they would call us. And in turn, if we had someone we had sober who needed a job, we could call them. We worked that out for several years in the 1940's, and it worked good. We even had a judge he [Dr. Bob] was involved with. This judge used to issue a summons for a guy to join A.A.

"There were arguments, of course—that was when the S—— boys [Paul and Dick] were fighting along pretty well— and we'd finally wind up having Doc settle it when we couldn't agree on it. He spent a terrific amount of time on A.A. And he went to New York quite a lot.

"Doc was extremely democratic," recalled Joe. "He'd go to a meeting, and he wouldn't sit up on the stage. He'd always sit in the second row or someplace like that. I always felt that he left off being officious and autocratic and ended up being extremely friendly. Still, he had to do a lot of finger-pointing to get this thing rolling."

"Doc used to play an important part in the Central Committee," said Dan K. "That was the steering committee for the office. We'd meet the first Monday of every month, and he always attended. There'd be a member from each group.

"During the meeting, sometimes, the words would fly like you were in a barroom. I'll never forget the time Dr. Bob got up. He put up his hands. You know—enough, stop! He said, 'Gentlemen, please. We're still members of Alcoholics Anonymous. Let's carry the principles of A.A. into these business meetings. You are servants of your group, here to take the ideas formulated by the committee. Let one man talk at a time, and let us conduct this business meeting as a service to the Lord and a service to our fellow members of Alcoholics Anonymous.' After that, we had no more brawls when Dr. Bob was around.

"We had groups start and break up. That was one of the most alarming things in those days. They didn't have connections with the steering committee."

Another alarming thing was slips. "When someone got plastered, that hurt Bob," said John R. "It didn't matter who it was, either."

"We were having a covered-dish dinner over in East Akron," recalled Emma K., "and when we got there, they told us that Wally G—— had fallen off the wagon. He was Doctor's right-hand man for many years. I was frightened for my husband [Lavelle]. He had always patterned himself after Wally. It was an awful shock to Akron."

"We used to sit around and argue about whether or not it was our fault if someone slipped," said Elgie R. "Had we gotten the message to him? For a while, we had it all down pat that it was our fault—until Wally got drunk. He was one man who knew all the answers and worked hard and never had any doubt about the A.A. program. That's when we realized that no matter how good we were or how hard we tried, if they hit a blind spot, that's where the guard had to go up."

"Wally was so against those who had slipped," said Sue Windows, Dr. Bob's daughter. "They should be excommunicated! Eventually, he had to eat his words. If he'd had his way, *he* wouldn't have been allowed back in."

"It took him a long time to get back," Joe P. said. "If it hadn't been for Annabelle [Wally's wife], I don't think he would have. She dragged him to meetings. Finally, he got sober again, and stayed sober until he passed away. Yes, his attitude did change."

"I think, at the beginning, we were kind of unaware that it was so serious," said Elgie. "For example, a man went and got a tooth pulled, and they gave him sodium pentothal. He came out of the office higher than a kite and went right into the first bar, because he wasn't aware that he was already drunk on that drug. Those were things we had to find out the hard way. There was a lot of experimentation, because we didn't have any sure answers."

As if to illustrate the danger, Jud O. noted that in 1969 he picked up a drink one week before he was to have his 30th anniversary. "I had retired as director of research for one of the big rubber companies, and taken a European tour. I had been fairly active in A.A. for a number of years, but then I got busy with my work and wasn't going to meetings. My wife was in the hospital, and I was feeling sorry for myself. . . ."

"That day when he came into the hospital, he was drunk," said Dorothy. "It was 11 in the morning, and it got me so upset, I asked for a hypo. When I woke up, I thought I'd had a bad dream. I couldn't believe it. I just couldn't believe it—30 years!"

"*Jud?* He was the Rock of Gibraltar," said Kate P., Duke's wife, on hearing about his slip nearly ten years after it occurred.

"When I came back to A.A., it was the same as I remembered, only more people and more meetings," said Jud.

"Some old friends and some new ones helped me, but getting straightened out was the hardest thing I ever did. It took three years. On the other hand, it convinced other people that the original idea was correct: No matter how long you don't drink, the next one is right around the corner. It never lets you go. Dr. Bob was right: 'The first one will get you.' "

xxv. Personal sidelights on his sober years

Dr. Bob's dedication to A.A. and its program was never at the expense of his family life; rather, it was an enrichment. Throughout the 1940's, he and Anne continued to live simply and without pretense in their modest home. Here, they shared the joys of parenthood, the sorrows, and the companionship of their friends.

"The way he loved his family, the devotion to his children and to Anne and to his home" impressed Dorothy S. M., she remembered. "He was one of the most devoted of family men. And his friends—those, too, he loved."

Until he retired, Dr. Bob's days were spent in the routine of the hospital, at his office, and at his club for recreation. During most of his adult life in Akron, Dr. Bob lunched at the City Club, where thick rugs and tapestries, paneled walls, fireplaces, and club chairs provided a retreat for rubber barons and professional people to nap, read their newspapers, play cards, or talk. In Dr. Bob's drinking days, he often went there to line up with the afternoon crowd in the bar or even to hide away in a room. But after he stopped drinking, he went to enjoy the company of his many friends outside the program.

Noon would almost always find him at the same table in the corner of the men's dining room. There, for more than ten years, he was served by the same waitress, Nancy. Dr. Bob always greeted her with "How's my chum today?" They were good friends. As Nancy served him his simple lunch of melon or grapefruit, soup, milk or coffee, and his favorite Boston cream pie, they discussed her problems. Once, Nancy, who was ill at the time, became uncontrollably angry and threw a cracker basket at another waiter. Dr. Bob admonished, "Now, now, chum, don't let little things bother you." The next day, he sent her copies of "As a Man Thinketh" and "The Runner's Bible."

Nancy always looked forward to serving Dr. Bob and his friends. Often, there would be discussion or argument at the table, and she would ask him why he didn't say something. He'd answer, "Too much being said already!" He was "such a good, kind man; he had such a simple faith in prayer," said Nancy.

After lunch, if time permitted, Dr. Bob joined his cronies for a game of gin rummy or bridge. He was expert at both, and he always played to win. But he never got angry. He had a habit of keeping up a steady chatter all through the game. His cronies said it could have been annoying except that it was always so funny, they had to laugh.

According to one anecdote, Dr. Bob often stated that it was silly to take the game of bridge seriously. When he and

Past the miseries of active alcoholism and the struggles of A.A. pioneering, Anne and Bob knew serenity together (next pages).

Anne were in Florida, he was airing this view to an agreeable stranger who later became his partner in a bridge tournament. They won that afternoon but upset their "serious" opponents so much that one of them remarked, "If you had bid right and played right, you never would have won!"

"Quite so," replied Dr. Bob, in his laconic way, as he accepted first prize.

On the other hand, Elgie R. remembered sitting down at a card table with Dr. Bob as a partner. "I played auction bridge and didn't know the first thing about contract," she said. "I made a bid, and he bid, and I thought he had a good hand. I started bidding to the sky. I'll never forget the look on his face. It was so pained. Finally, he got up and said, 'You know, I don't think I'm going to play bridge anymore.' Later, I asked him about it, and he said, 'Elgie, you have to concentrate on bridge. Sometimes when I'm driving, I picture bridge hands.' "

Perhaps he refused to take it seriously only when he was ahead. As the old poker axiom has it: "The winners laugh and joke, and the losers say, 'Deal!' " In any case, there was general agreement among those who knew Dr. Bob that he did not often play cards with A.A.'s. When he did, it was not for money.

Dan K. quoted Bob as saying, "Some of you jokers beat the other guy at cards, and he gets mad. And when he gets mad, you know what he does—he gets drunk." Therefore, Dan thought, Dr. Bob believed that card-playing and A.A. fellowship should not be mixed.

Elgie had another explanation: "He didn't play bridge very much with the A.A.'s because there wasn't anyone good enough to play with."

"He could tell you what you had in hand after three rounds," said Smitty, who noted that his father played with Sidney Lang, one of the foremost bridge experts of his time.

As for the Smiths' playing as partners, Elgie recalled, "Anne used to say, 'I wouldn't dream of it. Forget it!' She played with the other women when we were at get-togethers, but not with Doc."

Actually, Anne was regarded as quite a good bridge player herself, and she and Bob did play with Smitty and his wife, Betty, in later years. "They taught us some of the finer points," Betty said. "They were both very good."

For some obscure reason, Dr. Bob always carried a pocketful of silver. It may have been a carry-over from the insecure, squirrel-cage days of the eternal fight to keep enough money in his pocket to buy a quart, or it may have been just because he liked to hear the jingle. But there were times when he had as much as $10 in silver in his pocket. "I think he gave a lot of it away," said Sue. Often, the gift was more than coins. "He was always handing a fin [five-dollar bill] to someone."

Smitty wrote that his mother and father had a wonderful life in their last years together "Not only did they continue to give hope and encouragement to all who came to their door," he said, "but they were going around the country meeting members of some of the new groups, trying to help with growing pains and problems, which, of course, they had come through themselves."

On one of these trips, Bob ran into Dr. Philip P. Thompson, who had been his roommate at Dartmouth.

"About 40 years after graduation," Phil said, "I happened to become secretary of my class, and after writing letters to various men, I received this book from Bob on A.A. When I got a chance to look at it, I saw what wonderful work was being done. I wrote to Bob, who said he was glad that at last I remembered him. He had read in my notes about my going to Delray Beach [Florida] winters. He asked me about going down there and said he'd like to go with me. I told him what I could about Delray and forgot all about it.

"When my wife and I came down to Delray that winter and went in for breakfast in the dining room, the headwaitress said there were two people who would like to have us sit at their table with them, and I said to my wife, 'It may be Bob Smith, but I don't know how we'll get along.'

"We had an interesting breakfast. He was still lean, lanky, and restless and consumed large amounts of coffee. He talked the language of the gutter, much to the surprise and mystification of my wife. He referred to his wife as 'the skirt' or 'the little woman.'

"I became very much interested in his story. In Florida, Bob was called upon by many different people from all over the country, and all were charming people who adored him.

"He still continued with his language of the gutter. One day, we were sitting playing bridge when I saw a lovely woman peek in the door. Bob's back was to it, so he didn't see her, and she said, 'It's me,' and she rushed up to him and threw her arms around him and gave him a kiss, and Bob said, 'Who slipped me that slobber?'

"Another time, we were in a group of nice people who had their chairs together on the beach. We invited Bob and his wife to go down to the beach with us, and when Bob appeared in his bathing suit, we saw he was gloriously tattooed on his chest and both arms, with rather intriguing figures and snakes and so forth. My wife asked him what condition he was in when he got that last tattoo on his arm. And he said, 'It was a blazer.'

"His wife was practically blind and not a beauty in looks, but one of the loveliest characters I have ever known, and due to her, I think, he finally overcame this habit [alcoholic drinking].

"We met Bob and Anne again at Long Beach, California, where her brother, a prominent engineer, lived," Phil continued. "Bob was out there to address a large meeting in Los

Angeles. My remembrance is that at the end of that meeting, he told me he had to shake hands with at least 3,500 people.

"Bob always would tell us the number of months and the number of years and the number of days since he had his last drink. He visited us at our house once with his wife and once after he'd lost his wife, and we visited him at Akron.

"One of the outstanding incidents of my life is the Sunday we spent with him at his home in Akron. It was something like people coming to Lourdes—people he'd never seen or heard of. One was a dean of a large college in Ohio. Two people who stand out in my memory were a lawyer and his wife. They had driven all the way from Detroit to tell him what he had done through A.A. for them. This woman, who was charming, had been on skid row, and we couldn't believe it. She wanted to tell Bob, with tears in her eyes, how she went down to a reformatory in Detroit every Sunday and preached [sic], and she was very proud the last three Sundays She'd had practically the whole attendance of the reformatory, while the minister who had come out to preach a sermon had only two or three people.

"I don't know how many people came that day in Akron. There were seven or eight—entirely unknown to him before—who just came to his house to express their gratitude, and that was the way it was everywhere he went.

"In Florida, the people came from Miami, Fort Lauderdale, and Palm Beach and all around when they heard he was at Delray, and they were all of them people who were well worth saving. To me, it was amazing that they had ever been in the condition they must have been in."

At that time, of course, A.A. conventions and other local get togethers hardly approached the number found on today's crowded calendar. There was a two-week gathering in Minnesota that Dr. Bob attended for the four years it was held, through 1947. Called Founders Day, it was by invitation only—usually to those who were considered to be founders of groups in the Midwest.

"You were asked for one week, and there were about 40 people to each shift in the last year," according to Polly F. L., who said she thought it was stopped because it was not open to all and was thus against A.A. policy. (An A.A. from Chicago, Polly worked at one time in the General Service Office in New York.)

"Dr. Bob played bridge all the time," she recalled, "and those lucky enough to play the game saw more of him. He took walks and wasn't aloof at all. He was very approachable if you wanted to talk to him."

On one of these occasions, it was April and cold in Minnesota. Ernie and Ruth G., who stayed with Doc and Anne in one of the unheated cabins, recalled that they slept with their coats on, and on one particularly bitter morning, Dr. Bob sprinkled his chest with water and said that was going to be the extent of his sprucing-up for that day.

Though settled in Akron, Dr. Bob also had an abiding love for his native Vermont and made an annual trip to visit family and friends there.

While in Vermont, Doc also went to the regular meetings of the Fellowship Group in St. Johnsbury, and Ed G. recalled that Dr. Bob spoke at the group's first anniversary.

Eleanor E. wrote that, while she was a college student in Vermont, she was invited by Dr. Bob's niece to attend a meeting in 1946 at Burlington, where Dr. Bob and another man would tell some "interesting stories" at an A.A. meeting.

"I remember it clearly," wrote Eleanor, who knew about alcohol then but had never heard of A.A. "Unfortunately, it

Even fishing trips are more fun sober. Dr. Bob enjoyed socializing with fellow A.A.'s, as most members do.

took me 20 years to realize that I had, that evening, had the extraordinary privilege of hearing *both* founders of A.A."

Polly F. L. remembered that Dr. Bob was "a great joker" and everyone was quiet while he told a story. "Maybe they laughed even if it wasn't funny," she said, "but I think he had a good sense of humor. If you're an alcoholic, you *have* to develop a sense of humor to live in the world."

Gene C., another Chicago A.A., said Dr. Bob had a quality of happy sobriety and quoted him as saying, "If you can't be happy in this program, there isn't much use being in it." "He would loosen up a meeting by telling a story when it got too serious," said Gene.

The most risqué story (language standards were different then) elicited in all the interviews was one Bob reportedly told about the Cleveland drunk who heard there was a doctor in Akron who would help. "But when he learned I was a proctologist, he said, 'If that's the way he's gonna do it, the hell with it.'"

Several A.A.'s said that Anne would appear to get quite annoyed with Dr. Bob when he told one of his stories. Then, John R. mentioned a humorously caustic remark made by Anne in a private conversation. To the response that it didn't sound like her, he said, "Oh, she'd get off some dillies once in a while."

Smitty recalled how his father used to love to share the incidents and fun of his day—could hardly wait to tell some story picked up at the hospital. Dr. Bob would lean back in his chair and laugh until the tears streamed from his eyes. Then, with a familiar gesture, he would take off his glasses to wipe the tears away, still chuckling. "Our home was a happy one in those days," Smitty said.

The war, then marriage, took Smitty from home and to Texas, where he now lives. He laughed as he told of his father's first meeting with Betty, his future daughter-in-law.

Dr. Bob looked her up and down slowly, then remarked, "She's all right, son. She's built for speed and light housekeeping!"

Smitty once installed on the car belonging to the slightly accident-prone Betty specially ordered license plates reading "OOOOPS," then told the garage to keep one gallon of paint the color of Mrs. Smith's car on hand at all times. Like father, like son, as far as a sense of humor is concerned. But neither son nor daughter has had a drinking problem. Sue doesn't like hard liquor but drinks a glass of ale occasionally, "if I want to."

The younger Smiths have two daughters and two sons and now live in Nocona, Texas. Their youngest was born when Smitty was 47 and Betty was 45. "He thinks we're 34," said Smitty. At present, Smitty is a small independent oil producer and an antique-car buff.

Betty Smith recalled her first visit with Bob and Anne. "I flew with my Bob to Akron to meet his parents before our marriage in 1944. I had never heard of A.A. We went to a meeting that night, and I heard my first A.A. talk. I was almost overwhelmed. My father had a problem, and my mother and I were pouring liquor down the sink.

"I went home waving the A.A. book at my mother and said, 'We have the answer.'" Betty's father got sober and was later co-founder of a group in Clovis, New Mexico.

"I remember once telling Dad Smith, 'This is such a marvelous program,'" Betty said. "'You must be so proud.' I tell you truly, that was a no-no. He looked at me with his steely eyes till half of me melted right there, and he said, 'It is nothing *I* have done. I have merely been used.'"

Dr. Bob learned in later years to accept praise more comfortably, "even to appreciate it," said Smitty. "But he always tried to dispel the notion that he was a founder when talking to some new person. I remember him saying once that he thought it was just wonderful that so many people felt he had been of some help to them."

"I loved both Mom and Dad Smith very deeply," Betty said. "Dad Smith and I had a thing going about gin rummy. We would shout ugly words at each other, and we both had a marvelous time. His sense of humor was always at peak. Also, I do not know how many times he came up to me and slipped me a 50 and said, 'This is just between us—spend it any way you like.' I tried once not to take it, and that was a big mistake.

"Dad liked very good clothes. His suits were made with gorgeous material. He had a fondness for diamonds and other precious gems and wore them and bought them for Mom. When she died, he gave me a beautiful diamond that was hers, and I will cherish it forever.

"Once when she came to see us, she had a fur jacket," Betty said. "She wanted me to wear it when we went out for dinner. I did. Later, I found out she had never worn it. She truly treated me as a daughter.

"Anne was usually placid, but I once saw her disturbed. She went to her bedroom and came back after a short while. Her problem had been prayed away.

"She was a sheltered place for people in trouble," Betty said. "I doubt that any minister in any given week could have counseled more people, prayed with more people. In times of trouble, people rushed to her. She was a rock, a comforter with God's help—truly a person who went placidly amid the noise and haste.

"We *all* had talks about profound things. You know, Dad read for at least two hours every evening. Most unusual to have the great humor with the profundities. Or is it?"

Smitty, Dr. Bob's son, was sent to Texas during World War II service and now lives there with his family.

xxvi. His spiritual quest

Dr. Bob was a man in search of God, and it was in this area that he, like Bill Wilson, was probably among the least conservative of men. This is not remarkable when we consider that New England, politically and materially conservative as it was, still fostered many of the "new thought" philosophies and "mind cure" religions mentioned by William James in "The Varieties of Religious Experience." (The book, though not popular among Akron A.A.'s, was a favorite of Dr. Bob's.)

It is possible to theorize that Dr. Bob's search began earlier, but according to his own account, it started when he first contacted the Oxford Group, in early 1933.

Paul S. (the Akron pioneer whose brother, Dick, also joined the program) said of Dr. Bob, "At this time, he began his conscious search for truth through a concentrated study of the Bible over two and one-half years before his meeting with Bill. He felt that God had not heard his prayers for this entire period," said Paul. "And he could not blame Him. He felt that he was undeserving of any consideration. The revelation in Dr. Bob's life came when he made his second discovery: that spirituality couldn't be absorbed by someone emulating a sponge, but that one might find it in healing and helping to free those afflicted and in bondage."

This, of course, was what Dr. Bob meant when he said that Bill had brought him the idea of service. "I think the kind of service that really counts," Dr. Bob said, "is giving of yourself, and that almost invariably requires effort and time. It isn't a matter of just putting a little quiet money in the dish. That's needed, but it isn't giving much for the average individual in days like these, when most people get along fairly well. I don't believe that type of giving would ever keep anyone sober. But giving of our own effort and strength and time is quite a different matter. And I think that is what Bill learned in New York and I didn't learn in Akron until we met."

In another way, Dr. Bob's experience differed from Bill's. He never had the flash of light—the spiritual experience. One member recalled that he did not make any mention of this kind of awakening. Rather, it was spiritual growth that Dr. Bob talked about—in A.A., he said, his spiritual values changed as time went by.

He thought we were all seeking inner peace, said Smitty, but he believed that you had to work at something in order to be good at it.

As Dr. Bob himself said, "I don't think we can do anything very well in this world unless we practice it. And I don't believe we do A.A. too well unless we practice it. . . . We should practice . . . acquiring the spirit of service. We should attempt to acquire some faith, which isn't easily done, especially for the person who has always been very materialistic, following the standards of society today. But I think faith can be acquired; it can be acquired slowly; it has to be cultivated.

That was not easy for me, and I assume that it is difficult for everyone else. . . .

"We're all after the same thing, and that's happiness. We want peace of mind. The trouble with us alcoholics was this: We demanded that the world give us happiness and peace of mind in just the particular way we wanted to get it—by the alcohol route. And we weren't successful. But when we take time to find out some of the spiritual laws, and familiarize ourselves with them, and put them into practice, then we do get happiness and peace of mind. . . . There seem to be some rules that we have to follow, but happiness and peace of mind are always here, open and free to anyone."

According to Paul S., there was a period when Dr. Bob's faith wavered to the point that he was on the verge of a nervous breakdown. "There was gossip, and some sanctimonious people were citing his alcoholic experience to discredit him and have him removed from the staff at City Hospital," said Paul.

He went with Paul, against doctor's orders, to see the dean of Bible studies at Wooster College. "We learned there," said Paul, "that man will forsake us, but God never. We learned what was meant when Christ said, 'Therefore, if thou bring thy gift to the altar, and there rememberest that thy brother hath ought against thee, leave there thy gift before the altar, and go thy way; first be reconciled to thy brother, and then come and offer thy gift.'"

Dr. Bob was immediately healed, according to Paul. For two days, he spent his time apologizing to all those people who he had felt were persecuting him. The following Monday, he was back at his practice.

"Dad told me that what he was after was a spiritual revelation, which could come suddenly to some people," said Smitty. "He hoped it would be revealed to him in that way. He worked hard to attain it, and because it didn't come, he thought perhaps he was failing in some way. He studied for at least an hour every day on some religious subject. It was a long, slow process. The net result was that he had a wide and deep understanding of religious and spiritual matters. He had actually achieved the goal, although it was never revealed to him in a sudden manner."

"To the day he died," said Dorothy S. M., "he felt that if he only had more spiritual understanding, some way or another he could pass this message on."

Though Dr. Bob never had a sudden revelation, he did describe a moment at his desk to Betty and his son. "It didn't last long," he said, "but I had the most marvelous sense of peace, which transported me for a time. It was truly 'the peace . . . which passeth all understanding,' and I shall never forget it."

At the end, on his last trip to Vermont with Smitty and Betty, Dr. Bob had achieved a sense of peace—the feeling he had worked for "We would sit around on the bed at night and talk about it," said Betty.

Dr. Bob sought to discover and familiarize himself with the spiritual laws in great part through his reading, which was extensive. Dorothy S. M., in her conversation with Bill Wilson, said, "Remember that pile of books he had? Anne kept trying to move them up to the attic. And he had stacks by his bed and under his bed and everywhere else."

"He read everything," said Emma K. "I wish you could have seen the books. His son said to me [after Dr. Bob's death], 'Emma, you take care of them. I don't know what to do with them.' I gave the spiritual books to my minister and the medical books to two young doctors he helped get started. He was very kind to those young men when they came out of the service."

"He read about every religion," said Smitty, "not only the Christian religion. He could tell you about the Koran, Confu-

cius, even voodooism, and many other things. He read the
Bible from cover to cover three times and could quote favorite passages verbatim.

"I tried to read some of his books and couldn't understand them," said Smitty, noting one titled "Tertium Or-
ganum." "We have some others. There's 'The Varieties of Religious Experience.' He loved that. 'Confessions of St. Augustine.' 'The Robe,' by Lloyd C. Douglas (who, incidentally, was
a minister with a church in Akron in the 1930's). 'For Sinners
Only' (a book about the Oxford Group). 'Basic Teachings of
Confucius.' 'Teach Us to Pray,' by Charles and Cora Fillmore.
And 'Prayer Can Change Your Life.'"

"He recommended that I read 'The Art of Selfishness,' by
David Seabury," said Betty Smith.

"He also put a lot of stock in 'The Greatest Thing in the
World,' by Drummond," said Smitty.

But, Smitty noted, his father didn't come on strong about
philosophy or religion with others, because he didn't want to
scare them off. "He could see the funny side of it, too. I
remember once when Paul S—— referred to some fellow as
being a reflection of Christ, Dad said he thought he might
have a little dust on his mirror."

"The first thing he did was get me Emmet Fox's 'The
Sermon on the Mount,'" said Dorothy S. M. "Once, when I
was working on a woman in Cleveland, I called and asked
him, 'What do I do for somebody who is going into D.T.'s?' He
told me to give her the medication, and he said, 'When she
comes out of it and she decides she wants to be a different
woman, get her Drummond's "The Greatest Thing in the
World." Tell her to read it through every day for 30 days, and
she'll be a different woman.'

"Well, I don't know whether she was a different woman,"
Dorothy said, "but through the years, I still read it and reread
it. Those were the three main books at the time: that, *The*

Upper Room, and 'Sermon on the Mount.' Bob went on to explore every type of philosophy and religion, but he was pretty careful about recommending those to people for fear it might be disturbing," Dorothy added. "If people asked, he'd tell them, but he didn't push books at people."

"Dad was open-minded about religion," said Smitty, who recalled the period in their lives when their father took him and Sue to different churches.

In addition, Dr. Bob used to go to a Catholic retreat in Cleveland. "He'd go up there with his Bible and his pajamas and a toothbrush and check in for the weekend," said an A.A. member.

"He was even interested in people who claimed to have extrasensory perception and other forms of spiritual insight," said Smitty. "He felt that in far distant centuries, the science of the mind would be so developed as to make possible contact between the living and the dead."

This was an interest Doc shared with Bill Wilson and a number of other early A.A. members. Together and separately, they sought out mystical experiences.

John and Elgie R. recalled that in the late 1930's, Doc would talk for hours to a fellow named Roland J., "who believed in anything that came down the pike when it came to spiritualism. He could hypnotize you," said Elgie. Roland had studied many faiths in his search for sobriety, but never did stop drinking until he met Doc.

"I had several experiences with Roland J——, his wife, Doc and Anne, and Ruth T—— in Toledo," Elgie recalled. "We had a spiritualist séance one night, and an amazing thing happened: I became controlled, as it were. I was telling Doc about his father, who was a judge, and I didn't know anything about it.

"Afterwards, when I came to myself, Doc advised me to stay out of crowds. He told me I was sort of susceptible and liable to go into some sort of trance if there was somebody around who was upset. So for a long time after that, I just tried to stay away from crowds, because it scared me.

"I remember another time Doc, Anne, and I were sitting in the living room over at Roland's house one Sunday afternoon. Doc was reading the paper; Anne was sitting smoking cigarettes; Dorothy was out in the kitchen getting dinner; and Roland was sitting in a chair.

"All of a sudden, Anne started rolling her eyes, trying to get my attention. I looked in that direction. And so help me God, Roland had created the illusion of a beard on his chin. I didn't believe what I was seeing. When he saw that I was looking, he let it disappear. Doc just sat there and laughed. He believed that was the funniest thing he had ever seen."

"A lot of us believed in the spiritual thing," said Clarence S. "We'd go to Roland's on a Sunday night. He'd call in the spirits. It got spooky after a while—beyond what we should be monkeying with. Doc backed off, too."

Smitty agreed. "They got away from Roland J—— when they started to get bad vibrations," he said. "They felt it might be dangerous."

There was a similar feeling among Akron A.A.'s. "They were all against this spiritualist thing," said Sue. "Dad got to feel he was being criticized, and he was. They didn't approve. But I think what really got them was that they weren't included."

Sue also remembered meeting Roland, who told her, "I keep hearing a railroad train when I talk to you." "That was one of my memories," she said. "Walking down a railroad track with an older woman like a grandmother, before I went into the children's home. I was three years old."

Ruth G., wife of Ernie G. of Toledo, recalled that she had an illness for which she was trying to get spiritual healing, and that Dr. Bob "never once tried to discourage me. He encouraged it. He said that was what I was being guided to do. And Anne said the same thing. And he never once offered me his services or suggested what I could do. He always said, 'Give God a chance.'"

"Doc and Anne knew Ruth was getting a spiritual answer," said Ernie, "and they'd share books and things. This brought us closer together all the time."

"Of course, we knew that Doc had cancer long before it was generally known," said Ruth. "I thought he caught what I had, because we shared a cabin in Minnesota. We went over there, and he had just found out. He said, 'I haven't told this to anybody, but I have cancer. I have suspected it, but they've never been able to find it.' Some young doctor had visited him and, after questioning him, had made the diagnosis.

"Sometime later, however, Doc said, 'I think I've got the answer for you, Ruthie.' He had found out about someone else who had the same thing I had and about a doctor who performed an operation. 'Don't you think you ought to try that?' This was the first time he said anything medically, and it was after I had been turned away by the best doctors in Cleveland. I had been told by several surgeons that nothing could be done. I told him that I would have to pray about it. He told me to do what I felt guided to do.

"My Toledo doctor would not write a letter to the doctor in Cleveland, but Dr. Bob did," said Ruth. "He saved my life."

Dr. Bob also played a part in obtaining at least one spiritual healing, according to Virginia MacL., Dorothy S.'s sister, who had recommended that Dorothy take Clarence to see Dr. Bob in Akron. (Virginia, too, later joined A.A.)

The daughter of the MacL.'s, then four years old, had been ill since birth. "I had driven to Cleveland to take her to a children's clinic for an operation," said Virginia. "Roland had been instrumental in healing some children, and my sister, Dorothy, wanted me to see him first—to give him a chance at effecting a spiritual cure. I didn't have any belief in that sort of thing, and I thought she was too sick. Then Dr. Bob came in. This was the first time I had met him. I was impressed immediately—he was a doctor and knew what he was doing. Meeting him made all the difference.

"He took my daughter's temperature and said she was a very sick child. She couldn't even keep water down. Dr. Bob said he thought it [spiritual healing] would be worth trying. If it didn't work, she could still go into the clinic.

"I hadn't met Roland J—— before, either. He asked about my belief. I told him I didn't have any. He said I should go to a movie and keep my mind off it, so there wouldn't be interference from negative thoughts and they'd have a free field.

"When I came back two hours later, I could hear my daughter laughing before I even got into the house," said Virginia. "Then she called out to me, 'Oh, Mother, we're having such fun.' My daughter seemed completely healed, and she stayed well from then on."

Prayer, of course, was an important part of Dr. Bob's faith. According to Paul S., "Dr. Bob's morning devotion consisted of a short prayer, a 20-minute study of a familiar verse from the Bible, and a quiet period of waiting for directions as to where he, that day, should find use for his talent. Having heard, he would religiously go about his Father's business, as he put it."

Elgie R. recalled, "Doc told me that when he had an operation and wasn't sure, he would pray before he started. He said, 'When I operated under those conditions, I never made a move that wasn't right.' Dr. Bob never talked much about religion, but he was a very religious person. Whenever he got stuck about something, he always prayed about it. But that wasn't something he spread around. It was his own private attitude."

"He prayed, not only for his own understanding, but for different groups of people who requested him to pray for them," said Bill Wilson.

"I was always glad to think that I was included in those prayers," said Bill. "And I sort of depended on him to get me into heaven. Bob was far ahead of me in that sort of activity. I was always rushing around talking and organizing and 'teaching kindergarten.' I never grew up myself."

XXVII. Shadows—
illness and dissension

The happy years of Bob's sobriety were marred at last by Anne's illness and blindness. She developed cataracts that completely covered her eyes, so she could no longer drive a car. She could not recognize a person across the room and had to get up close or hear a voice before she could actually tell who it was.

Smitty felt that the love between his parents showed up more and more at this time, in the consideration they had for each other. And Betty recalled, "I was never around them for a day that Dad didn't hug her and say, 'How is our love today, Annie?' "

Anne had an operation for removal of one of the cataracts. When she was hospitalized, her only request was that Bob wouldn't be left alone. She felt that he would be lonely and worried, that he would need his friends around him.

That operation failed, and she would not permit a second on the other eye, in which she still had some vision. "It's better to see a little than not at all," she said. Smitty recalled that his mother had had a great deal of confidence in the operation. Later, he asked her what, in her opinion, was the reason for its failure. "I think it was because I did not have *enough* faith," she replied.

Dr. Bob then began to be her eyes as much as he could. Still in medical practice, he could not be with her every hour. He knew she needed daily care. He also knew she would be unhappy to think of herself as a burden to anyone. The solution that presented itself was a result of his own good work some years before.

In 1941, before Anne's blindness had become serious, Lavelle K. and his wife, Emma, who was a registered nurse, came to Dr. Bob's office for help.

"My husband was a new one—the second generation," Emma said. "He was assistant postmaster and had gone just about as far as he could go and still hold his job. Bill V——H—— talked him into going to see Dr. Smith. We thought it was for some kind of physical.

"Dr. Smith was the most marvelous man I ever knew. But if you didn't know him, he would frighten you to death, sitting there with his hands folded. I was paralyzed—he was so stern and gruff-looking. He gave up his entire afternoon to talk to us about A.A. We were spellbound.

"That was the way we first knew them. And we became very close. Oh, we had such good times! As long as Doctor was able, we would all go for a drive down the valley in the afternoon. Some nights, Mrs. Smith would call and say, 'Let's go off for a little ride. It's so hot!' She never sat in the front seat, even when they'd come after me to go into town. Lavelle would get in front. And we'd go across the railroad down along the Peninsula Road down through Portage Path. Doctor knew all the people who lived in the beautiful homes down there."

Emma also recalled the Smiths' generosity. "After Dr. Smith's mother died, Mrs. Smith said, 'Emma, I'd like you to wear this chain. It was Mater's.' Instead of saying 'Mother Smith,' it was 'Mater.'

"So I wore it and was very happy with it. Then, of course, I took it back the next day, and she said, 'Now listen. You like it, and it matches your ring. You keep it and wear it until I ask for it.' I still have it.

"I have a black onyx pin with three diamonds in it that Doctor gave me after Mrs. Smith was gone. She had such beautiful diamonds. He gave Betty—Smitty's wife—a beautiful diamond, and he gave Sue a beautiful diamond.

"They were always doing things like that for you. They couldn't do enough for you.

"Then they wanted to go on vacation. They had a dog, and they didn't want to leave him, and they didn't want to put him in a kennel. We had a little Boston also. So Dr. Smith came bounding up our steps one day and asked us if we would be willing to stay at their house while they were away.

"I didn't want to. But my husband said, 'We owe them something,' which we did. And that was the beginning of that. Whenever they wanted to go away, we just moved over there until they came back."

So, for eight years, Emma and Lavelle came from time to time to stay at Dr. Bob's house. Then, when it became necessary, Emma was with Anne most of the time.

"Mrs. Smith could see out of one eye, but she couldn't see well. She was having a very hard time walking, and her hands were cramped and swollen with arthritis," Emma recalled.

"I sometimes think everybody called her Anne but me," Emma said. "I couldn't do it. I called her Mrs. Smith. I was with her every day but Saturday and Sunday for three years. Of course, they had a housekeeper. And Doctor would be with her Saturday and Sunday."

At this time—1947-48, before Dr. Bob found out about his own fatal illness—Bill in New York began to think about A.A.'s future. What would become of the Fellowship when its founders died? It was Bill and Bob, chiefly, who linked the board of trustees and the General Service Office with the A.A. groups. If A.A. was to survive, Bill knew, the board and the office needed the moral and financial support of the groups. He approached Bob with the idea that the founders should give the groups full control of their own affairs through establishment of a general service conference, to which the groups could send delegates.

Bill thought this was vital, but the majority of the trustees wanted no such change. And many oldtimers in Akron, Cleveland, Chicago, and New York went along with them. Much as the Oxford Groupers were inclined to supervise the affairs of the early alcoholics, these same members—who had broken away from the Oxford Group—felt they should supervise the affairs of those who had come into A.A. after them.

Evidently, Dr. Bob was somewhere in the middle. In May 1948, he wrote Bill:

"However desirable many of these changes may be, I have the feeling that they will be brought about without too much sudden upheaval. If the trustees are wrong, they will hang themselves. I am just as interested in A.A. as you are, but am not 100 percent sure as to the wisest course to follow and the wisest ultimate setup. It does seem that for the moment, perhaps, 'Easy Does It' is the best course to follow. Maybe it would be wise to let the trustees act as trustees and perhaps insist that they do so, which might be effected with some outside pressure. The objection to the idea would be that they might mess things up badly while they attempt that. But they would surely get some unpleasant repercussions from the groups if they did. . . . Keep your shirt on for a bit,

and remember that whatever happens, we love you a lot.
Smithy."

This was the beginning, and while Bill evidently did keep
his shirt on for a while, the time would come when he realized
that "I must press for his [Dr. Bob's] consent." On the other
hand, there were those who felt they must press for his veto.
The result was that Dr. Bob came in for a great deal of pressure from both sides at a time when his health and strength
were beginning to fail badly.

Only a few months after Bill's letter, in the summer of
1948, Dr. Bob found that he had cancer. He closed his office
and retired from practice, so that he and Anne could live
their last days together quietly.

Later that year, just after Dr. Bob had one of several
operations, George H. stopped in to see him. George, a pro-
conference member from New York, had been surveying
groups around the country on their ideas about self-
government. After visiting Akron, he sent Bill a wire recording on which he included greetings from Dr. Bob and young
Smitty.

Short and to the point as usual, Dr. Bob's part of the
recording dealt noncommittally with his own condition: "Surgery varies a good deal depending on whether you do it or
whether it's done to you."

Smitty said, "Gave Dad a good lecture on exercise. It was
so good, I started taking it myself. But as yet, he hasn't."

George told Bill that Dr. Bob was in bed and predicted
that his time was limited to six months at the most. "His face is
drawn, and he is losing weight, and it is hard for him to get
around. He has good periods, then a lot of illness and pain.

"He overdid it when his son was here," George said. "He
should cut down on visitors and the length of time they stay.
Still, he's the old Bob—chin out and doesn't admit he is as ill
as he really is."

The rest of the recording reported the outcome of the survey. George devoted a good deal of his comments to the attitudes of oldtimers in Chicago, Cleveland, and Akron, who, he felt, were against change, "while all the rest of the United States—370 groups personally visited—feel control should be in a conference."

He said there was a feeling among these oldtimers that members in Chicago, Cleveland, and Akron were more entitled to serve on committees than were A.A.'s elsewhere. These pioneers were for a council of older members rather than a conference, and they favored use of the Steps only, regarding the Twelve Traditions (presented by Bill in a 1946 Grapevine article) as being too unwieldy.

George's personal opinion differed: "Length of sobriety isn't everything. You need to choose for planning ability and so forth.

"Bob and Annie are no longer young," he continued " They have arrived at definite conclusions and are not amenable to change." Stating that the best two words he could use to describe Dr. Bob were "meticulous workman," George noted that Bob had "intense loyalties. People he knew in the early days could do no wrong."

(Although it was not in regard to this specific point, Sue did agree that her father could be a friend "almost to a fault." Mentioning one or two people in Akron who acted in the interests of a few, rather than for the group as a whole, as well as one who was involved in some shady business practices, to the detriment of other A.A.'s, she said Dr. Bob stuck up for them even though they were wrong.)

George said that Bob's opinions were being molded by a few "whose ideas are warped"; that one oldtimer's "deviation from normal thinking has been obvious for the past two years"; that another was "using Bob as a tool to push things around as he wants them." He described one A.A. as "the

Crown Prince," who "has aspirations to the other title and
ambitions beyond" his hometown.

Both Bob and Annie, George said, were "much too ill to
think things out clearly" or to be "pushed and crowded as they
are being pushed and crowded now. We should leave them in
peace for the weeks and months they have left."

George suggested that "you two [Bill and Dr. Bob], who
really understand each other basically, make an open sort of
statement—a compromise involving a temporary advisory
board with names you both could agree on."

In listening to the wire recording, it is possible to detect
the impatience and the touch of condescension mingled with
respect and concern in George's description of Dr. Bob. This
implied attitude indicates one side of what was to be a growing controversy in A.A. over the next few years. The other
side was saying much the same kind of thing about Bill and
the "revolutionaries who wanted to take control."

George might have neglected to consider that, of all
those people from the early days who could do no wrong, Bill
was probably foremost as far as Dr. Bob was concerned. As
for Bob's unwillingness to change, it might have been one
thing for Bill to try to persuade him and quite another for a
"newcomer" from New York.

There was, and is to this day, a feeling that Dr. Bob and
Akron-Cleveland A.A. were never fully appreciated by "New
York"—meaning the trustees and the office.

"Dr. Bob wasn't acknowledged very much in New York,"
said Emma K. "That hurt Mrs. Smith. They went there for a
dinner one time, and she said, 'Really, Emma, there wasn't
anyone much who recognized Bob.' Of course, in Ohio, there
was nobody *but* him. I knew Bill—it wouldn't bother him. In
New York, it was Bill, I suppose. Probably, it didn't make any
difference to either one of them."

This dinner where "there wasn't anyone much who recognized Bob" might conceivably have been Bill's anniversary celebration in 1948. Al S., dinner chairman, recalled having been informed at the last minute that Bob and Anne would be there. "I was so flustered at having both founders and their wives there that I couldn't remember his name. I really muddled the introductions that night."

Emma, who saw Dr. Bob so often all during this period crucial to A.A.'s future, said of the co-founders, "They were as different as these two fingers. Bill would get off on a tangent, and Dr. Bob would say, 'Now look, Bill. Come on, let's talk about this a little bit more.' Bill was go-go-go, and Dr. Bob was kind of the soft pedal.

"Yes, I heard them talk about things quite a bit. However, you can see my position. I felt those two had so much in common and so much to talk about. I would go in and sit down and talk about different things with them, but to really sit and enter into their conversation . . . They always got along so well. So different, but in my opinion, more like brothers than anything else."

As Bob's condition deteriorated, Bill continued to press for his approval of both the Traditions and the conference. Most of their discussion on this matter probably took place in person and via the telephone.

In February 1949, however, Bill wrote a three-page, single-spaced letter once again outlining the need to transfer the board of trustees, the General Service Office, and the Grapevine "lock, stock, and barrel into the direct custody of regional representatives of the A.A. movement." The groups had already begun taking over their own affairs, Bill said, and there was no use "bucking the trend; the smoother the transfer, the better."

Aware of Bob's pivotal position, Bill concluded, "Most earnestly and prayerfully, I trust that you can and will lend us a hand. Your presence and influence are badly needed by all,

especially me. Your calm disposition and firm support may mean everything."

While not in direct response to Bill's letter, Bob's sentiments were expressed in a note to Bill, dated March 14, 1949, when he said: "Have been quite painfully ill since you were here . . . Do not have the feeling that this [the conference] is a particularly guided thing to do now. Maybe I am wrong, but that is the way I feel. Why don't you see if you can get the boys to put across this committee and let it go at that? Love, Smitty."

(The committee in question was envisioned as a "policy" or "joint headquarters" committee, designed to help in the A.A. publishing operation and to meet between trustees' meetings. By June 1949, it had been approved and was functioning, under the name General Service Committee.)

It was not until 1950 and Dr. Bob's last appearance at a large A.A. gathering—the First International Convention, in Cleveland—that he agreed to confirm the Twelve Traditions. A few weeks later, when Bill informed him that the trustees would probably consent to the idea of a conference, Bob finally agreed to endorse the idea as well.

Dr. Bob was not the only Ohio member whose attitude changed. Ed B. remembered when Bill Wilson came to talk to members in the area about the conference and the Traditions. "Bill D—— [A.A. number three] was opposed, and he was mad. He said, 'Ed, I'm going to that meeting, and I'm just going to tell Bill what I think of him!'

"I went with him, and Bill explained the purpose of those Traditions and the conference. He also mentioned that he and Dr. Bob were going to pass away, and if the members

Bill Wilson, upon hearing of Dr. Bob's serious illness, intensified the plans to safeguard A.A.'s future.

were going to take over, they should know *what* they were taking over.

"We both listened, and then we [Ed and Bill D.] went out to lunch. And I said, 'Well, Bill, what do you think?'

"He said, 'Ed, you know, he's got something.'

"'I think he has, too,' I said. Well, we went back to elect an officer that night, and Bill D—— was the first delegate [from Ohio to the First A.A. General Service Conference, in 1951]."

xxviii. Without Anne,
but with loving friends

In May 1949, Bob and Anne went on their last trip together—to Texas to see Smitty and his family. "That Smitty, he was a good guy," Emma recalled. "He was good to his parents. One day, he came up to visit, and of course, he went down to have lunch at the City Club with his dad. And Anne said, 'Emma, he had those old Texas boots on. I thought I'd die!' "

As they got ready for the long trip, Anne, who was very weak and tired, said, "You know, Emma, I don't really care to go, but Dad wants to. It will make him happy."

Of the same journey, Bob said, "I don't really want to go, but Mama wants it. It will make her happy."

"She usually called him Dad," Emma said. And he called her Mama.

"When they came back, he called me early one morning and asked me to come over. He said, 'Mama hasn't been well.' We both knew she was seriously ill. So we took her to St. Thomas. She lasted six or seven days."

Sister Ignatia remembered that Dr. Bob called requesting a bed for Anne. Their plane had been grounded for some time during a rainstorm, and Anne had contracted pneumonia, which was followed by a severe heart attack.

"On their arrival at the hospital, we noted that Doctor, too, showed the effects of the trip," said Sister Ignatia, "combined with anxiety about his beloved Anne. She lingered for several days, but finally, the last hour came." It was on June 1, 1949.

Following Anne's death, Sister Ignatia wrote Bob a letter in which she noted that Anne, as a patient, had been a model of calmness and had never been heard to complain. "In fact, she was more concerned about the well-being of her visitors than herself," Sister Ignatia said. "Even in her last illness, her great patience, courage, and strength were outstanding."

"I will miss Anne terribly," Dr. Bob said at the time. "But she would have had it no other way. Had she survived this attack, she would have been in the hospital for months. Then, there would have been months at home in bed. She would have hated being a burden; she could not have stood it."

"When Mother died, Dad was very much broken up, because they had been a devoted couple and he also knew at this time that he had not long to live," said Smitty. "And only after she was gone did it dawn on me that this deep, quiet, considerate person, who would do battle for what she believed or to protect her family, was the solid foundation which Dad needed to carry on his part of A.A.," said Smitty.

Through published reports of Anne's death, Dr. Bob's identity as a co-founder of A.A. was disclosed to the general public. In an editorial accompanying an obituary, the Akron *Beacon Journal* wrote: "It seems a pity Mrs. Smith's wonderful work could not have received the public's recognition while she still lived, but she must have known of the gratitude in the hearts of many people she had helped. . . . Akron should al-

ways be proud of the A.A. movement which was born here
and proud of the fine woman who did so much to foster that
movement."

"Dad was fortunate enough to have a lovely couple,
Emma and Lavelle, come in and take care of his needs and
home for him after Mother left," Smitty said. "They were a
wonderful inspiration to him and cheered him up when he
felt blue and took care of him and the house in a very efficient
manner."

"When Mrs. Smith died, Doctor didn't know what to do,"
Emma recalled. "I went home and got my husband and said
we'd better go over and stay overnight. Then we stayed
through the funeral.

"We stayed two or three weeks with him, and he was
looking for a housekeeper. And they [applicants] would come,
and he would sit and talk with them, and then he'd come in
and shake his head.

"We had to do something. He would say, 'Couldn't you
stay? Well, you can't ask your husband to give up . . .' It wasn't
fair, and he knew it wasn't fair. Yet he was so wonderful about
it. We knew we had to do something.

"One night—now, I haven't a superstitious bone in my
body—I dreamed Mrs. Smith said to me, 'Emma, please don't
leave Dad.'

"And when Lavelle got up in the morning, he said, 'I
have the queerest feeling. I don't know whether it was a
dream or what, but Anne kept talking to me. We can't leave
him.'

"We studied about it and talked about it. That evening,
we went and told him we would give up our home and come
there if he wanted us to.

"I will never forget the look on that man's face. Never!"

So the couple who once went to Dr. Bob for help came to
spend his last year and a half with him. They gave up their

home and lived with him until he, too, passed on. Lavelle, who referred to Dr. Bob as "the most lovable man I ever knew," said, "I was of the school that believed no house was big enough for two families; and for that reason, we kept our apartment for some time after we came to live with the doctor. But I believe that anyone who couldn't live with Dr. Bob would have a hard time living with himself."

"One of the things that hurt," said Emma, "was when he said, a few days after she died, 'We've got to get her a stone. Will you go with me?'

"We went to different cemeteries and different places and looked them over. When we decided on Mt. Peace Cemetery, I said, 'Surely, you're going to have something on the stone about A.A.,' and he said, 'Mercy, no.' "

This was a time when A.A. members were thinking about a monument for Anne and Bob. In fact, a collection had already been started. Hearing this, Dr. Bob promptly asked that the money be given back and declared against the Fellowship's erecting for Anne and himself any tangible memorials or monuments. He told Bill, "Let's you and I get buried just like other folks."

Dr. Bob watched the progress of his own disease each day. He knew that the malady was malignant and hopeless and accepted it with serenity and lack of resentment. He felt no bitterness toward the doctors who had failed to make an early diagnosis. "Why should I blame them?" he said. "I've probably made a lot of fatal mistakes myself!"

Between the times that Dr. Bob was forced to stay in bed or to go to the hospital for surgery, he lived his life as normally as possible and got as much enjoyment out of it as he could. After Anne's death, he and Dick S. (Paul's brother) flew to the West Coast and renewed old acquaintances.

Following their return from California, Dick wrote Bill that they had had a "grand trip and Bob really perked up," and that he looked better when they left Los Angeles than he had in months. Back home, Dr. Bob was able to go downtown for a haircut, but on Sunday "came those well-wishing friends — one in particular who stayed four hours and damned near drove him nuts.

"Monday, Bob went into St. Thomas, not because of anything serious, but for rest," Dick said. "Thought I'd give you the real picture in case you heard he was in the hospital with 'no visitors.' Scared hell out of me when I heard it first."

Emma reported that there were indeed a good many visitors after Anne died, and that they were, for the most part, uplifting. "There were many from out of town and so many that were close, right around in Akron," she said. "And we were never without a bouquet of flowers. Never!"

She did mention the "good friend who would sit and try to tell Dr.Smith, 'This is so, this is so, and that is so,' and just make Dr Smith . . . well, he didn't know what the man was talking about half the time.

"Then there was another A.A. member who came to see Dr. Smith every day. They would match half dollars. One day, he came, and Doctor couldn't see anybody. 'I'll have to do it for him,' I said. And for goodness' sake, I won! I never won anything in my life. I went upstairs and told him the fellow had been there, and he said, 'Did you bet with him, Emmy?' And I said, 'Yes. Here's your half dollar.'

"When A.A.'s came to visit, they sat in the kitchen, where they could all have coffee," said Emma. "You've seen that picture in the A.A. book ["Alcoholics Anonymous Comes of Age"]—I was pouring Dick S—— a cup of coffee when that was taken. I have poured gallons of it."

Following the trip to California, Bob and Dick visited the old home in Vermont and then went to Maine. Wherever Dr. Bob went, A.A.'s showered him with attention and kindness. Of this, he said, "Sometimes, these good people do too

much for me. It's embarrassing. I have done nothing to deserve it. I have only been an instrument through which God
worked."

Once again at home, Dr. Bob settled down to enjoying his
friends and the things he could do for them. Between his
serious attacks, he enjoyed Emma's good food. As she recalled, he didn't like hot food. He wouldn't drink his coffee
hot. When they went to the meeting at King School, he would
put five cups of coffee up on a little ledge in the kitchen and
let them cool.

"And he did not like to chew," Emma said. "If he could
have had his way, he would have had meat loaf every day of
the week. He'd say, 'Emmy, what are we gonna have today?'
I'd rack my brain trying to think of something to tempt him.
And I'd say, 'I think I'm going to have so-and-so.' 'Well, could
we have meat loaf tomorrow?' Really and truly, my poor husband never got more than two meat loaves after Dr. Smith was
gone. I can't eat it to this day.

"He was so fond of red raspberries. He had a neighbor
who would bring him four or five quarts when they were in
season. And he'd say, 'Now, do you know how to eat them?'
And I'd say, 'Sure, I know how. You put some sugar on them.'
'That's not the way, Emmy.' He would get a great big soup
bowl and fill it full of raspberries and pour ice water over
them and then sugar them.

"Lavelle and I had been talking about television, but I
heard Doctor say he didn't care for it. But we asked him
anyway. 'Well,' he said, 'I guess if you buy a television, I can
furnish you a chimney to put the aerial on.'

"But he wouldn't look at it [TV]. One night, it was real
funny. My husband and I were watching it, and he was way
over on the other side of the room lying on this very long
davenport reading the newspaper. Then I happened to
glance up, and here he was, looking over the top of his paper

at the television. That did it. I had to laugh. And he just grinned. At that time, they had good college wrestling on, and he was crazy about it. He'd say, 'We'll watch the wrestling tonight.' And I'd say, 'On one condition—that you go upstairs this afternoon and take a nice long nap.' And he would."

Then Dr. Bob acquired a convertible, a black Buick Roadmaster. He loved cars and had owned many of them through his life. But this was his favorite, "the car I always wanted."

"One day, as we all sat in the living room," recalled Lavelle, "he suddenly jumped up and went to the telephone. 'Hello, Russ. Doctah Smith at 855 Ahdmaw. Say, I see you have a convuhtible advuhtised. Bring it out, willya?'

"In due time, the convertible arrived," said Lavelle. "The doctor, being confined to the house, said, 'Abercrombie, get your shoes on and take a little drive, willya?' When I came back, he asked me how she percolated. I said okay, and that wrapped it up. He sat down and wrote a check for it."

Friends still remember his speeding through the streets of the city with the top down. "He was the most awful driver in Akron," said Emmy. "He got lots of parking tickets and for speeding, too. When he would get in the roadster, he would scoot."

Smitty agreed. "The older he got, the wilder he drove. He was a fright to ride with."

"He would go out in it every afternoon that he was able, down to play cards at the City Club," said Emma. "I'd say, 'Please don't go out with that old cap on,' and he'd say, 'Oh, Emma, that's style.' I could set the clock to the time he would get back. He would commence down that side street, and he'd get pretty near the house, and he'd put on the brakes and slide. He really was something—just like a young kid."

Through this period, Dr. Bob continued going to A.A. meetings at King School. Anne C. recalled hearing someone

asking him at this time, "Do you have to go to all these meetings? Why don't you stay home and conserve your strength?"

Dr. Bob considered the question for a time, then said,
"The first reason is that this way is working so well. Why
should I take a chance on any other way? The second reason
is that I don't want to deprive myself of the privilege of meeting, greeting, and visiting with fellow alcoholics. It is a plea-
sure to me. And the third reason is the most important. I
belong at that meeting for the sake of the new man or woman
who might walk through that door. I am living proof that
A.A. will work as long as I work A.A., and I owe it to the new
person to be there. I am the living example."

*Dr. Bob's dream car finally came his way in the last year of his
life —the convertible he had always wanted.*

XXIX. The last year

Members recalled that Dr. Bob's attendance at King School was fairly regular up to the time of his last talk, in Cleveland in July 1950. "Then," as one A.A. said, "he was conspicuous by his absence. That is, you looked to the seat where he usually sat—and it was empty."

"After they died, I thought so much about Dr. Bob and Annie that I hated to go to King School," said Bill V. H. "I'd be used to seeing them sit there. And it just kind of broke my heart not to see Doc there, because he had meant so much in my life. He always said a mouthful. I'd go a hell of a long way to hear him."

No one sat in Dr. Bob's place for a long time. Finally, a newcomer who didn't know sat there, and no one said anything. That, probably, is the way it should have been.

At the last, when Dr. Bob was getting ready to die, he had three things he wanted to do: He wanted to go to St. Johnsbury once more; he wanted to go to Texas for Christmas; and he wanted to make that appearance at A.A.'s First International Convention, in Cleveland.

As the days passed and the date of the Convention drew nearer, Dr. Bob began more and more to conserve his energy. Friends didn't think he should even try.

"He was not able to sit up," Emma recalled. "At noon, I said to him, 'Doctor, please don't go.' "

" 'I just have to go,' he said."

Al S., a New York member, drove to Cleveland with Dr. Bob. "All he said was 'I'm tired. Please excuse me if I don't talk,' " Al recalled. "I didn't think he was going to make it."

Thousands of people were there. Some remember how the waves of A.A. love seemed to lift Dr. Bob; others, how he held his side as he spoke. (At Bill's last Convention talk, 20 years later, there were those who remarked on the similarity of the circumstances.)

It was a short talk. Most people remember his advice on simplicity and quite often cite this to emphasize some point they themselves may be making. But Dr. Bob said a good deal more than that, and as he himself said about the Twelve Steps, none of it needs interpretation:

"My good friends in A.A. and of A.A., I feel I would be very remiss if I didn't take this opportunity to welcome you here to Cleveland, not only to this meeting but those that have already transpired. I hope very much that the presence of so many people and the words that you have heard will prove an inspiration to you—not only to you, but may you be able to impart that inspiration to the boys and girls back home who were not fortunate enough to be able to come. In other words, we hope that your visit here has been both enjoyable and profitable.

"I get a big thrill out of looking over a vast sea of faces like this with a feeling that possibly some small thing I did a number of years ago played an infinitely small part in making this meeting possible. I also get quite a thrill when I think that we all had the same problem. We all did the same things. We all get the same results in proportion to our zeal and enthusiasm and stick-to-itiveness. If you will pardon the injection of a personal note at this time, let me say that I have been in bed five of the last seven months, and my strength hasn't returned as I would like, so my remarks of necessity will be very brief.

"There are two or three things that flashed into my mind on which it would be fitting to lay a little emphasis. One is the simplicity of our program. Let's not louse it all up with Freudian complexes and things that are interesting to the scientific mind, but have very little to do with our actual A.A. work. Our Twelve Steps, when simmered down to the last, resolve themselves into the words 'love' and 'service.' We understand what love is, and we understand what service is. So let's bear those two things in mind.

"Let us also remember to guard that erring member the tongue, and if we must use it, let's use it with kindness and consideration and tolerance.

"And one more thing: None of us would be here today if somebody hadn't taken time to explain things to us, to give us a little pat on the back, to take us to a meeting or two, to do numerous little kind and thoughtful acts in our behalf. So let us never get such a degree of smug complacency that we're not willing to extend, or attempt to extend, to our less fortunate brothers that help which has been so beneficial to us. Thank you very much."

As he finished, those who watched could easily see that the exertion of saying the brief words had left him physically weak and spent. Try as he would, he was forced to leave. In consternation, thousands of eyes followed him as he left the stage.

"It was an awful struggle for Lavelle and me to sit there and watch him," Emma said. "We knew every breath was hard for him. His talk was beautiful. He didn't sit down on the podium when he was finished. He left. We got out of there as fast as we could. I was terrified. I thought maybe he would collapse. But we got home just about the same time he did, and he seemed all right again."

Al S., who drove back to Akron with Dr. Bob, said, "That one effort cost him so much that he could only lean back exhausted. He had literally given his all."

Al, who was editor of the Grapevine at that time and had much to do with the memorial issue for Dr. Bob (January 1951), said in an assessment of the founders in later years, "Without Bill's drive, there wouldn't be any A.A. Without Bob's balance, who knows what it would be like?"

"I had never heard Dad give a major talk before a large group of people," Smitty said. "Betty and I went to Cleveland. After this meeting, although Dad's health became very bad, we drove him back to Vermont, where we spent a week or so

"There, Dad looked up some childhood friends and old cronies and had a wonderful time. It was a trip Betty and I wouldn't have missed for the world, since we had a good opportunity to talk to Dad. We were interested in his religious experiences, and we both had some questions he helped answer."

Before leaving for Vermont, Dr. Bob had asked Lavelle which car he wanted to take on vacation. "Well, I had no thought of taking either car," Lavelle replied.

"Take the Cadillac," Bob said. "It's more comfortable for both of you. We'll take the roadster."

"We talked about it and talked about it," Emma said. "And when Smitty came, Lavelle said, 'Smitty, don't let him do that. There's so much room in the Cadillac. He can lie down, and he can stretch out his legs. And in the Buick, he can't do either.'

"They were gone ten days. And so were we, most of it in

Virginia. The last day before we started home, I was awful nervous, and Lavelle asked me, 'Are you fidgety?' I said, 'Are you?' And he said, 'Yes. I think we ought to go home.'

"We got home in the afternoon. About three or four o'clock, here comes the Cadillac. And when that blessed man walked up the sidewalk and saw the lights on in our house, I had to turn around and go in the kitchen, because I couldn't keep the tears back. He was so afraid we weren't going to be there."

Upon his return, Dr. Bob was admitted to St. Thomas Hospital for another of the minor operations that seemed to come along with such regularity during these last years. Afterward, he went home to the care of Emma and Lavelle.

This was in early September, and he lived until mid-November. "Then the pain was getting really bad," according to Emma. "Every day, he went down a little further. And he did so hate to go to the hospital. But there were things that had to be done to him, and they couldn't be done at home. So we would take him in, and maybe he would stay a day and a night. Then we'd bring him back home.

"We had good days, and we had bad days. I know one time he was in bed six weeks. Sometimes, he had to have five or six shots. And he always would say, 'Thank you kindly.'

" 'Thank me? For a thing like that?'

" 'Well, I do.'

"He was thin to begin with. It got so all I had was a little bit of skin in the calf of his leg to get my needle in. And never did he complain.

"My bedroom was catty-corner from the doctor's. He would sit on the side of the bed smoking a cigarette. Then he'd look all around the room and just sit there. And I'd think, 'You poor, poor dear. How can you go to sleep?'

"He never told us he had any pain, but it would have to be that. I know it was painful for him in bed. It seemed to be all through his stomach and hips. It started in the prostate. Had they discovered it two years before, they could have done something about it. But in searching, they didn't pick the right piece for a specimen [biopsy]. But he never felt bad about it. He said anybody could miss it.

"Yes, he *was* a fighter. And he liked to box. Whether he could box or not, I can't tell you. There was an old boxing glove and an old dog collar—their first bulldog's collar—hanging on Mrs. Smith's bed. It always hung there. I wouldn't have removed it for anything.

"You know, there was a deep sense of friendliness that allowed you to sit with him for hours and not speak, and he could put a world of wisdom into one sentence. But sometimes he would go on a regular talking binge. He'd talk for hours. When he was all talked out, he'd forget about it.

"I'd go upstairs for something when he'd be in bed, and he'd say, 'Aw, Emmy, leave it alone down there. Sit down and talk to me.' And he would talk and talk and talk—about things that were way over my head. But I would listen.

"Sometimes, I would have to go out to get my hair done, and he hated for me to go. One day I came home, and he said, 'Emma, do you have to go anyplace tomorrow?' And I said no. 'Oh, I'm glad you're going to be home.' And then I'd tell my husband, and he'd say, 'You're puffed up like an old toad.' It pleased me. It pleased me greatly.

"Yes, it was a responsibility. But we both felt very pleased to think that Smitty and Dr. Bob felt we were capable of being with him and knowing the things that should be done for him. And we felt it was a privilege to do this, because he saved my husband's life.

"He knew what was coming, but he was not melancholy. Oh, there's so many nasty little stories that go around about him—that he was getting too many pills and all of that when he was in the hospital. But his mind was as clear as yours or mine to the last. The night before he died, I had a permanent, and my husband said, 'Well, Dr. Bob, what do you think of the new hairdo you've got to live with?'

" 'That looks nice,' he said. 'You let her alone.' Don't ever let anyone tell you that he didn't know what he was talking about!"

Henrietta Seiberling visited Dr. Bob during those last months. "Bob, you and I are going to have a great adventure someday," she told him. "His faith was superb," she said. "He and Anne left no stone unturned when it came to growth. They were perfectly prepared when they died."

Dr. Tom Scuderi, who had known Dr. Bob since 1934, remembered talking to him on one occasion when he was in the hospital. "He said, 'I'll be gone in a short time to meet my Maker. I'm not afraid.' "

Anne C., who also had known Dr. Bob even before the start of his sobriety, remembered that he talked very freely about death. "You talk about dying like I talk about driving home in the afternoon," she said to him once. "No fear, no emotion, nothing. How come?"

"Anne," he replied, "have you ever been at the airport and watched the planes take off?"

"Many times," she replied.

"For a while, you see the plane, and then you don't see it," he said. "That doesn't mean that it has disintegrated or disappeared. It has just found a new horizon. That's the way I feel about death. I will have found a new horizon."

Before he could take his leave, there was one unfinished piece of A.A. business for Dr. Bob to complete. That had to do with the proposed conference—in a sense, his and Bill's bequest to all of the thousands in A.A. and those yet to come.

On the Sunday before Doc went into the hospital for what was to be the last time, Bill made yet another visit to 855 Ardmore—from which had issued a "measureless outpouring of grace since I first entered it." Bill remembered telling Doctor Bob that "if he and I did not act on this matter but continued our silence, we would *still* be taking action. . . . Everybody would suppose that the present state of affairs met with our full approval."

Bill thought "that we ought to call the conference anyhow, even if it was a failure at first. The movement's delegates could come down to New York and see what A.A.'s world affairs were really like. They could then decide whether they would take responsibility or whether they would not. That would make it a movement decision, rather than one taken in silence by Dr. Bob and me. . . .

"Finally, he looked up and said, 'Bill, it *has* to be A.A.'s decision, not ours. Let's call that conference. It's fine with me.'

"A few hours later, I took my leave of Dr. Bob, knowing that the following week he was to undergo a very serious operation. Neither of us dared say what was in our hearts. We both knew that this might well be the last decision that we would make together. I went down the steps and then turned to look back. Bob stood in the doorway, tall and upright as ever. Some color had come back into his cheeks, and he was carefully dressed in a light gray suit. This was my partner, the man with whom I never had a hard word. The wonderful old broad smile was on his face as he said almost jokingly, 'Remember, Bill, let's not louse this thing up. Let's keep it simple!' I turned away, unable to say a word. That was the last time I ever saw him."

"The last time," Emma said, "we took him to City Hospital, and they did a little more work. We went over there Wednesday evening, and he asked me to take him home. And I said, 'If you're permitted—of course.' He wanted me to stay with him, but I couldn't.

"About 11 o'clock the next day, I was getting ready to go to the hospital, and then I thought, 'I'll wait until Lavelle gets home.' Then the hospital called and said I'd better come at once. I had to wait for a taxi . . . and Sue didn't get there in time, either. He was gone.

"He had looked at his nails. They were blue — from cyanosis, when the blood stops. And he knew. He said, 'Call the family. This is it.' He knew it. He knew it the night before, when he wanted us to take him home.

"I felt so bad to think I didn't get there. But the doctor told me, 'Don't wish him back, whatever you do. He would have strangled before long. It was in his throat.' "

So, on November 16, 1950, Dr. Bob passed in pain from this life to "a new horizon."

"I came back to Akron for the funeral," Smitty said. "A great many of his old friends came to visit the funeral home. They were so grateful, for they felt he had helped them. It was a very moving experience for me."

The funeral service was conducted in the old Episcopal Church by Dr. Walter Tunks, whose answer to a telephone call 15 years earlier had opened the way toward bringing Bob and Bill together for the first time. Dr. Bob was "buried just like other folks," in Mt. Peace Cemetery. Next to him is Anne, as she was for so many years. Other than a simple headstone, there is no monument.

No monument?

Visiting the graves of Dr. Bob and Anne, Bill found no grand memorial, no mention of A.A. —just a "simple stone."

The Twelve Steps of Alcoholics Anonymous

1. We admitted we were powerless over alcohol—that our lives had become unmanageable.

2. Came to believe that a Power greater than ourselves could restore us to sanity.

3. Made a decision to turn our will and our lives over to the care of God *as we understood Him.*

4. Made a searching and fearless moral inventory of ourselves.

5. Admitted to God, to ourselves and to another human being the exact nature of our wrongs.

6. Were entirely ready to have God remove all these defects of character.

7. Humbly asked Him to remove our shortcomings.

8. Made a list of all persons we had harmed, and became willing to make amends to them all.

9. Made direct amends to such people wherever possible, except when to do so would injure them or others.

10. Continued to take personal inventory and when we were wrong promptly admitted it.

11. Sought through prayer and meditation to improve our conscious contact with God *as we understood Him*, praying only for knowledge of His will for us and the power to carry that out.

12. Having had a spiritual awakening as the result of these steps, we tried to carry this message to alcoholics and to practice these principles in all our affairs.

The Twelve Traditions
of Alcoholics Anonymous

1. Our common welfare should come first; personal recovery depends upon A.A. unity.

2. For our group purpose there is but one ultimate authority—a loving God as He may express Himself in our group conscience. Our leaders are but trusted servants; they do not govern.

3. The only requirement for A.A. membership is a desire to stop drinking.

4. Each group should be autonomous except in matters affecting other groups or A.A. as a whole.

5. Each group has but one primary purpose —to carry its message to the alcoholic who still suffers.

6. An A.A. group ought never endorse, finance, or lend the A.A. name to any related facility or outside enterprise, lest problems of money, property, and prestige divert us from our primary purpose.

7. Every A.A. group ought to be fully self-supporting, declining outside contributions.

8. Alcoholics Anonymous should remain forever nonprofessional, but our service centers may employ special workers.

9. A.A., as such, ought never be organized; but we may create service boards or committees directly responsible to those they serve.

10. Alcoholics Anonymous has no opinion on outside issues; hence the A.A. name ought never be drawn into public controversy.

11. Our public relations policy is based on attraction rather than promotion; we need always maintain personal anonymity at the level of press, radio and films.

12. Anonymity is the spiritual foundation of all our traditions, ever reminding us to place principles before personalities.

1879 August 8: Robert Holbrook Smith born

1898 Bob graduated from St. Johnsbury Academy

1902 Graduated from Dartmouth College

1910 Won M.D. degree at Rush University

1912 Dr. Bob started medical practice, in Akron

1915 January 25: married Anne Ripley

1933 Began going to Oxford Group meetings to cope with his alcoholism

1935 May 12: Dr. Bob met Bill Wilson
      June 10: Dr. Bob's last drink; start of A.A.

1937 Prospects came to Akron from Cleveland
      November: Dr. Bob and Bill realized "chain reaction" had begun;
      Akron A.A.'s agreed on need for book

1939 Alcoholics holding meetings in Detroit; group formed in Youngstown
      April: "Alcoholics Anonymous" (Big Book) published
      May 11: first meeting of Cleveland A.A. group (no Oxford Group
      connection)
      August: Dr. Bob and Sister Ignatia began treating alcoholics at St.
      Thomas Hospital
      September: group starting in Chicago
      October: articles on A.A. in Cleveland *Plain Dealer*
      November-December: Akron A.A.'s broke away from Oxford Group,
      began meeting at Dr. Bob's house

1940 January: Akron group found new home at King School
      September: first meeting of Toledo A.A. group

1941 March 1 *Saturday Evening Post*: article on A.A.
      Cleveland A.A.'s celebrated Doc Smith Day

1942 Dr. Bob and Bill accused of making undue profit on Big Book

1948 December: Dr. Bob's last major talk, in Detroit
      Summer: Dr. Bob found he had cancer, retired from practice

1949 March: Dr. Bob considered idea of A.A. conference premature
      June 1: Anne Ripley Smith died

1950 July 28-30: First A.A. International Convention, in Cleveland; Dr.
      Bob made last appearance at large A.A. gathering, joined other
      A.A.'s in approving Twelve Traditions
      November 16: Dr. Bob died
      December Grapevine: article (prepared earlier) signed by both Bill
      and Dr. Bob recommended establishment of A.A. general service
      conference

Sources

The following abbreviations are used in this section:

AA "Alcoholics Anonymous" (the Big Book)

Age "Alcoholics Anonymous Comes of Age" (book)

Alexander "The Jack Alexander Article" (pamphlet reprinting the *Saturday Evening Post* story)

C Cassette or other type of recording

Co-F "The Co-Founders of Alcoholics Anonymous" (pamphlet including Dr. Bob's last major talk, 1948)

Farewell "Dr. Bob's Farewell Talk" (parchment displaying excerpts from his last talk, 1950, which is available in full in cassette and typed-transcript form)

GV The A.A. Grapevine (monthly magazine)

L Letter

T Typewritten material, including transcripts of recordings

12&12 "Twelve Steps and Twelve Traditions" (book)

Material in the A.A. archives is identified by letters (enclosed in parentheses), which indicate the availability of each item, determined by the A.A. General Service Board and its Archives Committee, as follows:

(A-1) General—open to the public

(B) Classified—access requires review and approval of the Archives Committee

(C) Confidential—not available, for a specific time period or under special conditions

References to A.A. books and pamphlets and the A.A. Grapevine are followed by page numbers in these publications. Quotations from the Bible follow the wording of the King James edition, except where otherwise noted.

Pages	Lines	Sources
10	3-6	
10	20-29	C, T, 1954 (B)
10-12	30 to 1	Farewell, 1950
12	1-2	Age, 69
12	7-17	AA, 172
12-13	34 to 13	AA, 171
13	28-33	GV 1/51, 12
13-14	34 to 26	GV 6/74, 31
14-15	32 to 15	
15	18-25	GV 1/51, 12
15	26-29	GV 1/51, 13-14
16	15-21	GV 1/51, 14
17	21-32	C, T, 1977 (B)
18	14-32	C, T, 1977 (B)
19	3-14	AA, 172
19	19-24	L, 10/9/58 (B)
19-20	25 to 7	C (B)
20	15-26	C, T, 1954 (B)
20	27-29	GV 1/51, 14
20 21-22	30-33 10 to 4	C (B)
22	13-18	AA, 172
23	15-29	L, 10/9/58 (B)
24-25	14 to 2	C (B)
25	7-8	C, T, 1954 (B)

Pages	Lines	Sources
25	11-14	
25	23-26	
26	16-23	
26-27	28 to 1	AA, 173-174
27	1-5	GV 1/51, 17
27	6-26	AA, 174
27	27-34	GV 1/51, 17-18
28	7-15	AA, 174-175
28	15-18	C, T, 1954 (B)
28-29	19 to 10	AA, 174-175
29	15	GV 1/74, 32
29-30	21 to 2	
30	7-10	C, T, 1954 (B)
30	15-18	C, T, 1977 (B)
30-33	25 to 14	
33	27-30	AA, 175-177
33-34	34 to 3	AA, 188
34	4-10	C, T, 6/74 (B)
35-38	7 to 33	C, T, 1954 (B)
39	1-12	AA, 177
39-40	13 to 19	C, T, 1954 (B)
40-42	23 to 21	AA, 176-178
42-43	28 to 21	C, T, 1954 (B)
43	21-24	C, T, 1977 (B)
43-44	19 to 3	C, T, 1954 (B)

Pages	Lines	Sources
45-46	11 to 6	C, T, 1954 (B)
46	7-9	GV 1/51, 28
46	11-13	C, T, 1954 (B)
46	14-18	C, T, 1954 (B)
46-48	21 to 9	C, T, 1977 (B)
48	10-17	GV 2/77, 3
48	18-32	C, T, 1977 (B)
48-49	33 to 3	GV 2/77, 3-4
49	4-25	C, T, 1977 (B)
49-50	26 to 3	GV 2/77, 4-5
50	4-24	C, T, 1977 (B)
50-51	25 to 3	C, T, 1954 (B)
51-52	16 to 25	C, T, 1977 (B)
53	6-12	AA, 178-179
54	19-27	Co-F, p. 13
55-56	33 to 9	
56	19-20	
56	26-27	AA, 178
57-58	3 to 25	C, 2/26/78 (B)
58	27-28	Co-F, 9
58-59	31 to 16	C, 2/26/78 (B)
59	19-27	Co-F, 11
59	28-31	C, T, 1954 (B)
60	1-6	Co-F, 7-8

Pages	Lines	Sources
60	7-16	C, T, 1954 (B)
60	20-30	
64	8-17	C, 2/26/78 (B)
64	18-24	Age, 66
64-66	25 to 1	GV 1/51, 4-5
66	15-22	
66	25-32	Co-F, 6-7
66-67	33 to 5	C, T, 1954 (B)
67	6-14	Age, 67
67	20-28	C (B)
68	8-10	
68	12-19	Age, 68-70
68	22-31	AA, 180
69	11-21	C, T, 1954 (B)
69	23-30	C, T, 1954 (B)
69-70	31 to 1	C, 2/26/78 (B)
70	8-12	Co-F, 7
70	16-20	
70	27-30	
70-71	31 to 1	
71	6-9	L, 1935 (C)
71	10-13	
71	18-25	GV 1/51, 5
71-72	30 to 28	C, T, 1954 (B)
73	13-18	AA, 179
73	26-29	GV 1/51, 5
73	30-32	Co-F, 7
73-74	34 to 19	C, T, 1954 (B)

Pages	Lines	Sources
74-75	20 to 4	GV 1/51, 6
76	5-8	AA, 181
76	12-17	Co-F, 11-12
77	4-6	Farewell
77-78	20 to 27	L, 1935 (C)
78-80	29 to 15	
80	23-28	C, T, 1954 (B)
80-81	33 to 16	C, T, 1977 (B)
81	17-20	C, T, 1954 (B)
81-82	29 to 5	Age, 71
82	6	AA, 188
82	6-8	GV 1/51, 6-7
83	4-23	AA, 182-192
83-86	24 to 34	
87-89	11 to 22	C, T, 1977 (B)
90-91	1 to 34	C, 1975 (B)
92-93	5 to 20	C, T, 1954 (B)
93-95	21 to 3	C, T, 1954 (B)
95	12-18	C, T, 1977 (B)
95-96	19 to 13	C, T, 1954 (B)
96	19-21	C, T, 1954 (B)
96	22-28	
96-97	34 to 14	Co-F, 10
97	15-19	Co-F, 9
97-98	23 to 11	C, T, 1954 (B)
98	14-23	C, T, 1954 (B)
98-99	25 to 19	C, T, 1954 (B)
99	20-25	C, T, 1954 (B)
99	26-31	L, 1935 (C)
99-100	32 to 9	AA, 159-160
100	11-16	
100-101	29 to 8	C, T, 1954 (B)
101	11-21	C, T, 1954 (B)
101-102	22 to 1	C, T, 1954 (B)
102	24-28	C, T, 1977 (B)
102-104	33 to 18	GV 2/77, 5-6
104	26-28	Co-F, 9
104-105	31 to 15	Co-F, 8-9
105	18-26	C, T, 1954 (B)
105-107	27 to 30	C, T, 1954 (B)
108	8-12	
108	14-16	L, 1936 (C)
109	24-32	C, T (B)
109-110	33 to 14	C, T, 1977 (B)
112-113	4 to 23	
114-115	3 to 2	C, T, 1954 (B)

Pages	Lines	Sources
115- 116	19 to 27	C, T, 1954 (B)
116- 119	28 to 10	C, T, 1954 (B)
119	12-18	C, T, 1954 (B)
119- 121	19 to 25	C, T, 1954 (B)
122- 123	6 to 9	C, T, 1954
123 123- 124	11-23 29 to 23	Age, 145-146
126	3-10	(B)
126 126- 127	17-24 33 to 3	C, T, 1954 (B)
127	10-20	GV 1/51, 20
127	27-28	GV 2/45, 2
128	2-13	C, T, 1977 (B)
128- 134	31 to 30	2/23/38 (B)
134- 135	32 to 2	Age, 149
135- 136	8 to 2	8/11/38
137- 139	12 to 20	C, T, 1954 (B)
139 140	21 to 10	C, T (B)
140	12-32	C, T, 1954 (B)
140- 141	34 to 20	C, T, 1954 (B)
141	22-27	C, T, 1954 (B)
141- 142	32 to 7	C, T, 1977 (B)

Pages	Lines	Sources
142	8-17	C, T, 1954 (B)
142- 143	18 to 26	C, T, 1954 (B)
143- 144	27 to 25	C, T, (B)
144	26-27	Matthew 6:33
144- 146	28 to 4	C, T, 1954 (B)
146	8-12	C, T, 1977 (B)
146	13-17	C, T, 1977 (B)
146- 147	24 to 8	C, T, 1954 (B)
147	9-13	C, T, 1954 (B)
147	14-24	C, T, 1977 (B)
147	25-33	C, T, 1954 (B)
147- 148	34 to 6	C, T, 1977 (B)
148	10-15	C, T, 1977 (B)
148- 149	23 to 27	C, T, 1954 (B)
149- 150	29 to 4	C, 11/1/76 (B)
150	11-25	C, T, 1977 (B)
150- 151	30 to 5	C, T, 8/78 (B)
151	7-18	C, T, 1954 (B)
151	19-22	C, T, 1954 (B)
151 152	29-32 5-7	L, 6/38 (B)
152	10-15	C, 1975 (B)
152	20-25	C, T, 1954 (B)
152 153	26-30 5-9	C, T, 1954 (B)

Pages	Lines	Sources
185-188	6 to 29	
189	1-7	C, T, 1954 (B)
189	7-26	C (B)
189-190	32 to 2	C, 1977 (B)
190	3-9	C (B)
190-191	10 to 12	C, T, 1954 (B)
191-192	21 to 2	C, T, 1977 (B)
192	3-25	C, T, 1977 (B)
194 195-197	1-18 1 to 15	C, T, 1954 (B)
197	19-28	L, 12/24/49 (B)
198	23-25	T, 4/5/66 (A-1)
198-199	31 to 3	Cor. 1:27-30 (Douai)
200	2-13	C, T, 1954 (B)
200-201	15 to 4	L, 10/39 (B)
201	8-11	C, T, 1954 (B)
201	15-17	L, 6/4/39 (B)
201-202	20 to 16	C, T, 1954 (B)
202	19-24	L, 10/39 (B)
202-203	33 to 3	C, T, (B)
203	4-7	L, 10/39 (B)
203	14-23	C, T, 1977 (B)
203	24-26	C, T, 1954 (B)

Pages	Lines	Sources
203	28	Age, 20
203	29-32	C, T (B)
204	6-8	Age, 20
204	11-12	L, 1939 (B)
204-205	22 to 2	10/21/39 (A-1)
205	3-16	C, T, 1954 (B)
205	17-25	11/27/39 (A-1)
205-206	28 to 4	
206	8-20	C, T (B)
206-207	21 to 4	
207	27-32	C, T, 1954 (B)
208	5-25	L, 10/10 (B)
208 209	31 to 4	C, T, (B)
209	6-12	C, T, 1977 (B)
209	13-34	L, 11/10/40 (B)
210	4-8	C, T, 1977 (B)
210	18-27	L, 12/40 (B)
210-211	25 to 13	L, 12/12/39 (B)
211	14-34	Age, 21-22
212	3-4	Farewell
213 216	5-29 1-20	C, T, 1977 (B)
216 217	30-31 4-12	C, T, 1954 (B)
217	14-16	L, 12/39 (B)
217	21-28	C, T, 1954 (B)

Pages	Lines	Sources
217-218	29 to 8	
218	13-24	C, T, 1977 (B)
218	31-34	L, 1/2/40 (B)
219	10-13	C, T, 1977 (B)
219	21-27	L, 5/14/40 (B)
220-221	14 1	C, T, 1977 (B)
221	8-11	C, T, 1954 (B)
221	12-14	C, T, 1977 (B)
221	17-20	C, T, 1977 (B)
221	21-27	C, 1977 (B)
221	28-33	GV 1/51, 31
222	14-15	Co-F, 14-15
222	19-27	GV 9/65, 20
222-223	29 to 13	C, T, 1954 (B)
223	22-27	C, T, 1977 (B)
223	32-34	C, T, 1977 (B)
224	13-27	C, T, 1977 (B)
224-225	30 to 5	C, T, 1977 (B)
225-226	7 to 5	C, 7/5/75 (B)
226	7-8	C, T, 1977 (B)
226	9-23	C, 7/5/75 (B)
226	26-28	C, T, 1977 (B)
226	29-34	C, T, 1977 (B)
227	11-20	
227	25-29	GV 9/48, 1-2
227	31-32	C, T, 1977 (B)
228-230	21 to 2	C, T, 1977 (B)
230	13-21	C, T, 1977 (B)
231	4-6	C, 7/5/75 (B)
231-233	14 to 9	C, T, 1977 (B)
233	11-15	C, T, 1977 (B)
233	16-21	C, T, 1977 (B)
233-235	25 to 10	C, T, 1954 (B)
235	22-32	C, T, 1977 (B)
235-236	33 to 11	C, T, 1977 (B)
236	12-15	C, T, 1977 (B)
236-237	16 to 16	
238	1-2	
238	12-24	C, T, 1977 (B)
240	12-13	AA, xiv
240-241	23 to 1	12&12, 141-142
241	10-11	C, T, 1954 (B)
241	14-18	Age, 97-98
241	29-32	C, T, 1977 (B)
241-242	33 to 3	C, T (B)
242	7-19	
242-243	23 to 15	C, T, 1977 (B)
243	17-19	L, 11/40 (B)
243	23-31	C, T, 10/54 (B)
243-244	32 to 8	C, T, 1977 (B)

Pages	Lines	Sources
244	9-14	C, T, 10/54 (B)
244	15-18	C, T, 1977 (B)
244	19-32	C, T, 1977 (B)
244-245	33 to 4	C, 7/5/75 (B)
245	4-13	C, T, 6/74 (B)
245-246	15 to 7	C, T (B)
246	9-25	C, 7/5/75 (B)
246	27-34	C, T, 1977 (B)
247	1-9	C, T, 1977 (B)
247-248	11 to 8	C, 7/5/75 (B)
248	9-15	C, T (B)
248-249	16 to 2	C, 7/5/75 (B)
249	6-8	L, 1940 (B)
249	17-31	C, T, 1977 (B)
249-250	33 to 9	C, T, 1977 (B)
251-252	14 to 15	C, T, 1977 (B)
252	16-27	C, T (B)
253	9-24	C, T, 8/78 (B)
253	25-30	C, T, 1977 (B)
253-256	31 to 4	C, T, 8/78 (B)
256	5-5	C, T, 1977 (B)
256-257	16 to 4	
257-258	15 to 1	C, T, 1977 (B)
258	15-30	C, T, 1954 (B)

Pages	Lines	Sources
258-259	31 to 3	C, 7/5/75 (B)
259	6-16	Age, 25
261	2-16	C, T (B)
261-262	17 to 25	C, T, 1977 (B)
262-263	26 to 2	L, 1940 (B)
263	5-9	L, 9/40 (B)
263	11-14	L, 1/41 (B)
263	15-19	C, T, 1977 (B)
263	20-25	L, 1/41 (B)
263-264	29-33 4-19	C, T, 1977 (B)
264-265	29 to 2	CV 2/69, 11
265	3-16	C, T, 1977 (B)
265	17-29	C, T, 1977 (B)
267	1-8	C, T (B)
267	15-21	C, T, 8/78 (B)
267-268	26 to 11	C, T, (B)
268	31-32	6/42 (B)
269	9-13	L, 1941 (B)
269	26-29	12/42 (B)
270-271	16 to 14	C, 7/5/75 (B)
271	22-34	C, T, 1977 (B)
272	1-5	C, T, 1977 (B)
272	6-9	C, T, 1977 (B)
272	12-14	C, T, 1977 (B)
272	21-24	C, T, 1954 (B)

Pages	Lines	Sources
272-273	25 to 4	Co-F, 14
273	6-34	GV 7/44, 2
274-275	5 to 5	C, T, 1977 (B)
275	6-9	C, T, 1977 (B)
275	10-18	C, T, 1977 (B)
275-276	19 to 3	C, T, 1977 (B)
276	4-11	C, T, 1977 (B)
276-277	12 to 4	C, T, 1977 (B)
277	5-15	C, 1976 (B)
277	16-25	C, T, 1977 (B)
277 278	26-34 1-10	C, T, 1977 (B)
279	11-15	C, T, 1954 (B)
279	1-16	C, T, 1954 (B)
279-280	17 to 8	C, T, 1977 (B)
280	9-20	C, T, 1954 (B)
280	22-28	C, T, 1977 (B)
281	1-31	C, T, 1977 (B)
281-282	32 to 32	C, T, 1977 (B)
283 285	3 to 11	C, T, 1977 (B)
286 286-287	6-15 16 to 1	C, T, 1977 (B)
287	2-28	C, T, 1977 (B)
287-288	31 to 9	Co-F, 15-16
288	10-33	C, T, 1977 (B)
288-289	34 to 17	C, T, 1977 (B)
289	18-20	C, T, 1977 (B)
289	21-26	C, T, 1977 (B)
289	27-34	C, T, 1977 (B)
290	1-4	C, T, 1954 (B)
290	5-9	C, T, 1977 (B)
290	10-17	C, T, 1977 (B)
290	18-29	C, T, 1977 (B)
290	30-32	C, T, 8/78 (B)
290-291 292	33 to 6 7-10	C, T, 1977 (B)
293-294	5 to 7	GV 1/51, 34-35
294	8-17	C, T, 1977 (B)
296	24-28	C, T, 1977 (B)
296	29-31	C, T, 1977 (B)
296	32-34	C, T, 1954 (B)
297	1-4	C, T, 1977 (B)
297 297	5-8 14-23	C, T, 1954 (B)
297-299	24 to 29	C (B)
300	3-12	C, T, 1977 (B)
300	14-18	C, T, 1977 (B)
300-302	25 to 2	L (B)
302	3-7	C, T, 1977 (B)
302	8-12	C, 1975 (B)
302	21-24	C, T, 1977 (B)

Pages	Lines	Sources
302-303	25 to 7	
303-304	9 to 30	C, T, 1954 (B)
307	6-17	Co-F, 12
307-308	27 to 12	Co-F, 14-15
308	22-26	Matthew 5:23-24
308-309	31 to 6	C, T, 1954 (B)
309	7-9	C, T, 1954 (B)
309	7-9	C, T, 1954 (B)
309	13-14	Philippians 2:7
309	23-25	C, T, 1954 (B)
309	26-32	C, T, 1977 (B)
309-310	33 to 22	C, T, 1954 (B)
310-311	23 to 5	C, T, 1954 (B)
311	6-8	
311	13-17	C, T, 1954 (B)
311-312	21 to 18	C, T, 1977 (B)
312	19-31	C, T, 1954 (B)
312-313	32 to 25	C, T, 1977 (B)
313-314	30 to 19	C, T, 8/77 (B)
314	27-34	C, T, 1977 (B)
316	9-11	
317	1-5	C, T, 1954 (B)
317-318	15 to 34	C, T, 1977 (B)
319-320	22 to 2	L, 5/48 (B)
320	5	Age, 214
320-321	22 to 22	C, 1948 (B)
321	24-29	C, T, 1954 (B)
321-322	30 to 10	C, 1948 (B)
322	27-33	C, T, 1977 (B)
323	8-19	C, T, 1977 (B)
323-325	24 to 2	L, 2/49 (B)
325	5-10	L, 3/14/49 (B)
325-326	23 to 7	C, T, 1977 (B)
327	2-17	C, T, 1977 (B)
328	1-8	C, T, 1954 (B)
328	11-15	L, 6/49 (B)
328	21-27	C, T, 1954 (B)
328-329	31 to 3	6/2/49 (A-1)
329	4-9	C, T, 1954 (B)
329-330	10 to 14	C, T, 1977 (B)
330	20-21	Age, 136
330-331	34 to 9	L, 1949 (B)
331	10-30	
332-333	11 to 5	
333	10-23	C, T, 1977 (B)
333	24-25	C, T, 1954 (B)
333	26-32	C, T, 1977 (B)

Index